Journey into Darkness

JOHN UPTON TERRELL

Journey into Darkness

William Morrow and Company
New York   *1962*

To Donna
whose Spanish ancestors came by way of County Cork

Contents

Part Six

Part Seven

Author's Note

Historians long have called the journey of Cabeza de Vaca the most remarkable in the annals of American exploration. It was something more than that.

Cabeza de Vaca made a major contribution to the world's knowledge in his own time. He turned on a great light where only darkness existed. Moreover, he left a document that was of inestimable value to students, historians and scientists of later centuries.

Over a period of eight years, 1528-1536, he traveled up the peninsula of Florida by land, sailed by horsehide boat from northern Florida to the coast of central Texas, and with three companions crossed Texas on foot to El Paso, thence across northern Mexico to the Gulf of California, and southward to Mexico City. Altogether it was a journey of more than five thousand miles, virtually all of it country never before seen by white man.

De Vaca and two Spaniards and a Negro Moor were the only survivors of the three hundred men who comprised the Narvaez Expedition when it landed on the Florida shore near Tampa Bay. The last of the others died on the Texas coast.

These four men were the first to cross North America above Mexico, proving that the continent grew wider in the north, and that it was a solid land mass. Thus, they drastically changed all the maps of the Western Hemisphere.

De Soto did not discover the Mississippi River, as so many school children have been taught. He was the first to cross it north of the Gulf of Mexico, but the river's existence had been known for years before that time. It was shown on maps long before de Soto started out. The first white man known to have seen the river emptying into the Gulf was the Spanish pilot, Alvarez Pineda. He discovered the delta in 1519. Next came the disintegrating boats of the ill-fated Narvaez Expedition, one of them commanded by Cabeza de Vaca. They were driven out into the Gulf by the river's current in 1528.

Cabeza de Vaca's journal, or *Relacion,* was the first book to describe the immense territory, its inhabitants and flora and fauna, between Florida and the Gulf of California.

He was the first to write of such strange animals as the opossum, the armadillo and the Gila monster. He told the world for the first time about the buffalo. He described and located rivers, mountain ranges and deserts that were not known to exist. He was the first to see the pueblos, the first to carry the Christian gospel into the North American wilderness. He brought word to Mexico City of the fabulous Seven Cities of Cibola, and he broke the trail which Coronado later followed northward in search of them.

The basic and most authoritative material about Cabeza de Vaca is, of course, to be found in his own *Relacion.* Before it was published, however, he and two of his companions, Dorantes and Castillo, collaborated on a letter about the journey to the *Audencia* of Española. It was in the nature of a preliminary report. The Spanish historian, Gonzalo Fernández de Oviedo y Valdés, who made six trips to the Indies in Cabeza de Vaca's time, published the letter in his *Historia general y natural de las Indias.*

The *Relacion* first appeared in print at Zamora in 1542. Another edition was issued in 1555, and it included Cabeza de Vaca's account of his adventures in South America where, sometime after his return from Mexico, he served as Captain-General and *adelantado* of Rio de la Plata Province from 1540 to 1543.

In 1851, the noted scholar, Buckingham Smith, translated the *Relacion* into English, working from the 1555 edition. The next English translation came from Fanny Bandelier, the eminent authority on the history of the southwestern United States, in 1905. It was made from the original 1542 edition, and differs in some small respects from Smith's work.

The finest and most exhaustive study of Cabeza de Vaca's journey was published in 1907 by the distinguished historian and ethnologist, Frederick W. Hodge, of the Smithsonian Institution's Bureau of Ethnology. Working from an 1871 edition of Smith's translation, Hodge identified landmarks of the route. An authority on Indians and their culture, he was able to contribute footnotes which established Cabeza de Vaca's position at various stages of the long journey.

Later students have disagreed with some of Hodge's findings. The fact is, that it would be quite impossible to trace Cabeza de Vaca's entire course with accuracy. Hodge stated the case concisely when he said, "There are few Spanish narratives more unsatisfactory to deal with by reason of the lack of directions and distances."

However, there are details enough to establish the route with relative certainty. Two clues especially point to a line of march as stated in this book. On at least two occasions later Spanish explorers came upon Indian villages and tribes Cabeza de Vaca had visited. Also, the *Relacion* describes mountain ranges, canyons, minerals, trees, native customs and habitations which indicate his position from time to time.

Cabeza de Vaca's place in history is secure. His feats, his remarkable journey, will never be forgotten. Yet, there is something that historians generally seem to have overlooked in writing about him.

It is the creed by which he lived.

Like so many other Spaniards, he came to the New World to make his fortune. It is regrettable that he did not achieve that aim, for undoubtedly he would have used his riches beneficially and with justness.

In the face of terrible disappointment and hardship, however, he knew no bitterness, he never lost his courage, his spirit, nor his faith.

He neither stole, nor plundered, nor inflicted barbarities on the savage Indians he encountered. Instead he sought to inspire them with an understanding of the Christian God. He practiced goodness and kindness. He took for himself only what he needed for his own survival. He condemned his own people for the cruel and diabolical system with which they controlled the rich lands they had conquered only through brute force.

It seems to me that he should be honored for these accomplishments, too.

JOHN UPTON TERRELL

PART ONE

The Dream and the Shadows

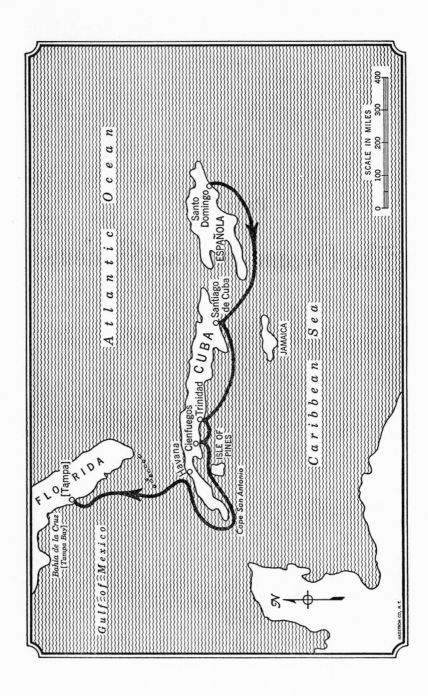

Bahía de la Cruz
[Tampa Bay]

FLO⸱RIDA
[Tampa]

Gulf of Mexico

Atlantic Ocean

Havana
Cienfuegos
Trinidad CUBA
Cape San Antonio
ISLE OF PINES

Santiago de Cuba
ESPAÑOLA
Santo Domingo

JAMAICA

Caribbean Sea

N

SCALE IN MILES
0   100   200   300   400

HAGSTROM CO., N.Y.

1

The Santo Domingo that Alvar Nuñez de Vera Cabeza de Vaca first saw in the summer of 1527 was a more important place than it is today. Yet, when the five ships of the Narvaez Expedition, of which he was the treasurer and provost marshal, anchored there some eight weeks out of Seville, it had been in existence only slightly more than thirty years.

Columbus discovered Española, which is now divided between the Dominican Republic and Haiti, in 1492. On the south coast of this big island, Santo Domingo soon became the main port of call for most of the galleons and caravels engaged in the incredibly profitable sea commerce between Spain and the new Western World. It was also the administrative and ecclesiastical capital of an empire established without any knowledge of its size or content by Pope Alexander VI.

In 1494, two years after Columbus had landed on San Salvador, believing he had reached India, Papal Bulls fixed a north-south line three hundred and seventy degrees west of the Cape Verde Islands. All new territory east of the line was given to Portugal, all to the west of it was awarded to the Kingdom of Castile.

The maps on which the arbitrary decision was based

3

provided nothing more than the portrayal of a round world as envisioned by poorly informed cartographers. Any relation between them and accuracy was purely accidental.

Portugal soon was dismayed to find that her share was the nose of Brazil, which extended a few hundred miles into the South Atlantic. Spain, with the scratch of a quill, had been made the ruler of two gigantic continents.

Their fabulous inheritance spiritually blessed, the Spaniards, inflamed by the few gold trinkets and gems Columbus had brought back, wasted no time in going after the fortunes which they were convinced awaited the taking. Before Santo Domingo had survived three wild decades and Cabeza de Vaca had arrived to take his place in the mad search for riches, the *conquistadores* had plundered virtually all of the Caribbean Islands and vast areas of the Central and South American mainlands.

They also had made secure for themselves a high place on the roster of the world's greatest barbarians, not outranked even by the early British settlers in Tasmania, who shot on sight the paleolithic men, women and children still lingering there and put out poisoned meat for them to eat.

The curtain had risen, and in 1527, Cabeza de Vaca could have traveled in almost any direction from Española to the sites of blood-chilling dramas. Between 1499 and 1516, starring roles had been played by Ojeda, Pinzon, de Lepe, Cabral, De Bastidas and de Solis along the coast of South America. Sailing there in this period was a distinguished geographer named Amerigo Vespucci who held a conviction that what had been discovered was not Asia but a New World—which was in time named for him.

In 1513 Balboa had fought his way across a tropical isthmus and had gazed down upon a great ocean never before seen by a white man.

The year 1519 had been important. Cortez had begun the systematic looting and destruction of an ancient civilization in a land called Mexico, growing fabulously rich as he advanced. A Spanish pilot named Alvarez Pineda had sailed along the entire coast of the Gulf of Mexico, from Florida to Vera Cruz. He crossed the mouth of a great unknown river flowing from the north. It was the Mississippi.

Juan Ponce de León, a true blue blood, had conquered Puerto Rico, but set his sights toward a greater conquest on an "island" called Florida which he had discovered in 1512. He returned in 1521 to establish a colony, and fell mortally wounded under a hail of Indian arrows. The same fate was suffered by Ayllon who, five years later, attempted to build a settlement in North Carolina, which he knew as Chicora. He and most of his men died of privation and disease.

The curtain had risen, but there was a part of the vast stage that remained empty and dark. That part was to the north, north of the faint candles Pineda and a few other pilots had lighted along the edge of the Mexican Gulf. What lay beyond those flickering tapers no one knew, and it was there the expedition of Panfilo de Narvaez was going.

The view of Santo Domingo and the luxuriant country surrounding it, which confronted Cabeza de Vaca as he sailed into the mouth of the Ozama River, could do no less than stir admiration in a man who had been so long at sea in a filthy ship. A closer look on shore later undoubtedly was not as inspiring.

The island was, as Columbus had reported somewhat ecstatically, extraordinarily beautiful. His description of it also would have been applicable for the most part to Cuba, Puerto Rico and Jamaica, as well as to a hundred other islands in the Greater and Lesser Antilles.

He made Española appear to be very close to a paradise on earth, calling it a "marvel," and writing: "The lands thereof are high, and in it are very many ranges of hills, and most lofty mountains . . . all most beautiful in a thousand shapes . . . and full of trees of a thousand kinds, so lofty

that they seem to reach the sky. . . . I am assured that
they never lose their foliage . . . some of them were in
flower, some in fruit . . . and the nightingale was singing,
and other birds of a thousand sorts. . . . In the earth there
are many mines of metals; and there is a population of incalculable number * . . . the mountains and hills, and
plains, and fields, and the soil, so beautiful and rich for
planting and sowing, for breeding cattle of all sorts, for
building of towns and villages . . . as well as many and
great rivers . . . many of which contain gold . . . there
are many spiceries. . . . The people all go naked, men and
women, just as their mothers bring them forth; although
some women cover a single place with the leaf of a
plant. . . . They have no iron or steel, nor any weapons
[other] than the stems of reeds . . . on the end of which
they fix little sharpened stakes."

Columbus spoke of them as a "wondrously timorous" people, and said they fled at the approach of his men. He gave
them gifts, attempting to win their confidence. "But such
they are, incurably timid. . . . Since they have become
more assured, and are losing that terror, they are artless
and generous. . . . Of anything they have, if it be asked
for, they never say no, but do rather invite the person to
accept it, and show as much lovingness as though they would
give their hearts."

He cites a good example of this generosity: "I forbade
that anything so worthless as fragments of broken platters,
and pieces of broken glass, and strap buckles, should be
given them; although when they were able to get such
things, they seemed to think they had the best jewel in
the world."

For the metallic tip of a lace, a Spanish sailor received
from an Indian half an ounce of gold. For a shiny *blanca*,
a coin worth about one third of a cent, he got several ounces

* It was probably about 250,000.

of gold, or fifty pounds of spun cotton. "They even took pieces of broken barrel hoops, and gave whatever they had, like senseless brutes. . . . I forbade it, and I gave gratuitously a thousand useful things . . . in order that they may conceive affection, and furthermore may become Christians . . . they know no sect, nor idolatry; save that they all believe that power and goodness are in the sky."

The Santo Domingo waterfront knew a bustling traffic the year around. Vessels of every size and description crowded the harbor: small, square-rigged caravels, light frigates, two-masted brigantines, bulky galleons, men-of-war.

Merchantmen arrived with luxury cargoes of wines, silks, silver and glassware, carved furniture and fine linens, as well as an array of ordinary foodstuffs. They departed with gold and silver bullion, rare woods, fruits, parrots, spices, maize, copper, tin, iron, diamonds, emeralds, pearls, opals and turquoise, hides, cotton, cacao, peppers and amber.

The slave trade was a continuing and profitable part of Santo Domingo's commerce. Slavers came in from Africa and marched columns of wretched, starved Negroes to the market place. Other vessels, with frightful odors preceding them to an anchorage, arrived from other islands and from Columbia, Venezuela, Panama and Mexico, carrying Indians half-crazed with fright, hunger and beatings to be sold to plantation owners, or to be taken on across the sea to Spain.

In the time of Cabeza de Vaca, the permanent population of the city numbered several thousands. Of course, only Spaniards were counted; those of Negro or Indian blood were considered chattels rather than human beings. They were bought and sold by the head, in the manner of cattle, swine and sheep.

Like most Spanish colonial towns, Santo Domingo, which was founded in 1496, was laid out in a rectangular pattern. The cathedral, built in the customary Spanish Renaissance style, dominated the central section. Begun in 1511, it was not yet completed when Cabeza de Vaca saw it, but it was even then an imposing and beautiful structure. Eventually it would contain three vast naves and fifteen chapels, and bones, reputedly those of Columbus, would be enshrined in a magnificent crypt.

Away from the cathedral, the narrow streets ran straight, intersecting at right angles, and interspersed with small plazas. Not far from the Cathedral Plaza was the palace built for Governor Diego Columbus, son of the discoverer of the New World. Adjacent were the government buildings in which His Majesty's representatives and the officials of the Council of the Indies had their offices. The Council exercised supreme administrative, judicial and ecclesiastical authority over all the Indies, and possessed supervisory authority over the *Casa de Contratación,* which governed commercial transactions, exports, imports and customs.

Most of the public buildings and mansions of officials, wealthy traders and planters, like the cathedral, were boldly executed in stone. Massive unbroken elevations lined the narrow streets, giving an overall drab effect, but behind them were brightly colored walls, and huge doors and windows looked out on lovely private patios and gardens.

A towering citadel built by Diego Columbus guarded the harbor approach to the city, and along each side of Santo Domingo rose thick stone bastions, giving the entire place the look of an impregnable fortress, which, indeed, in the day of Cabeza de Vaca, it was.

Some of Santo Domingo's streets were crudely paved with stones, but none of them were cleaned or swept. The residents freely emptied garbage pails and bed pots into them. The only street-cleaning forces were starving half-breed native children, buzzards, dogs and pigs, all of which lived in the gutters. Public latrines were established at strategic places, as they were in Seville, by merely painting crosses on walls. Despite the objections of clerics, the custom was applied to churches, as an accommodation to worshippers, the same as it was to other buildings.

This unattractive and unsanitary condition seemed to interfere not at all with the activities of the affluent, nor did it dampen their enthusiasm for publically displaying both themselves and their finery. A gentleman might be seen with a diamond rose or a cluster of pearls in his hatband. Behind him would trail several black slaves in bright livery with flowers on their bare feet. Gold and silver lace would cover the rustling silks of his lady, and topazes and pearls adorn her fingers, her throat, her ears and hair combs.

It was generally a gay, pleasant and satisfactory life, even if unclean and frequently interrupted by strange and deadly maladies. Personal hygiene was an unknown science, although the Indians had knowledge of a few of its fundamentals. They followed the queer practices of bathing and soaping the hair, but these were customs which remained incomprehensible to the Spanish.

Yet, if the Indians were cleaner than their masters, they were no more immune to sickness. Disease and pestilence traveled both ways on all roads. The Indians were not bothered by tropical fevers, but they were easy prey for syphilis, smallpox, measles and gonorrhea, which the Europeans imported along with their aristocratic airs and their religion.

Oriental magnificence dwelt with squalor. Cabeza de Vaca saw gold glittering in heaps on the gaming tables of Santo Domingo, and he saw beggars in verminous rags in the Cathedral Plaza. He heard the tale of the banquet at which the guests salted their meat with gold dust, and he heard the homeless urchins fighting in the streets for a scrap and a bone. He heard the sweet music of players brought from Spain, and he heard the screams of the tortured in rat-infested dungeons.

As an officer of the King and a gentleman, he dined with

officials, captains and lusty friars on sweetmeats, conserves, veal, beef, fowl, fish, *frijoles, tortillas,* green vegetables, venison, bacon, iguana and porcupine meat, eggs, honey, pineapples, rice, pears, peaches, oranges, lemons, and he drank chocolate and wine. The Indians, the slaves, got the leavings, the garbage, and their liquor was homemade *pulque* and *chicha,* which had a frightful stench.

Cabeza de Vaca had been a toddling child in Jerez de la Frontera on October 12, 1492. It was two o'clock on that morning when a lookout on the tiny caravel *Pinta* caught sight of a white beach shining in the light of a bright moon. Thirty-five years later, when Cabeza de Vaca reached the West Indies, of which that moonlit coral shore was a part, Columbus' "marvel" of the blue Caribbean and all the other islands had lost most of their paradisiacal atmosphere.

The destruction had been completed in that short span of time. Really, it had not taken that long to accomplish the spoilage, for not many moons had passed before the inhabitants were aware that the Spaniards had come from some other place than the sky. Not only the Four Horsemen rode through the mahogany and palm forests and lush valleys. With them sped the specters of torture, desecration, hypocrisy, lust, impiety, licentiousness and greed. The lagoons were mirrors of blood.

There is no surviving documentation to show that Cabeza de Vaca registered a protest at the time against the barbarities of his people. Yet, that he was a man possessed of a pronounced humaneness was to be dramatically demonstrated in later years. He could not have escaped from witnessing countless atrocities, and there is evidence that he understood the sinister aspect of affairs in the New World, recognizing the unsoundness and precariousness of economic and social structures built upon nothing more substantial than the bones of the conquered. Perhaps the heavy responsibilities of his post, the shortness of his first stay in

Santo Domingo, the ordeals which the expedition encountered in the beginning, were factors which contributed to his *official* silence. His voice was to be heard.

The Spaniards had not found the kind of people they had expected to meet as they progressed through the islands. They did not see even one man with a long tail, nor did they come upon one with a single eye in the center of his forehead. They looked in vain for the Amazons, although Columbus did report seeing three mermaids, which were not as beautiful as commonly painted, and which disappointed him.

The cinnamon-colored Arawaks who came from the dank green forests on the larger islands to greet the incredible strangers with gifts of value and gestures of friendship were ordinary Mongoloids. They wore no clothes. Some of them were cannibals. Their faces were gross and hideous, their nostrils large and distended. Their foreheads were low. Their bodies were hairless. Their teeth were dirty and black. Their eyes were fierce and protruding. As infants their heads had been flattened by their mothers with the pressure of hands or by the use of small boards. Their skulls were so thick that Spanish swords often broke over them.

The only other people encountered were the Caribs, fewer in number and comparative newcomers to the area. In contrast to the Arawaks, who were sedentary, the Caribs were travelers and raiders who had migrated northward and had captured some smaller islands, mostly in the Lesser Antilles.

The Caribs were the best physical specimens, but no less primitive. They were handsome, of medium stature, and given to habitual smiling. Most of them displayed extremely white teeth. Their skin was an olive shade. Their noses were flat, crushed by their mothers during the suckling period. A wide flat nose was considered a mark of beauty. They were lovers of cleanliness, bathing thoroughly every day. The Carib women wore a small apron called a *gueyu* suspended from strings tied about the waist.

Dressing for a feast or a dance, both sexes painted themselves in wild patterns of various colors. The men shaved parts of their heads, leaving other parts covered with long tufts of hair. These weird adornments, which signified individual distinction and wealth, were in the eyes of the Spanish not only ridiculous but indicative of an inherent madness.

It was as much a strain on the mental processes of the invaders to think of the islanders as belonging to Homo sapiens as it was for the Indians to believe their own eyes and ears when confronted with their resplendent visitors. They could do no more than stare in terror and awe at the horses, the shining breastplates, the tasseled lances, swords and crossbows. They shook violently when the guns talked. Great Lombards which hurled twenty-five pounds of iron to shred big trees, muskets, firelocks, harquebuses, falconets, were weapons that only gods could conceive, and were beyond the powers of mortals to create.

In the ingrained view of the Spaniards, all the natives were heathens and undeserving of any kindness or consideration. Certainly there could be no friendship between Christians and such pagans.

Not only were the Spaniards consumed by the blind bigotry which had been instilled in them by long religious wars, but they had no curiosity. They had not come to study scientific subjects, to observe the habits, mores and physiognomy of an ignorant, primordial race. They had come for one thing alone: gold.

So the slaughter began. And the timorous, artless, jungle primitives helplessly watched their wives being raped by gangs of armed soldiers, their children held aloft on spears, their homes and meager possessions being destroyed, their gods being desecrated.

Those who were permitted to survive for a time were robbed, enslaved and baptized, whether they accepted Christianity or not. Most of them accepted it. They would have accepted any creed if it would have alleviated their suffering.

But this was not the case. The God of the conquerors brought them no succor. In the end, with all hope gone, and unable to endure longer the brutality, they took their own lives. They cut out their own hearts. They hung themselves together, by tens, by scores. Whole families died at one time, in some villages thirty, forty or fifty of them in a single day.

Of the two hundred and fifty thousand Tainos who lived on Española when it was discovered, less than thirty thousand were alive twenty years later. Soon after that they were extinct.

The padres, comparatively few in number at first, were swept aside by the vicious onslaughts. They saw their own reward chiefly in the saving of souls, but opportunities to carry on that commendable work swiftly decreased. Their parishioners were mostly corpses.

Columbus had taken for granted the enslavement of the Indians, although assertively opposed to unnecessarily cruel treatment of them. Most of the clergy took a similar position. It was a padre, Bartolemé de las Casas, who advocated increasing the importation of Africans to halt the wanton destruction of the island natives and at the same time relieve the critical labor shortage on Española. The good man was to regret making the proposal when he saw the misery and suffering of the blacks.

However, if the padres opposed the inhuman treatment, they recorded few official protests against the *encomienda,* a semifeudal institution which made medieval serfs of both the red and black people caught in its net.

Each native was obliged to pay tribute to the Crown. It was Columbus, as the first governor of Española, who authorized the acceptance of labor in lieu of gold dust. As most Indians were paupers, having been robbed of what little they might have owned, they were forced to surrender to the *encomienda,* or be tortured.

In the beginning the Spanish Crown had looked upon this arrangement as a means of acquiring the labor needed in mines and plantations, and thereby contributing to the desired economic development of its colonial empire. Laws were enacted to force the *encomienderos,* or proprietors and contractors, to pay their workers wages, once the annual tribute had been earned. The Indians so employed also were to be considered free men, and were to be treated with justice.

As it turned out, theory had nothing in common with actual practice. The laws were ignored. The Indians were forced to labor for nothing, lashed if they complained, killed if they made bold demands, and thoroughly exploited in every way.

Mostly the system contributed, not to the government, but to the wealth of the *encomienderos,* and only misery and death were the rewards of the unfortunate captives. Royal officials, towns, and the Church itself established profitable *encomiendas.* In some places the priests ruled over enormous holdings and hundreds of slaves.

Cruelty and the incorporation of slavery were no more innovations of the Spaniard in the Indies than his disdain for work was a new development in his character. He had practiced both for centuries, and his church had sanctioned both. The religious laws of Christian Spain prescribed terrible penalties for heretics, even for minor violations of the papal creed. It was an approved custom to mount the heads of Moors on saddle bows or poles, and toss them to boys in village streets for playthings. The bodies of Moorish children were thrown onto church steps to be torn apart and eaten by scavenging dogs.

The Spaniard was merciless to the infidel because he had been made to believe that his Lord commanded him to pursue such a course. When he reached the Indies, he had only a short time before been victorious in a terrible religious war with the Moslem, and he was fanatical, wholly unwilling to tolerate beliefs differing from his own. Being an ascetic who knew the pain of flagellation, he had no hesitancy in torturing others.

His cruelty was entangled in his religion, and in the oppressive environment of the tropics, under the pressure of an inordinate surge of greed, that cruelty opened the gates to sadism, immorality and wantonness.

He crucified thirteen Indians in a row in honor of Christ and His Apostles, and slowly killed them with sword pricks. He held the natives to be bestial, with no standing in the eyes of God, and so he beat them and slashed their flesh and murdered them. He considered Indian girls unchaste, so he raped them and forced them into prostitution, and if they produced half-breed children, he let the spawn run loose like packs of hungry mongrels.

He burned a hundred men alive in a single thatched council house because they distrusted his offer of friendship. Condemned for the terrible deed by a priest, he cried:

"Oh Father, you know they are only savages and have no souls."

He worked the bestial people until their strength failed and they fell in agonized death. Then he demanded more slaves to replace the fallen, and the raiders brought them from newly discovered islands. They, too, were starved and worked and, when useless, thrown into unmarked graves.

Father las Casas, who found the time while he struggled

to protect the Indians to write very good histories, told of a frenzied *cacique,* or chief, pleading with his people:

> *We must get rid of the Spanish God!*
> *I know him.*
> *His name is Gold!*
> *He is more powerful than any other god.*
> *Wherever the Spaniards go, they seek him, and it is useless to hide it, for they have marvelous ways to find it.*
> *If you swallow it, they will disembowel you for it.*
> *The bottom of the sea is the only place they will not go for it.*
> *When we have no more gold, they will leave us alone.*

The chief and his desperate people threw what little gold they owned into the sea. Hearing of their act, the Spaniard caught them and burned them alive.

As the chief was put to the stake, a padre pleaded with him to accept Christ, so that he might be received into heaven.

The chief refused, answering, "If that is where the Spanish Christians go, I have no wish to see it."

The curtain had risen.

Spain, a poor and infertile country, in less than half a lifetime had achieved a position of incomparable wealth and prosperity. With its monopoly of the seemingly inexhaustible gold and silver and the rich bounties of limitless forests and fields in the new Western Hemisphere, it dominated the world.

If the *conquistadores* could not know with certainty that even more great discoveries were to be made, they had every reason to believe that time, in its own inexorable way, would bring them.

Panfilo de Narvaez, Cabeza de Vaca, and all the others—either noble and accomplished, or common and ignorant—who were members of their expedition justifiably could hold such a conviction.

They looked northward, where there was nothing but

darkness, an immense unknown void. What that void held
for them they could do no more than imagine or surmise,
but hopes demanded no premium, and no penalty was ex-
acted for secret dreams.

2

Panfilo de Narvaez was tall, courtly, proud and well-
mannered. His complexion was fair. His beard resembled
curled copper wire. He had a voice that was deep and
resonant, and in moments of anger it sounded as if it came
out of a cave. He had lost an eye in a fight with Cortez in
Mexico, and he wore a silk patch over the empty socket.
After that misfortune, his surviving orb had developed a
fierce and penetrating gleam.

He was an old hand in the Indies when he brought his
expedition into Santo Domingo, having spent more than
twenty years in His Majesty's service. Mines, lands, con-
cessions and privileges awarded him for his victorious
campaigns against the Indians had made him wealthy. Still
in his forties in 1527, he might have enjoyed years of splendor and ease. He might have returned to Spain and lived in
Seville or Valladolid, his birthplace, with a large retinue of
Indian and Negro slaves to serve him. Or he might have
lived in luxury on his expansive and beautiful Cuban estate.

Neither of these possibilities appealed to him. He was too
much of an adventurer to be satisfied with a sedentary life,
no matter how comfortable, how affluent, it might be. The
fever of conquest still burned in him as it did when he first
sailed westward. He could no more rest on his laurels than
he could stifle his dreams.

The dreams had come to dominate both his thinking and his actions. They were born of two sources. One was geographical. Rather, it was an unknown quantity in the geography of the western world, a kingdom above the peninsula of Florida into which no European had ventured. He was the new governor of that kingdom.

The second source of his dreams was his own greed. He was rich, yet his greatest desire—actually an obsession—was to acquire more gold, more jewels, more of everything that had monetary value. This craving was complicated by a marked penuriousness. He was a celebrated pinch-penny.

Narvaez's reputation as a competent and thorough campaigner was established by 1510, at which time he was an officer in Jamaica. Competency in his case was more the result of superior fire power—guns against sharpened reeds and arrows—than it was the product of military genius.

He was mentally alert, but there was a clearly discernible limit to his intelligence. He also was excessively bullheaded and lacking in compassion. As to his thoroughness, its cornerstone was the belief that the best way to pacify a province was to destroy the inhabitants. Certainly it was the simplest way.

He had adhered to this conviction as the lieutenant of Juan de Esquivel in the subduing of Jamaica, winning wide acclaim as one of the best butchers among the *conquistadores*.

This valorous conduct brought a promotion. He was made field commander of the forthcoming Cuban campaign, which gave promise of presenting extremely difficult problems.

Besides the fact that it was an immense island, some seven hundred miles long, very little was known about Cuba in 1511, although nearly twenty years had passed since its discovery.

Diego Velasquez, a wealthy gentleman who had been a

close friend of Columbus, was given the task of bringing it into the economic sphere of the Spanish Empire. This required the dispatch of a strong expeditionary force, and Velasquez was neither much interested nor very efficient in military operations. He placed that phase of the project under the direction of Narvaez, and gave his attention to the establishment of towns, ports, *encomiendas* and mines, all undertakings more to his liking.

As far as being a good job of work, the reduction of Cuba was unsurpassed. Landing on the southeastern shore, the invaders moved steadily westward, leaving in their wake wide areas of devastation, burned villages and dead natives.

That Narvaez was both a man of courage and a good student of his enemies was demonstrated early in the invasion, when seven thousand Indians gathered at one place in the jungle and launched a night attack on the Spanish encampment.

Clad only in his nightshirt, Narvaez mounted his horse when the alarm sounded. He was unarmed, but he carried a set of cowbells. Charging directly into the advancing Indians, he waved the bells wildly over his head. The attackers, terrified by the clamor, fled in mad confusion. Narvaez went back to bed.

The advance continued. One evening the force came upon a large village with nearly three thousand inhabitants. They offered the Spaniards *casava* bread and fish. During the meal a soldier suddenly drew his sword and ran it through an Indian. At once, as if by a silent command, the others began a vicious attack on the helpless villagers.

Father las Casas, who was present, reported that within a few minutes not a person, young or old, was left alive. During the terrible slaughter, las Casas saw Narvaez calmly sitting on his horse, as if he "were made of marble."

Narvaez called out to the priest: "And what does your worship think of what our Spaniards have done?"

In fury las Casas answered: "I offer them and you too to the devil!"

Governor Velasquez had taken with him to Cuba as his private secretary a young man of good education named Hernando Cortez. In time he made him an *alcalde*. Differences over personal affairs and policies developed between them, but the breach was not critical enough to prevent Velasquez from appointing Cortez to head an expedition to conquer Mexico in 1518. It was still a land unpenetrated to any extent, but scouts Velasquez had sent out from Cuba previously had made landings, and their discoveries served to bring it under his domination.

Cortez stuck a plume in his bonnet, and set sail with a formidable force of eleven vessels and more than five hundred soldiers. He had no more than feasted his eys on the fabulous riches of the Mayas and Aztecs before ambition overcame him.

He decided to establish a new colony, ignore Velasquez, and make himself a captain-general and a *justicia-mayor*. In such a capacity he would be required to report only to the court in Spain.

Intelligence which reached Velasquez in Cuba in 1520 concerning the brash activities and ambitions of Cortez infuriated him. Cortez was not only defying his authority and disobeying his orders, but was getting rich on Mexican plunder. His former secretary had to be stopped, and Velasquez could think of no better man for the job than Narvaez.

With twice as many men as had accompanied Cortez, Narvaez reached San Juan de Ulea in April, 1520. It wasn't long before he realized he had met his match.

The emissaries he dispatched to Cortez with an order to surrender were courteously received, given gifts of gold, and informed that fortune awaited any of Narvaez's men who cared to transfer their allegiance. The strategy was highly successful. When Narvaez's soldiers contrasted his stinginess with the generosity of Cortez, the matter of loyalty was quickly settled.

Convinced that Narvaez's troops would not oppose him, Cortez struck in the night. He was correct. Only a handful of faithful followers stood with Narvaez. He led them in a stubborn defense for a short time, then was forced to take refuge on a native sacrificial pyramid. Suddenly his hollow voice was heard crying out in the darkness:

"Holy Mary protect me!"

He had been blinded in one eye. Death for him and the few loyal soldiers remaining was imminent.

Cortez stopped the fight. He took over Narvaez's command, clapped him in jail, and held him for two years.

According to contemporary accounts, when Narvaez was released he fell on his knees and would have kissed the hand of Cortez had he been permitted to do it. Cortez merely embraced him, and offered him a chair.

The story does not seem to be in accord with Narvaez's character. Whatever the case, Cortez presented Narvaez with a pouch of gold pesos, and sent him home.

During his absence from Cuba, Narvaez's wife, Maria de la Valensuela, had been doing quite well there by herself. She had been diligent and thrifty in operating his properties, exploiting his Indian slaves in the manner of a ruthless *encomiendero*, and she presented him with a small fortune as the fruit of her industry.

Narvaez was pleased but not much impressed. The uncountable gold, silver and precious stones he had seen in Mexico had created an uncontrollable lust in him. Life in Cuba, even on a grand scale, now seemed like a grubby and unprofitable existence.

Tortured by dreams of amassing wealth to surpass that of Cortez, and occupied by illusions of himself as the governor of domains so vast that Mexico would appear as a dooryard, he managed to grace his wife's life for a year, but at the end of that time he could contain himself no longer. He sailed away to Spain, hoping to have an audience with the king, and to be rewarded for his long and faithful service to the Crown.

It so happened that at the time the Council of the Indies, which in fact was supreme ruler of the colonies, was investigating the activities of Cortez. Narvaez was happy to co-operate as a witness for the prosecution. His appearance before the council not only afforded him an opportunity to discredit and malign Cortez, but gave him a chance to present an account of his ignominious defeat in Mexico that was highly favorable to himself. Also, it so happened that since the debacle in which Ponce de León had been mortally wounded, no further attempts had been made to settle Florida. Juan Ponce de León had sailed along both coasts of the peninsula in 1513. He had received bitter receptions from the Indians, but had departed with a head full of dreams intact. Not the least of them, according to legend, involved a fountain of eternal youth, believed to be somewhere in the unexplored jungles. By 1521, he had obtained a royal patent which made him governor and gave him the right to colonize the vague province to which, on Easter Sunday eight years before, he had given the name Feast of Flowers. He went back, but the Indians were as unfriendly as they had previously been. He was driven into the sea, soon to succumb to his wounds.

The office of Governor of Florida remained unfilled until in 1526 Narvaez, undaunted by the experiences of Ponce de León, and filled with dreams even more fantastic than those which had stirred the man of the lion's heart, set out to secure the highly promising post for himself.

Narvaez's petition to the king contained strong inducements. For one thing, he was rich enough to finance the conquest with his own money. For another, his record was evidence of his extraordinary experiences, personal courage, honesty, and ability as a field general.

How good an impression Narvaez really made at court cannot be determined. If the king held a personal dislike for him—and that may have been true—it was offset by his financial standing, and the references he presented removed responsibility from the royal shoulders. The fact seems indisputable that rewarding Narvaez with the governorship of Florida cost King Charles V, who was given to keeping a close watch on the Spanish purse, little or nothing.

The historian Oviedo clearly pointed out that such seemingly magnanimous appointments were notoriously inexpensive: "The prince may be deceived like the poor vulture, and I have noticed one thing that is not to be forgotten: and that is that Their Majesties almost never put their property or money into these new discoveries, but only paper and fine words, and they say to those captains: 'If you should do what you say, we will do this or that,' or 'our gratitude will be given you.' And they give him the title of *adelantado* or governor, with license and authorization to go wherever it may be by grant with those who from ignorance will accompany him with their persons or goods, taken by the sweet smell of his false nobilities."

Oviedo, the irrepressible, made other forceful and pointed comments concerning the petitioning of the Spanish court for a governorship or permission to launch a new conquest, and he cited Narvaez as a specific example of petitioners whose motives were frequently deceptive. Educated at the court of Ferdinand and Isabella, Gonzalo Fernández de Oviedo y Valdés was a fiery patriot. In 1523 he was appointed Historiographer of the Indies and went to Santo Domingo. Altogether he made six journeys across the sea to the New World. His patriotic bias, however, was too obvious to be misleading, and the historical narratives he wrote were both trustworthy and interesting.

A man of reputation and importance from the Indies who sought royal favors, said Oviedo, "utters a flood of promises among those who know nothing of it, and all those who listen to him think that he knows and has seen and has visited and explored everything there is out there . . . these loud speakers don't fail to talk in such a way about everything. And the ignorant people, hearing them, imagine . . . the Indies must be like . . . Portugal or Navarre, or at least a compact and narrow country, wherein every inhabitant knows everybody else and can communicate with the same ease as from Cordova to Granada.

"Thus, letters arrive [in the Indies] from ignorant mothers and wives seeking and writing to their sons and husbands . . . and they are addressed thus: 'To my beloved son Pedro Rodriguez, in the Indies,' which is like saying, 'To my son Mahomet, in Africa,' . . . which is as good as saying, 'In the next world.' . . . many people come to these Indies just as benighted as those who addressed the letters I spoke of, not knowing or understanding whither they are bound. And Narvaez caught plenty of them . . . because the poverty of some and the greed of others and the craziness of nearly all doesn't let them realize what they are doing."

Oviedo made no effort to conceal his contempt for the methods employed by promoters like Narvaez. "The organizer . . . comes to Seville with less money than he would like. He sends out a drummer and a couple of friars or a few priests, who join him under color of the conversion of the Indians, and go here and there upsetting people's minds and promising riches that they know nothing about."

While the victims were being lured into joining the company, the promoter was busy borrowing money and buying ships which Oviedo declared were "old and worn out," and which had reached port only "by the grace of God and double pumping."

Once they had sailed away again, these dilapidated hulls would never "bring back to Castile a report of the cargo [human or other kinds] they had carried out."

Speaking of Narvaez as well as other ambitious captains, Oviedo had this to say: "He sends out a young man who is appointed his 'secretary,' and who has never learned what a 'secret' is, with other cunning and smooth-tongued fellows, the best schemers the captain knows, who know how to talk over the poor volunteers and persuade them to two things:

"First, to lend the captain money on the vain hopes they are promised, and on a receipt which the recipient thinks to be like a bank note. Thus, the poor volunteer gives up the little money that is left him, and if the trap is well sprung, he will sell his cape and his doublet and go in his shirt like Guillote, because he thinks that when he comes to the tropics he will be finely dressed . . .

"The other thing is that . . . volunteers . . . shall obligate themselves . . . to pay each one at a certain time ten or twelve ducats or pesos of gold for their food and transport . . . but what they get can only be told by . . . dupes who have returned to Spain, and they are few . . . the voyage is long and life is short . . . most of those who come there . . . never return."

In Santo Domingo the cynical and wise Oviedo admonished a group of young men who had just arrived from Spain with these words: "Don't say that you come to the Indies to serve the king and to employ your person and your time like valorous gentlemen, since you know that the truth is just the contrary, that you come only with the desire to get more wealth than your father and your neighbors."

In view of what was to occur within two years, some of the provisions in the patent given to Narvaez in 1526 are worthy of note. Also, they illustrate the humaneness of

Charles V, and make apparent his strenuous efforts to establish sound economic and beneficial social structures in the Spanish colonies.

The northern boundary of the territory over which Narvaez had jurisdiction could not be delineated, simply because no one knew where it might be. Its southern extent was easier to define. It was the shore of the Gulf of Mexico, all the way from the Florida Keys to the River de las Palmas, about a hundred miles north of the present city of Tampico.

Narvaez was commanded to establish at least two permanent settlements, with no less than a hundred men in each, and to build three forts. His annual salary was two hundred and fifty thousand *maravedis,* about $1,000, but this was an insignificant feature. He was to receive four per cent of the tax levies, and in a rich and prosperous colony—which of course Florida would soon be—that would be a fairly tidy sum. There was nothing in the document to prevent him from establishing his own systems of graft.

He was to select a private estate for himself and his family twenty-six miles square, more than four hundred thousand acres. This would provide him with enough land to assure a large supply of meat, grains and vegetables for his table, and for export; vineyards and orchards; shooting grounds and gardens; and other requisites of a man of such high station. Another, and very important, special privilege gave him the authority to make slaves of rebellious Indians.

The word rebellious was underscored. The warrant sternly admonished him to be considerate of the rights of natives. Cruelties which were known to have been practiced in some other colonies were vigorously denounced and forbidden in Florida.

Any brutality reported was to be investigated by the Council of the Indies, and the perpetrators were to be punished. Obedient natives were to be treated as free men, and were not to be forced into slavery or made to labor against their will, as long as they paid their annual tribute to the Crown.

Clerics were ordered to be present at all times to protect the Indians from mistreatment at the hands of unscrupulous civil or military authorities. There was to be no forced barter. War was not to be declared against the natives without the consent of the clergy. Free Indians were to be paid wages, and only with the permission of a padre could they be assigned as an *encomienda*.

The sovereign's intentions were commendable, but he had never been to the Indies. Narvaez was an insular veteran, and no man held a better understanding of the way of things in those remote lands. If he did not look with approval on some of the patent's provisions, the objections remained unregistered.

He willingly affixed his signature to the documents, and set out to recruit a private army, hire craftsmen, purchase ships and supplies, and complete the plans for the expedition.

He must have smiled as he considered the king's naïveté and the government's ignorance, and his one eagle eye must have shone with an especially bright gleam of cunning satisfaction.

3

The family of Alvar Nuñez de Vera Cabeza de Vaca was prominent rather than distinguished. Neither on the side of his father nor that of his mother had an event occurred which gave the clan the mark of an illustrious house. Until he himself became famous, the greatest honor bestowed on

any of the family branches came through a royal command
which changed the name of his mother's ancestors.

The incident is important only in that it throws light and
shadow on the character of the one Cabeza de Vaca who was
to win for that name a secure place among the greatest explorers and trail-breakers in the history of the New World.
Had it not been for his incomparable feats, the origin of the
name Cow's Head would have remained a minor legend in
the voluminous chronicles of Spanish wars.

It happened this way:

In July 1212, the Christian Army of the King of Navarre,
pressing southward against the Moors, reached the Sierra
Morena, north of Seville. The heathens had taken up strong
positions in force on the mountain slopes, and a direct assault on them would have been suicidal. Patrols found no
opening into which an advance might have been attempted,
until they came upon a shepherd whose name was Martin
Alhaja.

Alhaja informed them there was a little-known pass
through the mountains near-by, and he offered to direct the
king and his men into it. He had marked the entrance with
the skull of a cow.

The route allowed the Christians to pass through the barrier unmolested, and the decisive battle of Las Navas de
Tolosa followed. Not only were the Moors defeated, but the
engagement marked a turning point in the Reconquest.

A few ducats probably would have been more appreciated
by Martin Alhaja as a reward for his services than the one
he received. Having no say in the matter, however, he was
obliged to submit to having his surname changed by the
grateful King of Navarre from *Jewel* to *Cow's Head*.

Pride in the honor remained strong through generations
of Cabeza de Vacas. If anything, it seemed to increase with
the passage of three centuries, and it appeared to burn with
a bright flame especially in the heart of the boy Alvar.

On the side of his mother, Teresa Cabeza de Vaca, some of his forebears had risen from lowly rustic pursuits to positions of political and commercial rank. Among these were the builder of the Jerez de la Frontera wall; a captain of that city's fleet; an *alférez mayor* of Navarre, and a Grand Master of the Order of Santiago.

His paternal ancestors achieved equal local prominence, but far more notoriety. They included a councilman of Jerez, a prison warden, a First Lord of Cadiz, and a *Caballero* of the Golden Scarf, but no notable monuments marked their earthly paths. Whatever their accomplishments, they were outshone by the tempestuous careers of his grandfather, Pedro de Vera, and his Uncle Hernando.

Pedro de Vera conquered the Canary Islands for Spain near the close of the fifteenth century. If coming events cast their shadows before them, the subjugation was an accurate depiction of many conquests to take place a few years later in a far-off western world then unknown.

Pedro de Vera was fearless, sadistic and without conscience. While serving as a courtier of Henry IV, he tore out the tongue of a critic of the king with his bare hand, and threw it to a crowd of noble spectators. This fiendish act he considered proof of his loyalty to his sovereign.

He fought the Moslems for Ferdinand and Isabella, until his extracurricular brawling became insupportable. With the hope of quelling his turbulence, and at the same time using his talents to better advantage, the king and queen suggested he conquer the Canaries for the Empire, and become the first governor of those islands.

Though he was obliged to pay the cost himself, Pedro de Vera welcomed the opportunity to lead a major campaign and secure such a high and lucrative post. He sailed away in 1480, landed on the Grand Canary, most populous of the seven islands, and soon demonstrated that he had embarked on an undertaking for which he was well suited, that of torturing and destroying a simple and helpless people.

The Canaries were inhabited by descendents of the ancient Numidians of the Carthaginian Empire, but probably ten centuries had passed since they had fled their homeland. Isolation and a new way of life had buried their original culture beyond the reach of memory. They wore skins and palm leaves, plowed the earth with goat horns, and worshipped the image of a naked woman.

Pedro de Vera found the taking of the islands considerably more difficult than he had anticipated. He captured the native chief, pierced him with a lance, and appointed himself godfather of the dying man as a priest baptized him. Despite this loss, the Guanches refused to capitulate. Like most savage people, however, the structure of the Canary Islanders' unity was weakened by serious factional quarrels. De Vera took advantage of the circumstances, and played the cards as they fell into his hand.

With the conquest going badly for him, he called for a cessation of hostilities, and with that accomplished he offered to aid the Grand Canary natives in an attack against their political and religious adversaries on the mountainous island of Teneriffe. He swore before them on holy bread that he would lead them to victory and lift them to a place of dominance over all the people of the islands.

The offer was irresistible, and the best fighting men of the Grand Canary boarded de Vera's ships. He quickly locked them below decks and sent them off to Seville and a miserable life of slavery.

Guilt for this deception weighed not at all on him, for the holy bread on which he had sworn had not actually been consecrated by a priest. Therefore, the promise he had made was void, and his absolution was assured.

More disconcerting was his pressing need for funds. To relieve this condition, at least temporarily, he pawned his two sons, Hernando and Francisco, to a wealthy Moor as security for some supplies.

Proceeding in his conquering under more favorable conditions, he moved to the island of Gomera. There he engaged in the pastime of pulling the legs off all males over the age of fifteen with horses, and selling the women as prostitutes and slaves. This put more money in his purse, and helped to pay off the debt for his sons.

When a priest protested the enormities, he commanded him to hold his tongue under pain of having a red-hot metal skull cap clapped on his head. The padre was silenced, but only until he could get to Spain and secure an audience with the king and queen. He told a story which appalled them, and Pedro de Vera was recalled.

He was assigned once more to fighting the Moors. When this conflict was concluded in 1492, he was restored to the governorship of the islands, but he did not return to them. Pedro de Vera's strength at last was failing him. He remained in Jerez, and there, in 1500, he died.

While Don Pedro had been off spilling blood in the Canaries, Cabeza de Vaca's Uncle Hernando, having been pawned and redeemed, was enjoying some interesting if less glamourous adventures. He was gifted as a poet, and he employed his pen as ruthlessly as his father did the sword.

Uncle Hernando wrote some verses anonymously about King Ferdinand and Queen Isabella. They were not preserved for posterity, but there appears to be no question that they would have been more appropriate for the wall of a *retrete publico* than for parlor recitals.

The king and queen were not amused, and dispatched agents to apprehend the literary culprit. Uncle Hernando deemed it wise to move his residence. He took refuge for a time with a lady friend, found out she was scheming to betray him to ingratiate herself with the queen, and vanished into parts unknown.

Failing to track down their quarry, the monarchs held the entire city of Jerez, the scene of the crime, responsible. The lieutenant of the city was beheaded in the plaza, and several prominent civic leaders were banished into exile.

Some time later, Pedro de Vera managed to obtain a pardon for his son. Uncle Hernando was sent away for safekeeping to Barbary, and there he died, presumably comforted little by his literary talent.

The other son of Don Pedro, also freed from the bonds of his pawnage, was the father of Cabeza de Vaca. Francisco de Vera did not make much of a name for himself. His greatest, if not his only, claim to distinction was a never-ending clash with the government. He was something of a political renegade, objected violently to whatever new laws were enacted, and resisted all forms of authority. At one time he was condemned to lose his property for contumacy, although the decree was not enforced. He died in 1512.

Alvar Nuñez de Vera Cabeza de Vaca was born in Jerez de la Frontera about 1490. Neither the exact year nor the day of his birth is known. No vital statistics were kept in Jerez until a hundred years later.

He was the eldest of four children, and he was named by his mother for his great-great-grandfather Alvar Nuñez, once the captain of the city's fleet. His mother died when her three sons and one daughter were still young. His father married a second time, and the children were placed in *curatela*, a kind of guardianship.

Even as a youth, Alvar chose to call himself simply Cabeza de Vaca, and it was by that name he was popularly known throughout his life. Whether this preference for the matronymic name sprang from an antipathy to his difficult father, or was alone the result of inherent pride, cannot be determined. In view of later incidents, the latter seems to be the most logical reason for the choice.

Little that has been authenticated about Cabeza de Vaca's

early life has come to light, but despite the lack of biographical details some of the influences which were brought to bear on him are apparent.

He was only about ten when his grandfather died. At least until that time the household was served by numerous Guanche slaves. He heard their songs of the islands, their nostalgic tales of the great mountains that rose from the sea to the clouds, and he knew their loneliness and heartache. The fierce old warrior regaled him with blood-chilling stories of the conquest, most of which undoubtedly contained morals proclaiming the slaughter of heathens to be holy and righteous, which excoriated compassion, and which condemned those who failed to show a scorn for death.

Warfare, religious intolerance and conquest were subjects as much a part of his education as the writing and fundamental mathematics he was taught. He was a diligent and attentive student. His rapid progress and the posts he secured as a young man attest to the high level of his intellect. He was physically strong, and in his nature were an enthusiasm shaded by cautiousness, a geniality, a courteous manner, and a courage which appeared to be unadulterated.

As a boy he was frequently in Cadiz and Seville, in both of which relatives of the de Veras and the Cabeza de Vacas resided. There is reason to believe he was inspired by the sight of Columbus passing in the streets. He saw American Indians being trained as interpreters (those enslaved in Spain did not live long) and watched them playing their curious game of *pelota.*

He hurried with hundreds of others to the docks along the Guadalquivir when vessels arrived from the Indies, gazing in fascination at their strange cargoes of painted savages, parrots, lizards, animals and plants. He tasted pineapples and sweet potatoes, and he watched the drays carting off heavy loads of gold and silver bars to the Crown treasury.

It was an exciting time. Spain was growing fabulously

rich. The nation's commercial tentacles continuously reached farther out, gaining a stranglehold on the world's trade. Young men were set to studying the swiftly advancing sciences of cartography and navigation. Books were being written in great numbers, and, what was more, were being widely read. Intelligent youths were encouraged to acquire knowledge of painting, design, architecture and alchemy.

Unfailingly the pursuit of culture and science, at least for a great many persons, was interrupted by war. It came with the regularity and certainty of taxes. In 1511, Cabeza de Vaca was recruited for service with the troops dispatched by Ferdinand to Italy in response to an appeal from Pope Julius II.

He fought at Bologna and Ferrara against the French invaders. Although badly hurt, he survived the terrible battle of Ravenna, in which twenty thousand men died and the Spanish were driven from the field. Gallantry in action won him a lieutenant's bars, and he was stationed in an administrative post in Gaeta, near Naples.

A handsome young officer who might, if prevailed upon, display his scars, Cabeza de Vaca returned to Seville at the end of three years' service. He married a young lady of whom nothing is known and whose name has been forgotten. Through the influence of friends, possibly those of his wife, he obtained a position as *camarero* to the Duke of Medina Sidonia. In this capacity he was required to serve both as a steward and a soldier, but military actions occupied more of his time than the work of a gentleman aide.

He rendered valuable service in throttling rebel factions which opposed new financial decrees imposed by Charles V. During the ensuing years, under the duke's banner, he fought the *Comuneros* at Tordesillas and Villalar, and the French in Navarre. Holding the confidence of his employer, he was frequently entrusted with missions which brought him in touch with members of the king's court. These were fateful assignments.

He came to know distinguished *conquistadores* back from the Indies and living in splendor on the returns from their slave trading and gold finds. He met Magellan, who soon was to embark on the greatest voyage of discovery in all history. Most important of all, he met Panfilo de Narvaez, and heard about the proposed conquest of the unknown province of Florida.

Cabeza de Vaca was tall, slender, and had the bearing of a gentleman, but it is doubtful if his good appearance had much to do with securing for him the appointment as treasurer of the Narvaez Expedition. The King and his close advisers were not swayed as much by an applicant's looks or size as they were by his ability to perform required duties with honesty, dispatch and thoroughness.

As far as the king himself was concerned, the position of treasurer was the most important one in any expedition. The treasurer was responsible for collecting the king's five per cent of all discoveries of intrinsic value, such as gold, jewels and other minerals, and only a man of established sobriety, diligence and integrity, and whose arithmetic was without fault, was acceptable.

In addition, it was the duty of the treasurer to collect rent on salt works and other establishments, duty on imports from Spain, and income due the court from fields and livestock. He also was obliged to pay the salaries of officers, and devote himself, when he had time, to subduing recalcitrant savages and helping to build a prosperous colony.

That is not all he had to do. He was required to submit regular reports telling how efficiently and obediently all royal commands were being carried out. The reports had to recite in detail the extent to which the Lord was being served.

For the privilege of assuming these arduous tasks, he was obligated to post a bond of two thousand ducats.

Perhaps as further assurance that Cabeza de Vaca would have adequate authority to carry out his work without interference, he was made provost marshal, which placed him in charge of military discipline.

Under the law, the king had the prerogative of accepting or rejecting any priest assigned to the Indies by the church. It is particularly significant in this case, as well, that in addition to appointing the treasurer, the king also exercised his right to name the other chief officials who would accompany Governor Narvaez.

Father Juan Xuarez was accepted as the leader of the five Franciscans who would sail with the expedition. He also was made commissary. Father Xuarez already had seen service in the New World, and had been for a time with Cortez in Mexico. He was highly intelligent, his record was illustrious, his devoutness unqualified, and his experience invaluable. The king considered him a distinct asset.

Alonso Enrriquez was made comptroller, and Alonso de Solis was given the post of assessor. Both were efficient and trustworthy men. With Cabeza de Vaca and Father Xuarez they completed a staff which warranted the king's faith.

What adventures lay in store for these loyal officers, and what bearing their acts would have on the course of history, then were locked in the impregnable vault of fate, but these secrets soon were to be disclosed.

Not all members of expeditions to the Indies were chosen with such thought and care, or were as politically well-informed, educated and trained. Stupid nephews of cardinals and the illegitimate offspring of ladies-in-waiting frequently were got rid of in this manner.

Narvaez acquired five ships. While they were being loaded in Sanlúcar de Barrameda, at the mouth of the Guadalquivir, Cabeza de Vaca paid a last visit to his home town, Jerez de la Frontera, which was hardly more than fifteen miles away to the southwest.

He said farewell to his family and friends, visited his childhood home, his school, and strolled through the old streets in which he had played as a youth.

He knelt in the ancient chapel, where his mother had carried him as an infant, and he asked for God's protection and guidance.

Then he returned to Sanlúcar to begin his long journey into darkness.

4
—

The five creaking vessels left Sanlúcar on June 17, 1527.

Into them were crammed more than six hundred men, at least ten wives, and an unknown number of Andalusian horses, hunting dogs, goats, swine, sheep, cattle and sea-going rats.

The two months' trip across the Atlantic was nothing less than a constant nightmare. In each of the leaky, little ships, none of which exceeded a hundred tons burthen, some one hundred and twenty men were crowded together, with no more space to move about than the penned livestock.

Even in comparatively calm seas, the stubby, clumsy caravels pitched and rolled tremendously. A victim of seasickness had no choice but to vomit where he stood or sat, usually over himself and those packed against him, for it was quite unlikely he would have a chance to reach the lee rail, even if he had the strength to do so.

Any attempt at cleanliness was futile. Any form of sanitation was inconsequential. Neither water sloshed from buckets, nor seas surging over the rails, were very efficient sewage disposal systems. They did help to alleviate some odors temporarily, but the vermin were not affected by these spasmodic showers, and throve with increasing immunity to all assaults. Bilge rats stood at bay like wild boars.

The penuriousness of Narvaez, so well known in the Indies, soon made itself felt on shipboard. He had been niggardly in purchasing supplies. Food was not only inadequate but of poor quality. Cooking was done, weather permitting, in a brick galley, where, sailors maintained, cockroaches achieved the size of ocean wild fowl.

The basic rations customarily dispensed in ships engaged in the West Indies trade consisted of a pound and a half of biscuit and a quart of wine a day to each person. On Sundays and Thursdays each received, in addition, a pound of meat and two ounces of cheese. On Tuesdays, rice soup, two ounces of salt pork and oil, garlic and vinegar were added to the menu.

On Mondays, Wednesdays, Fridays and Saturdays, bean and chick pea soup, and a third of a pound of salt fish were distributed.

This diet, unsubstantial as it was, was not always maintained. Narvaez's table, however, was weighted daily with such luxuries as roast pork, breast of fowl, green vegetables, suitable condiments, pastries, fine cheeses, fruits and vintage wines.

By the time the grubby flotilla came in sight of the brilliant green shores and misty blue mountains of the island of Española, one hundred and forty of the men had had all they wanted of the conquest of Florida.

These *conquistadores* who had sailed so bravely and hopefully westward across the great ocean were disillusioned, frightened out of their wits, homesick and hopeless. They now presumed that when Columbus called the island a "wonder," he meant simply that it was wonderful to be on it and out of his ship.

As fast as they could, they made for shore, and vanished into the saloons, brothels, inns and cool shaded patios of Santo Domingo.

They deserted.

With a quarter of his contingent lost to the paradise of Española, Narvaez made an effort to recruit replacements, but he met with small success. He was irritated by the high cost of supplies there. It was a seller's market. Ships could not put into unknown seas without adequate provisions, and suppliers were not averse to bleeding captains for every penny the traffic would bear.

Narvaez managed to purchase another small ship and a few head of horses to replace those which had died on the crossing, but at the end of forty-five days, extremely annoyed by the situation, and seeing no hope of securing more men, he put his flotilla of six vessels out into the Caribbean. His destination was Santiago de Cuba where, he had been informed, he might procure at less severe prices the additional arms, mounts and foodstuffs he needed.

They turned the westernmost point of Española Island and set a northwest course up the Jamaica Channel. It was the hurricane season, and the pilots maintained an anxious watch for signs that would warn them to race for the closest sanctuary.

Santiago was the chief Spanish port on the southern coast of Cuba. Narvaez was on home ground there. Hardly three years had passed since he had departed for Spain, a man of wealth, property and wide reputation. Now he was returning with even greater distinction. He was a governor, the commander of a small army, on his way to richer and larger conquests.

A number of men came forward to throw in their lot with him. They were good men to secure, for they had tasted life in the islands, they had jungle experience, they knew what they were doing and what they could expect.

The cost of supplies was, as he had hoped, more favorable. He bought food, horses and men. And when a message arrived offering to *give* him a quantity of provisions if he would call at Trinidad for them, he hastened to take advantage of the opportunity.

The message had been sent by a friend, Vasco Porcallo de Figuroa, who, incidentally, was to become de Soto's lieutenant general ten years later. Trinidad was a small town on the Cuban coast some two hundred miles west of Santiago. The ships set out for it under calm conditions, but they had not sailed half the distance before the weather deteriorated.

The adverse change prompted Narvaez to turn the fleet into the harbor of Cabo Cruz. As winds abated and skies cleared again, he ordered two vessels to proceed onward to Trinidad while he bided his time in the safety of the port. One of the ships dispatched had for its captain Juan Pantoja, Lord of Ixtlahuaca, who had been with Narvaez on the abortive mission to Mexico and was his friend and loyal supporter. Cabeza de Vaca was in command of the second ship.

At Trinidad, Cabeza de Vaca, the superior officer, sent Captain Pantoja and some thirty men ashore for the supplies, remaining on board himself. It was a poor port, affording little protection. The pilots, scanning the skies and tasting the wind, advised that speed in leaving it was essential. Should a severe blow occur, there would be little chance to escape. A number of ships were known to have gone to their graves in the place.

The weather steadily worsened. By morning heavy rain was falling, and the seas were mounting over the shallow harbor bar. As Cabeza de Vaca nervously paced the deck, a canoe paddled by Indians came out from shore. It brought word that a problem regarding the provisions had arisen and that his presence was required in the town.

He disliked to leave the ships under the menacing conditions, and he delayed going, hoping that whatever difficulty his emissaries had met would be solved without him. At last, under the urging of the frightened pilots, who thought he might be able to speed the loading, he agreed to go. He gave orders that in the event of impending disaster, the sailors were to beach the ships, and think first of saving their lives and the valuable horses.

Several men whom he invited to land with him declined with the excuse that it was too cold and wet to venture out. They promised that, should the weather improve, they would go ashore the next day. It would be Sunday, and they would have an opportunity to attend Mass.

Cabeza de Vaca went alone. On the beach he mounted a horse which had been brought from the town for him, and disappeared on the jungle road.

No one attended Mass that Sunday. The hurricane roared out of the Caribbean upon the land, venting its fury in screaming wind and thundering deluge. The houses and the church of Trinidad crumbled under the terrible battering. Clinging to each other to keep from being blown away, the men fought to reach the jungle and escape the disintegrating stone walls and timbers of the doomed town. Trees were uprooted and crashed about them, and they huddled through the night beneath fallen logs and in cavities dug in the earth by the cataclysmic force.

Some of the townspeople and men from the ships were killed, many were grievously injured, and all suffered from exposure.

At the height of the storm, obviously terrorized, Cabeza de Vaca heard strange noises. There came to him "a tumult and great clamor of voices, the sound of timbrels, flutes, and tamborines, as well as other instruments."

The hurricane ceased with the coming of dawn. Taking some men, Cabeza de Vaca set out for the harbor. The country was "in a condition piteous to behold; the trees prostrate . . . there being neither grass nor leaf."

The ships were gone. All that remained to signify that they had existed were two buoys floating in the water. Searching the flooded shore, they came upon bits of wreckage. The bodies of two sailors were found, so badly disfigured from being beaten against the coral that they could not be identified. A coat and a coverlet, both shredded, were picked up. That was all.

Sixty men and twenty horses had perished. Cabeza de Vaca sent a messenger overland to Cabo Cruz to apprise Narvaez of the tragic loss. He also commenced the preparation of an "authenticated account" of the storm to be sent to His Majesty in Spain. It was the first official descriptive report of a West Indian hurricane ever printed.

The disaster at Trinidad occurred in October. Governor Narvaez arrived at Cabo Cruz with the four ships which had safely ridden out the blow on November 5.

If Narvaez intended to continue on the way to Florida with the equipment left to him, he soon learned that his plan had to be drastically altered. The heart had been blown out of his men. Uppermost in their minds was a desire to stay ashore until all danger from hurricanes had passed. They meant to do it, too.

In the face of this determined attitude, Narvaez announced that the expedition would spend the balance of the winter in the comfort and protection of a shoreside retreat. He placed Cabeza de Vaca in command of both men and ships, sending them to a large and more weatherproof bay at Cienfuegos, a few miles to the west. Then he took himself off overland to spend the coming holidays with his wife, look to the condition of his Cuban properties, pick up what funds had accrued during his absence, and otherwise enjoy himself.

Sometime during the winter he journeyed up to Havana,

where he bought another ship, engaged a captain named Alvara de la Cerda, and left him in charge of forty infantrymen and twelve cavalrymen he had induced to join his expedition.

Hearing that a brigantine was lying in wait for a buyer at an attractive price in Trinidad, Narvaez returned there. He bought the ship and drummed up a crew among the residents, most of whom were only too willing to leave the stricken place. A stranded pilot named Diego Miruelo also was signed on. He swore that not only did he know well the location of the River de las Palmas in Mexico, having been there, but that he was thoroughly familiar with Cuban waters and had sailed along the Florida coast. The gross dishonesty of these assertions was soon to become manifest.

It was the nineteenth of February 1528, when Narvaez returned to Cienfuegos. He was happy to find his army intact and to learn that his men had recovered their courage and were eager to resume the conquest.

There being no reason for delay, he ordered sails hoisted the following day. Four hundred and eighty men, six or eight wives, and eighty horses were aboard the four caravels and the brigantine as they passed out of Cienfuegos Bay.

The immediate destination of the fleet was Havana, where the sixth vessel awaited them. Miruelos, the pilot from Trinidad, set the course. Two days later they were solidly hung up on the shoals of Los Cannareos off the Isle of Pines.

For fifteen days they were caught there, the keels of their ships scraping the jagged coral bottom. Near the end of this period their peril was increased by a storm which came out of the south. Death seemed imminent, and the men crossed themselves, confessed to the padres and were resigned to meet their Maker.

This time, instead of being destroyed by a Caribbean tempest, they were saved by it. The wind drove so much water over the shoals that the ships were freed.

Bad weather persisted. They came close to being driven on reefs at Guaniguanico, and were obliged to take refuge for three days in the lee of Cape Corrientes to escape a severe blow. At last they doubled Cape San Antonio, the westernmost point of Cuba, and beat against northerly headwinds.

They were within sight of Havana harbor when the wind suddenly reversed and blew so fiercely from the south that they were helpless before it. It was as if a new pilot, Adversity, had taken full command. The green coast of Cuba vanished over the stern.

It was Holy Week, but the sailors were too busy trying to keep the ships upright, and most of the others were too sick, to give themselves to devotions. The best they could manage was an occasional Hail Mary.

On Tuesday, the twelfth day of April, they came in sight of some mangrove islands. The winds withdrew, as if in defeat. The sun shone brilliantly on a smooth green sea. Shore birds flew over them. They saw long reaches of white sand, and palms held their plumage against an azure sky.

They were looking at the southwest coast of Florida.

PART TWO

Blind Decision

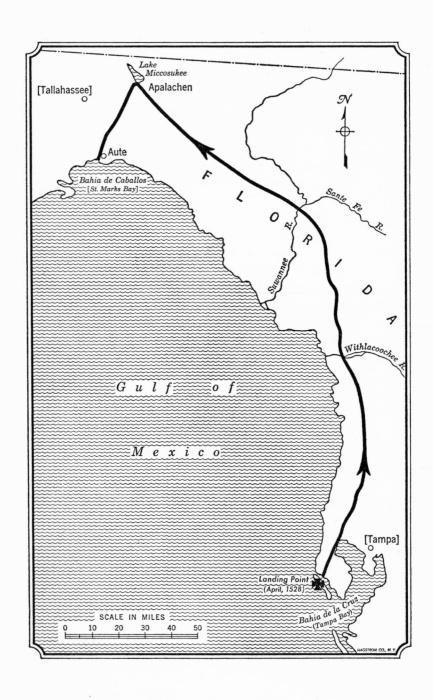

[Tallahassee]

Lake
Miccosukee
Apalachen

Aute

Bahia de Caballos
[St. Marks Bay]

F L O R I D A

Sante Fe R.

N

Suwannee R.

Withlacoochee R.

Gulf   of

Mexico

[Tampa]

Landing Point
(April, 1528)

Bahia de la Cruz
(Tampa Bay)

SCALE IN MILES
0   10   20   30   40   50

HAGSTROM CO. N.Y.

1

On Holy Thursday of the year 1528, the four ships and one brigantine of the Narvaez Expedition rode easily at anchor on the clear placid waters of a Florida lagoon. Near-by a small pass opened through the sand dunes, palmettos and marsh grass of a narrow island to the shimmering immensity of the Gulf of Mexico.

The smoke of fires over which the foot soldiers, sailors and cavalrymen cooked crustaceans and bottom fish they had caught in the adjacent shallows traced dark patterns across the hot sky. Eastward, behind the mounds of white oyster shells about a deserted Indian village, was a forest of live oaks, palms, magnolias and pines which created a green backdrop marking the wandering contours of the mainland.

As they had sailed northward along the western coast of the peninsula, the pilot, Diego Miruelo, had watched for a large bay which he had sighted on a previous voyage. It would, he declared, be an excellent place to land and a safe haven.

Strangely, the bay, which was to bear the name of Tampa, was not sighted from any of the vessels, although they sailed directly across its mouth. They landed instead on the arm west of the bay, in the vicinity of what is now known as Clement's Point or John's Pass.

Alonso Enrriquez, the comptroller, had been the first to go ashore. A ship's boat took him to a small village on the mainland. There he spent some time in an attempt to convince the Indians with gestures and signs that their new governor desired only peace and friendship. The head tribesmen presented him with some fish and venison, but obviously were unconvinced of his sincerity. Once Enrriquez and the sailors had returned to their ship, the entire village fled into the jungle.

It was on Good Friday, April 15, that Narvaez, Cabeza de Vaca and a contingent of soldiers landed and searched the *buhios* of the village. Considerable excitement was caused by the finding of a "tinklet of gold" among some fish nets.

Narvaez ordered the main body of his forces to land on the following day and formally took possession of the country for the King of Spain.

This was not a simple ceremony. It was burdened by rigid formula, tortured by protocol and adulterated by court red tape, political deceit and ecclesiastical humbug.

First came the raising of the Spanish flag while the padres were engaged in setting up a cross. Then Cabeza de Vaca and the other officers laid their commissions before the governor. He acknowledged each one in turn, and returned it to its owner. The notary, Hieronymo Alaniz, worked furiously to record each act as it took place, as if without such a running account written on the spot the whole procedure might have been forgotten and the taking of Florida would have been conducted without the proper legal sanction. When he had finished his work, he presented it to the participants for their sworn signatures.

All that accomplished, the stage was set for the governor to issue an official proclamation and to make a speech to the Indians. That there were no Indians to be seen in no way altered the convention as prescribed by law.

The inanities contained in this *Requirimento* are without precedent. Indeed, the whole undertaking was inconceivably absurd.

Parts of the document Narvaez read to the audience of trees in his hollow voice were known as the King's Summons to the Indians. It was a standardized proclamation read wherever *conquistadores* landed on a previously unclaimed shore. Other sections were creations of his own twisted mind.

It went something like this: "In behalf of the Catholic Caesarian Majesty of Don Carlos, King of the Romans, and emperor ever Augustus, and Donna Juana his mother, Sovereigns of Leon and Castilla, Defenders of the Church, ever victors, never vanquished and rulers of barbarous nations, I, Panfilo de Narvaez, his servant, messenger, and captain, notify and cause you to know in the best manner I can, that God our Lord, one and eternal, created the heaven and the earth, and one man and one woman of whom we and you and all men of the world have come, are descendants and the generation, as well will those be who come after us: but because of the infinity of offspring that followed in the five thousand years and more since the world was created, it has become necessary that some men should go in one direction and others in another, dividing into many kingdoms and provinces, since in a single one they could not be subsisted nor kept."

Narvaez stated that the Pontiff in Rome, who was called Papa, was King, Lord and Superior of the Universe, and supreme father and governor of all men, had given Florida to the King and Queen of Spain. He offered to produce written documents to prove the claim, but none of the natives expressed an interest in seeing them.

Narvaez then commanded the Indians to recognize the

Church as their mistress, and the king and queen as their masters. If they complied willingly and obediently, he declared, "I will receive you with love and charity, relinquishing in freedom your women, children and estates without service, that with them and yourselves you may do with perfect liberty all you wish . . . you will be converted to our Holy Catholic Faith, as nearly all the inhabitants of the other islands have done."

Perhaps their Majesties meant every word of the interminable proclamation which the conquerors were obliged to read upon entering a new land. Perhaps the king and queen fully intended that its promises should be fulfilled. The men who disseminated it did not. They made it a mockery, and purposefully turned it into a completely deceitful, disgraceful and cruel declaration.

So Narvaez threatened what he fully intended to do in any case, no matter how submissive the Indians became.

He told them: "If you do not do this . . . I will enter with force, making war upon you. . . . I will subject you to obedience to the Church and yoke of Their Majesties, and I will take the persons of yourselves, your wives, and your children to make slaves, sell and dispose of you."

As far as is known, the *Requirimento* was first used in 1514 by Pedrarius de Ávila during a landing on the Isthmus of Panama. It is alleged that the bishop accompanying this expedition remained in safety on a ship while Ávila went ashore to carry out the formalities.

Returning to the ship in disgust, Ávila is reported to have told the bishop: "My Lord, it appears to me that these Indians will not listen to the theology of this Requisition, and that you have no one who can make them understand it. Would your Honor be pleased to keep it until we have one of these Indians in a cage, in order that he may learn it at his leisure and my Lord Bishop may explain it to him?"

Some Spanish invaders purportedly complied with the

law by crawling close to an Indian village in the dead of night and reading the *Requirimento* in a whisper to the trees, after which a notary witnessed it and impressed his seal upon it. That accomplished, the soldiers, waiting in the forest, fell upon the sleeping village and murdered its inhabitants.

If any of the natives who dwelt upon that lonely Florida shore did hear Narvaez, they gave no sign of it. The only applause came from the little waves lapping the white beach and from startled birds in the green forest beyond the lagoon.

Perhaps a few of the Timucuans observed the ritual from their places of concealment in the swamp grass. It does not matter. Even if they could have understood the words, they would not have complied with their demands. They had no intention of submitting to any invader.

Thirty-eight of the horses had died on the rough trip from Cienfuegos, and were rotting in the ships. The remaining forty-two still alive were so exhausted and lean as to be almost useless.

On shore man and beast ate and rested, enjoying the peacefulness of the island, the feel of steady land beneath their legs, the deliciousness of the fresh seafood. The tinklet of gold had revived hopes that had been jettisoned in the tempests at sea.

Then out of the jungle came several Indian emissaries. Narvaez gave them an audience, but all spoken words were wasted. The men in shining breastplates talked, and the naked red men talked, and neither understood what the other was saying.

But if words were incomprehensible, the gestures of the Indians were not. No other form of communication was needed to make unmistakable the warning that moving hands and arms wrote on air: Go or die.

The Indians vanished as silently as they had come. Narvaez, the veteran jungle fighter, the conqueror of Cuba, laughed and knew no fear. More than a few angry threats was needed to stir even mild apprehension in him. In days past, he simply would have cut the bowels out of the emissaries and have forgotten the incident. He had chosen to let them go unharmed, for his thoughts at the moment were not on killing natives or even conquering them. He was interested in learning what his kingdom contained. The savages would be taken care of in good time.

Having formulated no definite plan of campaign, Narvaez elected to reconnoiter the surrounding area. Taking Father Xuarez, De Solis, Cabeza de Vaca, thirty-four men on foot and six cavalrymen, he set out northeastward. The company advanced through the day until the hour of vespers, when it came in sight of a large body of water that appeared to reach far into the mainland.

They made camp for the night, unaware that they had stumbled upon old Tampa Bay, the western arm of the fine harbor for which they had been searching.

Returning to the ships the next day, Narvaez ordered the pilot, Miruelo, to sail in the brigantine northward along the coast in search of the elusive bay. Miruelo obeyed, but he was a man as much in the dark about his whereabouts as Narvaez and the others. Not only had the brief land incursion brought them to the bay, but its entrance lay less than half a day's sail to the south of them. But Miruelo went north as he was told.

His orders were to examine the coast for a reasonable time, and if the bay were not found to sail directly for Havana. There he was to join the ship of which Alvara de la Cerda was in command. Both were to take on full loads of provisions, and return to Florida.

Restless and undecided as to the proper steps to be taken, Narvaez, with the same contingent that had accompanied him on his first reconnoitering trip, set off once again to look at the country. They had gone no more than ten miles when horsemen ran down and captured four Indians who had been observing them.

The captives were shown some maize and asked by signs if they knew where a supply of it might be obtained. They readily led the Spaniards to their own village, which stood at the head of Old Tampa Bay. The only corn there, however, was not ripe, but of transcending importance was the surprising discovery of numerous articles of Spanish origin among the meager possessions of the villagers.

There were several wooden cases of the kind used to ship merchandise from Spain to the Indies. In each case was an Indian corpse wrapped in painted deerskin.

Father Xuarez was incensed by the sight of them. This was idolatry that he could not tolerate, and he made a pyre of the cases and burned them, bodies and all.

A search through the thatched houses produced pieces of Spanish shoes, canvas, broadcloth, iron utensils, linen and hat plumes, and most significant of all, several small pieces of gold.

Replying to the interrogations of the excited Spaniards, the Indians indicated they had obtained the goods, except the gold, from a ship which had been wrecked in the bay. Then for the first time Narvaez and his men heard the fateful name of Apalachen.

Apalachen, said the Indians, was a province which lay far to the north. It was inhabited by a powerful tribe. Its gold resources were great, and there was a bountifulness of all the other things which they knew the Spaniards desired, such as food—oh, the maize was unlimited!—and precious stones.

If the natives on the shore of Old Tampa Bay understood what the invaders desired, it was probably not due to previous contact with other Spaniards. Their story of plundering a wrecked ship was very likely untrue. Much more likely is the assumption that they had obtained the goods through trade with Indians who lived farther south. Natives of the West Indies crossed the Straits of Florida in canoes. An Arawakan colony—the Indians inhabiting the Caribbean Islands—was known to exist on the coast of southwest Florida in the fifteenth century. Clothing and household articles purloined from the Spanish in Cuba could easily have been transported as trade goods to the Florida peninsula.

Gold, of course, also could have reached Florida in such a manner. But not the gold Narvaez held in his hand. That came from Apalachen, which could be reached overland by trekking straight north.

That was all Narvaez wanted to know.

Because he and his little company were hungry, he was obliged to waste two days in hunting up some edible maize. The captured Indians guided him to it, a distance of ten or twelve leagues away,* but once stomachs were satisfied, Narvaez wasted no time setting out for the ships.

2

In the eight or nine days since the expedition had landed in Florida, no untoward incident had occurred. The Indians had made some threats, but had done nothing more than spy on the invaders from the safety of the swamps. The horses were beginning to recover their strength. The men were rested and comparatively well fed on the seafood, game and fruit obtained near the island camp and which was a beneficial supplement to the unwholesome

---

* The Spanish judicial league equaled 2.634 English miles. Cabeza de Vaca frequently overestimated distances.

ship stores. Altogether it had been a peaceful and sometimes enjoyable period passing under the rich light of their great dream.

Now there could be no peace and little rest. Now they saw themselves on the verge of having that dream fulfilled. There was gold in Apalachen. They had seen samples of it.

Soon after returning to the ships, Narvaex summoned Cabeza de Vaca, Father Xuarez, Alonso Enrriques, Alonso de Solis, the notary Heironymo Alaniz, and a sailor, Bartolomé Fernandez. The presence of an ordinary seaman at the high council remains unexplained. Perhaps Narvaez was using him as a secretary or personal attendant. The record does not show that he participated at all in the discussion.

Listening to Narvaez speak, Cabeza de Vaca soon became filled with a profound foreboding. This state of mind had its source in the plan which he understood had taken firm root in the disorganized brain of the governor, a plan predicated on nothing more concrete than a few puny pieces of gold and an insuperable self-confidence.

Narvaez was proposing to leave the protection of the ships and set off blindly into the unknown interior of a land no white man had ever penetrated, a land of which he had no knowledge whatsoever, and in which he had arrived in precarious condition less than a fortnight before. All other considerations appeared to have become inconsequential in Narvaez's muddled thoughts.

Cabeza de Vaca, being in full control of both his emotions and his senses, in spite of the disappointments and hardships already experienced, viewed Narvaez's proposal as beyond the bounds of impracticality. It belonged in the realm of sheer irresponsibility, if not complete madness.

Cabeza de Vaca did not forget to take into consideration the fact that Narvaez had spent many years in the unknown wilderness of the New World, while he himself was a neophyte in the Indies, but he also remembered that he was a trained soldier who had known the horror and bloodshed of battle. He had received a thorough schooling under the exigencies of international conflict. He had learned the vital importance of avoiding unnecessary exposure, of maintaining a certain haven of retreat to meet the demands of unexpected reverses, and he knew the peril of advancing without established lines of communication and supply. In Narvaez's plan he found only complete disregard for every fundamental of field operation, and he was appalled by the prospect it presented.

The overall picture was even darker when he considered events which had transpired since their departure from Santo Domingo. In the record of those months he could find nothing which might be grasped as a promising sign, nothing that might be used as a foundation for a resurgence of hopes, and least of all, nothing to support a conviction that the Narvaez force was invulnerable.

He could cite numerous reasons for adopting a contrary attitude. Not the least of them was a warning by a Moorish woman fortuneteller of Hornachos in Castile that only disaster awaited the Florida expedition. The sinister prognostication had been made to the wife of one of the gentlemen adventurers, and during the voyage out from Spain she had repeated it to Narvaez and the other officers.

The governor had dismissed it as a piece of nonsense unworthy of consideration. He and his men were going to fight and conquer nations wholly unknown, and it was to be expected that in subduing savage countries some would lose their lives. The rewards to be gained were worth such a gamble, for whoever survived would return a rich man.

As hardships and reverses mounted, however, the prediction had taken on more significance, until it hovered over many of the people like a shadow of doom, its dark portent inflicting despondency that even the strength of their great dream could not completely remove.

Now they had reached the fabled land, the waters about them were serene, and the words of Narvaez coupled with the gold he held in his hand were inspiring men anew. Once again, as it had been in the beginning, eagerness and zeal were welling up in them, causing them to grumble about delays, blinding their judgment.

Cabeza de Vaca could find no justification for such spirit, such feeling, such enthusiasm. In reality, the future promised nothing. There was nothing they might believe, nothing they knew to be true. Even if he forgot the woman of Hornachos, forgot the trials of the past months, his burden of foreboding remained.

In Santo Domingo and the other ports at which they had called, a considerable amount of intelligence had been gathered. Some of it was valuable and obviously had a basis in fact, but most of it was patently false. A man could hear anything he wished to hear in those places. A great deal of talking was done only to please ears. Santo Domingo especially abounded in good storytellers, adventurers with a penchant for romancing and plain diabolical liars. The best a man could do was to accept tentatively only that which seemed reasonable to him, and ignore everything else. In most instances, he would do better if he relied on nothing but his own judgment and experience, and put his trust in no one but the Lord.

Cabeza de Vaca attempted to follow that admonishment. The result was he found that all the knowledge and experience he had gained during his life served only to increase his apprehension.

The Indians about them were the same people who had mercilessly driven off and mortally wounded Ponce de León. Was there any reason to believe that Narvaez would be spared by them? The attitudes of those few with whom they had attempted to treat indicated otherwise. Trouble with them appeared to be inevitable.

They were Timucuan Indians. Almost all the knowledge of them available had been brought back to Santo Domingo by survivors of the de León venture.

They were tall, well-made people, elaborately tattooed. Their villages were compact, and surrounded by stockades of palm and pine logs. The houses were circular and thatched with palmettos. They scalped and mutilated their dead. Human sacrifice was a regular part of their religious ritual, and the victims were not always captured enemies. Sometimes they were infants of their own tribe. They occasionally indulged in cannibalism.

Not a very pleasant picture to contemplate. With it and the memory of what happened to de León in mind, Cabeza de Vaca concluded that it would be folly, if not suicidal, to enter the country of such a treacherous and uncivilized people without adequate supplies, dependable equipment, and proper preparations. Yet, that was exactly what Narvaez intended to do.

The story of the clash between the incompetent and ruthless Narvaez and his able and practical lieutenant on that lonely Florida island is historically important. Had the argument not occurred, or had it not resulted as it did, not only the course of events in that theater would have been greatly altered, but the conquest and settlement of the United States unquestionably would have been swifter.

Narvaez set forth his proposal much in the manner of an ultimatum. It was a simple one. He would lead his entire force northward by land. The ships would sail along the coast until they found a good harbor. There they would wait until contact was made with the land expedition.

How long were they to wait? Who could say, but the other vessels soon would return with supplies from Cuba? Then other ships might be sent back to Havana on similar missions. By this system sufficient food and ammunition would be kept at hand.

How was he to know where the ships had anchored? How was he to find them? Well, that would be done. It was not a problem that needed to be considered at the moment. Perhaps he would send out scouts periodically to locate the ships.

Condescendingly Narvaez inquired if anyone else held any views pertinent to the plan.

Cabeza de Vaca had quite a few, and he disclosed them in an emphatic manner. Under no circumstances should they separate themselves from the ships until an adequate harbor had been located. As for the pilots, they were virtually useless and not to be trusted with such a vital undertaking. They had lost their confidence, could not agree on any point, and had no idea where they were.

Cabeza de Vaca had other comments to make. The horses were not yet in condition to travel long distances. If they could be grazed on shore for a few more days, while a search was made for a suitable site for a main base, their full recovery would be achieved.

Also, said de Vaca, the distinguished governor and loyal servant of his Majesty was advocating a journey into a land inhabited by savages with whom he had no way of communicating. An effort should be made to train an interpreter. As it was, they were precluded from learning what they must know of the country, if they were to be successful. It was hardly necessary to point out that they knew nothing of the country's character, nor did they have knowledge of other wild people who might inhabit it.

To be blunt, they didn't have any more idea of where they were or what might confront them than did the helpless pilots. In addition, it should be remembered that their food supplies were insufficient to sustain a force of several hundred men setting out with no goal or destination, know-

ing not how long they would be required to march before
additional food was found, indeed, knowing not whether
they would ever find any at all. He, for one, did not enjoy
the prospect of starting off with only a little biscuit and
dried pork into a wilderness no other Christian had ever
seen. Cabeza de Vaca did not mention, although he must
have been tempted to do so, that had it not been for the
governor's previous shortsightedness and parsimony, their
larder would not have been in such a state of depletion.

He offered a counterproposal: Embark once more and not
only find the desired harbor but determine if there was not
a part of the country in which the soil was better than that
about them. It might be possible to locate not only a good
port but an advantageous site for a settlement which could
be developed into one of the two colonies which Narvaez,
under the terms of his agreement with the king, was obliged
to establish in the Province of Florida.

Driven by delusions of grandeur, not to mention illusions
of immeasurable wealth awaiting his coming, Narvaez was
not only adamant before Cabeza de Vaca's protests, but
resentful and insulting. His one eye glared with fury. He
sneered at de Vaca, and asked the opinion of Father Xuarez.

The padre was opposed to re-embarking the entire expedition. He expressed faith in the pilots' belief that a good
harbor was not far off, obviously to the north of them as
they had passed none to the south. He thought it might be
feasible to march northward, but always keeping in close
proximity to the coast, while the ships made a similar
search. The two-pronged advance would undoubtedly produce a suitable place. Whichever found it first, the ships or
the land company, would wait for the other.

Presumably the padre had had enough of the sea to last
him a lifetime, but he concealed personal feelings behind
a doctrinal declaration. He pointed out that after so many

adversities and tragic losses to take again to the ships might be indefensible defiance of the will of the Almighty.

Narvaez appeared to see some merit in Father Xuarez's suggestions, but he did not commit himself to accept them. Were there any others who wished to address themselves to the matter?

There was one other, Alaniz the notary. He revealed his courage by standing squarely with de Vaca. Before abandoning the ships, he declared, it should be ascertained that they were anchored in a safe bay to which the land explorers could retreat, if the need arose. With that done, the governor could do whatever he pleased in comparative safety.

If Narvaez had been a more responsible and a saner man, he would have recognized the extent of his rashness, and would have understood that his resentment of de Vaca's opposition sprang as much from envy as from any other source. De Vaca had served with Narvaez long enough for him to have a measure of the younger man, and in comparison he had found himself wanting. De Vaca's courage was unquestionable, and his ability as an officer had been amply demonstrated.

The governor was deeply agitated by the situation. If de Vaca were permitted too much leeway, he might find himself confronted by an unpleasant situation. His disastrous experiences in Mexico, if they had done nothing else, had made him extremely sensitive about his own shortcomings. The advantage to be won in throttling lieutenants before they had an opportunity to illustrate their superior capabilities had become all too apparent to him.

With stern finality he announced they would proceed to carry out his plan. That was both his wish and his order.

It was a decision which surprised none of those present. Knowing Narvaez as they did, they had understood that he

intended to march, and that his request for their views had
been made only as a sop to their egos.

Cabeza de Vaca bowed to the command, too good a soldier to do more than savor the thought of insubordination,
and recognizing the futility of violence. The arm of royal
authority could not reach into that far place, and an outcast
would have little chance of survival. He had not abandoned
the hope of returning to civilization some day.

Yet, de Vaca did not turn submissively away.

In the light of what the following years brought, his next
act appears not a little uncanny. It was as if he could sense
the nature of things to come, and was aware how the decision, made there beside the still Florida lagoon on that
last day of April in 1528, would so dramatically affect the
terrible path of life he was to know.

In the name of his sponsor, the King of Spain, de Vaca
demanded a certificate, done under the hand of the notary,
stating that he had advised against the Narvaez plan. He
requested an unequivocable report of the conference in
which his position was recorded in unmistakable words,
a report sworn to and bearing an official seal, so that posterity might know the unvarnished truth.

Narvaez seemed to realize at once the danger to himself
that would be inherent in such a document, and he protested that he was doing no more than abiding by the opinion of the majority. He pointed out that Father Xuarez had
not opposed him, but had merely offered some amend-
ments. The comptroller had not opposed him, nor had the
assessor.

Four to two in favor of the land expedition.

Narvaez understood, as well, that he would find little, if
any dissatisfaction about going among the men of the ranks.
They, like he, had come to Florida for one purpose, and
that was to share in the fortunes to be found there. Gold,
rubies, pearls, and emeralds, and all theirs for the taking.

Already an unbelievable amount of wealth had been ex-
tracted from such places as Mexico and Panama and other
parts of the Indies. His blood raced at the thought of it.
The patent he had received might provide that he was to
colonize Florida and convert the natives to Christianity, but
unless the padres were stronger men than he, those orders
would be the last to be carried out. He could not conceive
of himself pausing to build a settlement and a church before
Florida was stripped bare of its great wealth.

If he couldn't completely control Cabeza de Vaca, he
could the notary, and he ordered him to refuse the request
for a report. De Vaca's demand, however, had given him
an idea, and cleverly he turned the situation to his own advantage.

Narvaez instructed the notary to prepare a certificate for
him. It was to state that as there was no means of subsistence in their present location, it would be impossible to
maintain a settlement there. Nor was there a secure haven
for the ships in the immediate area. Therefore, he felt it
incumbent upon himself to move his entire company in
search of a more favorable place.

This artful maneuver accomplished, Narvaez turned vi-
ciously on de Vaca, excoriating and insulting him in the
presence of the others. Since de Vaca was so strongly opposed to the land march, declared Narvaez, it was obviously
because of timidity. Perhaps de Vaca would prefer to remain
with the ships. That would be a very suitable arrangement.
De Vaca could have command of the flotilla, and all those
on board. Of course, that included the women. Meanwhile,
he would explore the interior, facing whatever dangers
might await him.

The meeting concluded on that unpleasant note, but if
Narvaez believed he had gotten rid of de Vaca, he soon
realized his mistake. Had he been able to order de Vaca to
remain with the ships, the matter would have been settled,

but he had no such authority. De Vaca was treasurer of the expedition by royal decree.

In his journal, de Vaca says simply that he requested to be excused from taking command of the ships, but later entries show there was more to the situation than that.

Narvaez persisted in urging de Vaca to accept the assignment, and even sent others to argue with him. When these overtures failed, Narvaez himself approached de Vaca again, demanding to know from de Vaca's own lips the reasons for his objection to remaining behind. He heard them.

Here once more de Vaca gazed into the future with extraordinary perception, forecasting events to come with phenomenal accuracy.

The land expedition, he told Narvaez, was never to see the ships after leaving them. Yet, the question of his remaining or going with it had no bearing on his conviction that disaster lay ahead in the Florida bush. It had now become a matter of honor. His motives had been questioned, his personal courage had been assailed. That he would not tolerate. No amount of entreatment could persuade him to remain with the ships. He not only intended to take his chances with Narvaez, but he intended to vindicate himself from the accusations cast upon him. Narvaez and all the others would come to understand that the aspersions were without foundation. Risking his life was preferable to security under the cloud of Narvaez's insults.

Narvaez gave up, and named an *alcalde*, Caravallo, to head the sea forces.

On the eve of the start, the woman who had warned him previously of the Moorish clairvoyant's dire prediction, again approached the governor and beseeched him not to go. The journey, she said, would end in disaster. He and all the others would be lost. If any of them did happen to return, it would be only by virtue of great wonders performed by Almighty God.

Once again Narvaez laughed, and rejected her entreaties. The land ahead was incomparably opulent. Only a fool or a coward would hesitate to take the fortunes awaiting them. He was neither.

The next day the march into the unknown began.

Two hundred and sixty men on foot, forty on horses, set off on the first overland expedition to enter the continental United States.

Plumes and banners waved in the damp tropical breeze. Breastplates and arms gleamed in the sunlight. Strung out in a long line, weaving through the scrub growth, palmettos and reeds, the soldiers with their weapons, knives girding thighs, and the horsemen with lances aloft and swords rattling an accompaniment to the jingling of spur chains, presented a formidable array.

The officers were no less than grand in their colorful costumes. Fluttering bright silks, shining soft leather boots, glittering armor, fine linens, silver buttons and gay plumes adorned them, and in their personal saddle kits were thick woolen blankets, down coverlets, and capes of heavy cloth and soft fur.

Somewhere along the line was the little band of padres, a dream of conversions to come lighting their eyes, a prayer for the salvation of the company touching their lips. Their cassocks gathered dust and burrs as they plodded dutifully along.

If the edibles carried were meager, enthusiasm was plentiful. The stores of the ships had permitted the distribution to each marcher of only two pounds of biscuit and half a pound of bacon, hardly enough to give a man a feeling of well-being in the face of unpredictable circumstances.

The slender margin of safety frightened Cabeza de Vaca. For Narvaez, who was too stupid and too obstinate to be concerned about such things, matters were turning out as he had believed they would. He could see delight in the faces of his men. The great adventure had begun. When it was over, and all were rich, the soldiers could go back to the taverns and the Indian and Negro girls in lovely Santo Domingo. He would live in his Florida palace.

Ignorance, unquenchable self-esteem, irrepressible confidence pictured for him the glories to come. As for the natives, no number of jabbering savages could stand before him. That they probably would not make the attempt was indicated by their complete disappearance. Not even a lone terrified wretch was dragged from the bush by the scouts and outriders.

On the column moved toward the northeast, skirting the northern end of Old Tampa Bay. On through the sandy reaches, splashing through the swamplands, the saw grass cutting their fine boots and tearing their clothes, slashing their hands and faces, and the mud tarnishing the bright armor. On through the endless stretches of palmettos, the jungle thickets, the pine forests and palm groves, wading, plunging, struggling through the dark waters of the uncountable streams.

Silence pressed upon them, a silence broken only by bird calls, by their own subdued voices, by the snorts of the Andalusian horses, by the rattle of sabers.

It was the silence of the ages, the silence never before broken by a foreign invader, the silence of the unknown.

It drew a curtain about them, and it swallowed them.

3

Today a super-highway cuts its smooth stream along much of the route which the Narvaez Expedition followed northward from Tampa Bay, but a great deal of the country is the same as it was in May of 1528.

One sees swamps in which age-old cypress trees with enormous boles lift their bare gray arms in eerie supplication. Seemingly endless thickets reach away in each direction in dismal dampness. Dark palms stand in groves like ragged islands in the ooze of bogs. For miles on end it presents forlorn wastelands, changed from their original state only by garish advertising signs and pennants marking the worthless lots of fraudulent real estate developments.

But the few modern touches and occasional interruptions by clusters of filling stations do not prevent one from imagining this dreary land as it was when Cabeza de Vaca saw it. Only a few feet away from U.S. 41 it appears to be impassable. Rattlesnakes and moccasins, poisonous spiders and alligators still infest it. Marshland and mud, palmetto and pine, sand and sink, flies and fever, it repels one.

Eight years later, Cabeza de Vaca was to remember well the difficulties encountered, and recalling that at the start of the march each man's rations consisted of two pounds of biscuit and half a pound of bacon, he was to set down these words in his invaluable *Relacion:* "We traveled on the allowance we had received fifteen days, without finding any other thing to eat than palmettos which are like those of Andalusia. In all that time we saw not an Indian, and found neither village nor house. Finally we came to a river."

Measuring the distance as the highway would have taken them, they traveled less than a hundred miles. But they trekked much farther than that, for they were obliged to search for fords in the countless creeks, to circle numerous swamps, ponds, lakes and jungle growths.

Both the heat and the insects were unmerciful. There was no relief, no escape night or day, from either. The earth steamed, and green mold covered equipment, and a man felt as if he were rotting before he had died. The necks and shoulders of the horses were sheaths of blood. So great and thick were the clouds of flies that the column was hidden in them. Some of the torturers were the size of bees. The faces of the men were swollen into grotesque shapes by the bites of mosquitoes, which came in such swarms that a man could not avoid breathing them. Gnats filled a man's ears and nose, every crevice in his skin, and the bites of some persecutors made a man jump as if he had been stuck with a red-hot needle.

The same conditions prevail in the Florida woods and swamplands today.

The river they reached on the fifteenth of May was the Withlacoochee. It was deep and had a strong current. Some of the men took off their armor and clothes and swam across, but rafts had to be built to carry equipment and those who could not swim. An entire day was consumed in the crossing.

Then the Indians, so long absent, suddenly reappeared. Two hundred tribesmen surrounded the camp. Narvaez's signs of friendship were rejected with vulgar replies. They made indecent gestures at Narvaez when he sought to talk with them, and threatened him with their bows and arrows.

The fight that followed was brief. A few gun shots, apparently into the air, sent the Indians off in a panic. Six of them were captured. To save themselves, they offered to guide the Spaniards to the village in which they lived. It was only little more than a mile away.

Near the huts was a large field of ripe maize. The men fell furiously upon the golden grain while giving thanks to the Lord for succoring them in their great extremity. Not only were they wearied almost beyond endurance, but they were on the verge of collapsing from hunger.

For three days they stuffed themselves on fish, corn and roots. On the third evening of their stop at the Withlacoochee, a delegation called on the governor. It consisted of Cabeza de Vaca, Enrriquez, de Solis and Father Xuarez. Their mission was prompted by the gravity of the company's situation.

They requested Narvaez to send men to look for the sea. He laughed at them. Stop thinking of the sea, he told them, for it was far away.

De Vaca reminded him the captured Indians had indicated that the river flowed into a large harbor not far to the west. The vessels might very well be there. Narvaez capitulated, and told de Vaca to go, although he had no conviction that a search would produce anything but more poor country. He was already beginning to reveal his disappointment in the province over which he was the supreme ruler.

De Vaca departed on the following morning, the eighteenth of May. With him he took a foot company of forty men commanded by Captain Alonzo del Castillo. Keeping to the right of the Withlacoochee, passing the site of the present community of Yankeetown, they came at noon to sea sands. For five miles they walked knee-deep in tidal water. The bottom was covered with oysters which badly cut their feet. They were finally prevented from going on by deeper water, and turned back toward their camp. It was apparent that only by crossing the Withlacoochee farther upstream could they follow it to its junction with the sea.

Acting on this information, Narvaez ordered an officer named Valencuela to take forty soldiers and six horsemen on a second search. They crossed the river at the camp. Returning at the end of two days, Valencuela reported that he had reached the mouth of the river. It emptied into a bay so shallow that no ship could enter. Several large canoes carrying Indians who wore plumed headdresses passed across the bay as Valencuela and his men watched from shore.

On May 21, disappointed at not meeting the ships,* but somewhat recovered from their hunger and weariness, the

* The vessels presumably were still safely anchored in the vicinity of Tampa Bay, although this cannot be definitely established.

expedition moved once more northward in quest of the fabled town of Apalachen. The captured Timucuans were taken along as guides, but they were of little assistance, if any at all. The ordeals of the previous fifteen-day march were repeated, but on this leg of the journey they struggled through the forbidding wilderness almost twice as long— twenty-eight days.

The distance covered in that period, if measured in a direct line, was no more than seventy-five or eighty miles. In all probability, their route, affected by numerous natural barriers which forced them to detour, was a third longer. Indians were sighted from time to time, but no contact was made with them. It was not until the seventeenth of June that they were approached by natives. On that day a tribal chief was borne into their camp on the back of a servant. His regal rank was denoted by the painted deerskin he wore, and by the large contingent of musicians who pre-ceded him, playing weird melodies on reed flutes.

De Vaca recorded the chief's name as Dulchanchellin. For an hour he sat in council with Narvaez. They talked by means of signs, gestures and ground drawings. The dis-closure that the expedition was en route to Apalachen brought from the dignified *cacique* the declaration that the people of Apalachen were his enemies and he would join the Spaniards in subduing them.

Gifts were exchanged, Narvaez presenting his caller with much-prized beads and hawk bells, and receiving in return the royal painted deerskin. The Spaniards then followed the Indian chief and his contingent of warriors and mu-sicians on a trail to the north, and in the evening reached a wide and deep river with a swift current.

It was the Suwannee. Forty-eight days had been spent in traversing a distance over which an automobile travels in little more than three hours. Almost each of those days had been one of peril and ordeal. They had suffered terrible fatigue in the fierce heat. They had been maddened by clouds of insects. They had known excruciating hunger.

The record hardly commends their facility for self-preservation, but they were not woodsmen. Most of them had never seen a jungle before reaching the Indies, and they had received no training to prepare them for their adventure. Least of all were they good hunters.

Florida abounded in wild game, but they were able to obtain little of it. Most of the time they could not get close enough to a deer to shoot it. Even rabbits and squirrels eluded them, for they traveled with a great commotion and noise. Animals vanished ahead of them, and they did not possess enough ingenuity to stalk them. The Spaniard did nothing quietly in the wilderness. Not until they had spent months in the bush and had observed the stealth and cunning with which Indians hunted did they achieve any success in securing the wild meat they so badly needed.

They were able to pull a few fish from creeks with hook and line, but if they ever thought of using nets, they didn't do it. They were dirty and evil-smelling, but they made no attempt to cleanse themselves with the wild soaps that were obtainable. They suffered from ticks and lice and insect bites, but they had no soothing lotions or other remedies which they could have obtained from the Indians. The people of the wilderness could have taught them much, but the Spaniards were not inclined to be either diplomatic or kind. They disdained to associate with savages, to ask favors of them. The natives may have been made in man's image but they had no standing in the eyes of God.

The exact site of the Suwannee crossing is not known. Presumably it took place in the vicinity of the present Branford, probably a few miles south of the town near the confluence of the Santa Fe River with the larger stream.

The first death of the journey occurred during the crossing, which was achieved with what appear to be unnecessary difficulties. For some reason, they decided that rafts would not suffice, and built some sort of a canoe. The men were ferried across a few at a time, the operation requiring a full day.

Impatient at the slow progress, a cavalryman named Juan Velasquez, whose home was in Cuellar, rode his mount into the river. The current swept him from the saddle. He gripped the bridle reins, pulling the horse's head beneath the surface, and both were drowned.

The Indians recovered the bodies. Velasquez was interred with appropriate ceremonies, having achieved the dubious honor of being the first white man drowned in what is now the United States. Although saddened by the loss of their companion, the soldiers enjoyed eating his horse for supper.

Chief Dulchanchellin provided them with a supply of maize, but after that his friendship mysteriously cooled. A trooper going to the stream for water was shot at, the arrow narrowly missing him. When the expedition left the Suwannee, after a sojourn on its bank for two days, not an Indian was on hand to bid it farewell. Apparently the chief had changed his mind about joining in an attack on Apalachen.

Later in the day a few natives were sighted. They looked ready to do battle, but made no assault. Narvaez detailed some horsemen to remain behind in ambush. They succeeded in capturing four Indians who were taken along as guides.

At this point in the de Vaca journal occur several conflicting statements that cannot be reconciled.

He relates that they entered a country very difficult to travel through but "wonderful to look upon." It was a land of great pine forests, the trees of immense girth and astonishingly tall and majestic. So many had fallen that their way was constantly impeded and passage was achieved only with "a considerable increase of toil."

In the next paragraph he reports that they came in sight of the long-sought village of Apalachen on "St. John's Day." St. John the Baptist's Day is June 24th. Apalachen was at least seventy-five miles in a straight line running north-northwest from the Suwannee crossing. Yet, only six days at the most had elapsed since they left the river. Obviously they had not traveled in a straight line through a country which was a jungle of fallen trees. They must have gone a hundred miles, but assuredly not at the rate of seventeen or more miles a day.

The discrepancies, however, are of little consequence. More important is the understanding that over a period of fifty-five days they had broken a trail through an unknown land probably three hundred miles in length, an average of more than five miles a day. This was accomplished in the face of extreme hardships, and on rations hardly sufficient to sustain the life of an inactive man. Only one soldier had been lost, and his death was the result of an irrational act.

Their goal had been reached.

4

Any description of the disappointment registered in the weary eyes of the gaunt Spaniards as they gazed at the town of Apalachen must be an understatement.

It consisted of forty low thatch huts scattered along the shore of Lake Miccosukee, near the present community of Monticello in Jefferson County, Florida. It appeared dilapidated, dirty and deserted. Across an arm of the lake a smaller village could be seen, offering an equally unpromising prospect.

The surrounding country was hilly, covered with groves of immense pines, walnut, laurel, cedars, savins, live oaks and liquidamber or sweet gum which produced a fragrant balsam called copalm. The fresh water lakes in the area were larger than any encountered on the northward march, and there were countless ponds and marshes surrounded by tangles of fallen trees and impenetrable thickets.

If the spectacle was profoundly discouraging to all, it was no less than heart-sickening to Narvaez. He knew an overwhelming despondency. Not only was his great dream shattered, but he had stripped himself of the fortune he had accumulated through so many bloody years in the Indies. He had now seen enough of Florida to realize that it contained none of the riches he had expected to find. It contained nothing. He was governor of a worthless kingdom, a miserable land in which even an effort to survive taxed a man almost to an unendurable limit.

In place of the colorful, enthusiastic expedition which had set out from Tampa Bay for the golden land of Apalachen, Narvaez saw only a beaten army. Emaciated from hunger, his men were ragged, bruised, bleeding and sick. Many had galled shoulders from carrying heavy armor. Unconquerable fatigue caused them to drop gasping on the ground, to lie virtually helpless, their bodies covered with bites and scars, too weak to fight off the insects which constantly tortured them.

If there was a hope left, it lived only in the prayer that God would let them live long enough to escape the terrible land. Life was more precious than all the gold in the New World. Pearls could not give the strength and courage they must have to survive. Only food could provide that. If Apalachen would give them this sustenance, they would ask nothing more.

Narvaez told Cabeza de Vaca to take the grubby town. He and de Solis led nine horsemen and fifty infantry in the assault.

There was no resistance. Long before aware of the approach of the invaders, the tribesmen had fled into the forest. Only terrified women and children were found crouching in the filthy huts.

If Apalachen had no gold, it had a fine supply of maize. It stood ripened in near-by fields, and quantities were stored in cribs. Within a few minutes the captive women were put to work cracking it in stone mortars for the starving soldiers. If any man thought of raping an Indian girl, he had neither the inclination nor the strength.

Suddenly an arrow drove through the horse of de Solis, killing it, and the Apalachees launched an attack from the surrounding trees. The Spaniards formed to repulse it, but as suddenly as they had appeared, the Indians vanished. De Solis' horse was quickly cut up and added to the menu.

The main contingent entered the town. They had hardly time to wolf a meal before a small group of natives emerged from the bush and made gestures signifying they wished to approach in peace.

They were permitted to enter the camp. Their request that the women and children be allowed to leave was granted, but Narvaez ordered that a *cacique* with the truce party be held as a hostage. The other emissaries, taking the village families with them, departed, but they made plain with signs their resentment at the seizure of the chieftain.

For the first time on the journey, the Spaniards received a full taste of the type of Indian warfare that was to inflict disaster on so many expeditions penetrating the American wilderness during the next three centuries. The stealthy approach, the swift attack, the silent retreat—tactics which American frontiersmen both understood and employed, but which seemed incomprehensible to most Europeans. The French *coureurs de bois,* opening the north and the far west on their fur trading missions, adopted them, but not the British. They, like the Spaniards, advanced into battle in rigid columns, and four and six abreast, in brightly colored uniforms, flags flying and trumpets sounding, and they were slaughtered by foes they never saw.

The Apalachees were jungle fighters of the first rank. The warriors were mostly men of good stature and great strength. They were cunning and courageous. Cabeza de Vaca wrote that at a distance they appeared like naked giants, but this description may have been influenced by psychological factors. The Spaniards were haunted men.

Bows used by the Apalachees, he reported, were as thick as an arm, eleven or twelve palms in length, and arrows were shot from them at two hundred paces with great precision. The razor-sharp flint and bone points of the thin shafts tore through Spanish armor. He tells of seeing two red oak trees, each the thickness of the lower leg, pierced through by Apalachee arrows. One that passed closely to him drove nine inches into the butt of an elm.

In the dawn of the second day after the Spaniards' arrival at Apalachen, the Indians struck. They came with such silence and swiftness from the forest that they had set fire to several houses before the sleeping men could emerge from them. By the time the troops had rallied, several were wounded, and before a counterattack could be launched, the Indians were vanishing into the lake thickets. Pursuit was in vain. The soldiers could neither see nor hear them. Only one Indian was slain.

A single native casualty was the result of a similar dawn attack which took place the next morning.

Most of the men had never known the fire of battle, and only a very few of them had engaged the mysterious natives of the New World. Probably no more than a score, including Narvaez, had any real experience in jungle warfare, and in northern Florida, even they faced a situation never before encountered.

The major campaigns in the islands had been carried forward with large numbers of men, adequate arms, troops of cavalry, and sufficient provisions. The conquerors of such places as Jamaica and Cuba and Española were comforted by the knowledge that both reserves and supply ships were within comparatively easy reach of them.

The false confidence and unqualified egotism of Narvaez had influenced him to give little consideration to the matter of logistics. Now circumstances made his wantonness cruelly apparent.

For Cabeza de Vaca, the memory that he had argued strenuously against advancing without proper safeguards brought small satisfaction. Neither time nor the distances traveled could be recovered. The course upon which they had so stupidly set out was the only one open to them. It was go forward on it or die.

His accounts of the clashes with the Indians and of the endless tribal warfare served as valuable guides to some of the explorers and fortune hunters who came in his wake.

He viewed the strategy with which the Indians protected themselves as comparable to that of Italians reared in the continual bloody feuds of that ravaged land. In making the comparison he was speaking with the voice of experience.

When the Indians traveled in a part of the wilderness in which an enemy attack might be expected, de Vaca later wrote, they placed their mat and skin houses "on the skirt of a wood, the thickest and most tangled they can find, and near it make a ditch in which they sleep."

A camping place was prepared for the women and children deeper in the woods, and about them, in the ditches, the warriors concealed themselves beneath grass and brush so cleverly "that if come upon they are not discovered."

Fires were kept burning in the houses throughout the night to give the impression they were occupied. In the event of an assault, the men leaped from the ditches, launching counterattacks from several directions.

When no woods were available in which ambuscades

could be built, trenches were dug in open ground and covered with vegetation.

The Indians lived with the wariness of animals, ever suspicious, ever watchful for possible danger. "If they fear an enemy they are awake the night long, each with a bow at his side and a dozen arrows. He that would sleep tries his bow, and if it is not strung, he gives the turn necessary to the cord. They often come out from their houses, bending to the ground in such a manner that they cannot be seen, looking and watching on all sides to catch every object. If they perceive anything about, they are at once in the bushes . . . and there they remain until day. . . . When the light has come, they unbend their bows until they go out to hunt. The strings are the sinews of deer."

Significantly Cabeza de Vaca pointed out that crossbows and harquebuses were of little value in fighting men who refused to stay longer than a moment in one place, who slipped through the thickets with the quietness of rabbits and the speed of deer, who could conceal themselves like burrowing rodents. Clumsy matchlocks which had to be supported for firing by a hook were virtually useless against moving targets, and even the vaunted crossbows were ineffective against shadows in the form of men which appeared from behind trees or out of the tall grass only long enough to discharge an arrow and then vanish again into concealment in which they could not be detected.

The Indians scoffed at these weapons. They were so "effectual in their maneuvering that they can receive very little injury."

It was not the guns, not the Spanish bows, not the Spaniards themselves, the Indians feared. It was the horse.

They dreaded the horse. The sight of it filled them with awe, and they were struck with terror when the inconceivable monsters charged upon them. They fled from the horse.

Cabeza de Vaca set down a few words of advice that

were born of his gruesome and bitter experience in engaging the Indians: "Whosoever would fight them must be cautious to show no fear, or desire to have anything that is theirs; while war exists they must be treated with the utmost rigor; for if they discover any timidity or covetousness, they are a race that well discern the opportunities for vengeance, and gather strength from any weakness of their adversaries."

They possessed not only the cunning of animals, but the endurance and hardiness. "Oftentimes the body of an Indian is traversed by the arrow; yet unless the entrails or the heart be struck, he does not die but recovers from the wound."

In his estimation, they saw and heard better and had "keener senses than any other in the world."

Perhaps the comparative bountifulness of the food in Apalachen stirred a spark of new hope in Narvaez. There were daily skirmishes with the tribesmen, but there were also daily meals of good maize, squash, roots and fish. It must be presumed some wild game was shot, but Cabeza de Vaca does not mention eating it. He does, however, describe the wild life of the country, stating that three kinds of deer, hares, lions (panthers), bears and other beasts were seen. Strangely, he does not include alligators and wild turkeys, but he does tell of seeing a strange animal "with a pocket on its belly, in which it carries its young, and if it should happen that they should be out feeding and anyone come near, the mother will not run until she had gathered them in together." This is the first known allusion to the American opossum.

Rations also must have been supplemented by various kinds of fowl, for Cabeza de Vaca states that geese, ducks and partridges abounded. Falcons, ger-falcons, sparrow-hawks, merlins, fly-catchers, herons and numerous other birds were observed.

Taken altogether, it was a diet which might revive some spirit in men who had been on the verge of dying from starvation. Certainly, combined with a reasonable amount of rest, it would give them new strength. This apparently was the case, for three incursions were made into the northern Florida wilderness. Probably the scouting parties visited the site of Florida's capital, Tallahassee, and they may well have entered the rolling lands of southern Georgia. The border is only a few miles from Lake Miccosukee.

But if hopes were renewed, they were soon destroyed again. It was a land of "poverty," proffering little more than a few maize and pumpkin patches. The hit-and-run warfare of the natives was unceasing. Among those killed by the deadly arrows was the Aztec prince with the unpronounceable name whom Father Xuarez had induced to join the expedition.

Men who went to drink at the lake were wounded. The horses were easy targets for ambushers. Almost invariably the Indian shot at the Spaniard from concealment, and retaliation was impractical if not impossible. A man couldn't shoot something he couldn't see.

Had Narvaez been willing to free the *cacique* who was taken prisoner on the first day of their stay in Apalachen, the Indians might have been willing to treat with the invaders, but Narvaez was a stubborn man, a frustrated, bitter, sick man, and he refused.

The chief demonstrated that he was shrewder than his counterpart. When Narvaez demanded information from him, he concocted a tale he believed the governor would eagerly swallow, and his judgment was soon shown to be correct.

The largest town in the region, said the chief, was Apalachen. There was no use wasting time looking for others, for none existed that were worthy of the governor's consideration. Nor was there gold to be found, except in minute quantities, and any pearls discovered would be of such poor quality as to be virtually worthless. Northward, eastward and westward the inhabitants became less numerous and even poorer than the Apalachees, and going in those directions one would find nothing but dense forests, more impassable lakes, immense deserts and vast solitudes.

But what of the land directly to the south?

Ah yes, the south. That was the place to go! It was a land rich in maize, beans and pumpkins. Being close to the sea, fish were plentiful. The people were friendly. Just nine days' journey from Apalachen was a prosperous town called Aute.

This encouraging intelligence resurrected a vision that once had dominated the thoughts of Cabeza de Vaca, but which, like all other dreams, had been long in its grave. It was the vision of hopeless and lost men being saved by ships.

Cabeza de Vaca prayed that God, in His infinite wisdom, would see fit to guide them to this salvation.

If the same thoughts occupied the mind of Panfilo de Narvaez, he did not disclose them, but he came to the conclusion that their present position would bring no advantages in the future. Each day, by reason of dwindling supplies if not because of losses of men and horses, it was becoming more untenable. The country to the south could be no worse, and the chief, now given his freedom, had spoken glowingly of it.

Perhaps the governor's hopes were, after all, unquenchable. Certainly his *naïveté* was indestructible.

They left Apalachen on July 20, after a stay of twenty-six days, and plunged into the forbidding land. During the first day's march they advanced unmolested, and they gave haven to the assumption that the Indians, glad to see them depart and having recovered the chief, had no more interest in warring upon them. The invalidity of this conclusion was demonstrated the following day when they were in the middle of a swamp whose water came up to their paps.

From the protection of fallen trees and tall grass, the Apalachees rained arrows on them. Men and horses went down in the slimy green water with cries of pain and screams of terror. Blood stained the ooze. Nor did the Indians halt the attack when the swampside was finally gained. On through the underbrush and thickets the fight continued. Several times the Spaniards rallied and attempted to counterattack, and each time the Indians vanished. They could find no one at whom to fire, no one to charge with lance or sword. Like wraiths the Indians came again and again, sending their arrows through leather and metal into flesh, and like wraiths disappearing once more.

The cavalrymen were forced to dismount, their horses being of little use in the soggy earth and dense brush.

At last, the Indians departed. Cabeza de Vaca concluded they had run out of arrows, and were forced to halt the assault until a new supply could be obtained. He was probably right, but evidently the needed arrows were brought to the field during the night, for the attack was resumed spasmodically the following day.

The wounded made progress slow and difficult. Some of the injured had to be lashed to horses. Others stumbled forward under their own power on clear ground, but had to be assisted through the marshes and over the tangles of fallen trees that eternally barred their way. The Indian assaults came on their flanks, from the front and from the rear. Defense preparations were futile, for no one knew whence the next would come. It was like running an endless gauntlet of death.

Cabeza de Vaca suffered a minor wound in one of the few clashes which occurred on open ground. In this brief fight, being under conditions more favorable to them, the soldiers managed to kill two natives and wound several. Once more in the woods, however, they found themselves helpless to prevent surprise attacks.

In a sudden rear guard action, a *hidalgo* named Avellaneda ran back to assist his serving boy, who had been wounded. The brave act brought his death. An arrow struck him at the edge of his cuirass, passing through his neck.

"In this manner," wrote de Vaca, "we traveled eight days."

When they reached the village of Aute, they found the houses burned, the people of the village gone. But in the little fields the corn and the beans and the pumpkins waited to be harvested. And the sea was not far away.

5

The country directly south of Tallahassee, bordering immense Apalachee Bay, is one of the most miserable in the United States, if not in the entire Western Hemisphere. A motorist traveling through it on U.S. 98 for the first time on a bright day might be prompted to remark in admiration of its pine forests, its palm-fringed inlets, and the islands that lie a short distance offshore against the blue Gulf of Mexico. A brief pause in such a journey, however, would remove this deceptive guise of beauty and reveal the ugly truth of things.

It is an insect and vermin paradise. During the summer months—the Narvaez Expedition reached it in the latter part of July—it is swept almost daily by violent thunderstorms and torrential downpours. The heat and humidity, night and day, engage in a bitter race for the hundred-degree mark, but one seldom outstrips the other for any length of time.

In the winter months, however, dampness is frequently the victor. Temperatures often drop near the freezing point, and sometimes considerably below it. Sharp winds combine with the unrelenting wetness to chill the bones.

Today, except for a few civilized enhancements, most of them provided by the Federal Government, it is changed little from the time when Cabeza de Vaca described its wretchedness. The Indians are gone, but it would be difficult to find either intellectual, moral or social qualities superior to theirs in the people who have supplanted them.

Poverty is rampant. Backwardness is standard as a way of life. There are only a few forlorn, unpainted clapboard towns like Apalachicola, Carrabelle and Sopchoppy to prove that a few stump-grubbers, white trash, swamp rats and fishermen can survive there. People with respect for their own welfare, or those possessing pride and ambition, shun it. Only those remain who have no means of escape.

One of Cabeza de Vaca's great fears was that he would die there, and death "coming in such a place was . . . all the more terrible." He wondered what worse fate a man might suffer than to go to his eternal rest in a land "so remote and malign, so destitute of all resource" that a man could not "live in it or go out of it."

From the town of Apalachen on Lake Miccosukee to the site of Aute would be hardly more than forty miles in a cross-country march. It had taken them eight or nine days (here another discrepancy occurs in de Vaca's account) to traverse the distance.

They followed a course running slightly toward the southwest. It took them generally along a large stream to which they gave the name River of Magdalena. Now it is called the St. Marks River. It flows into St. Marks Bay, at the head of which stood the Indian village of Aute. The little oil port town of St. Marks occupies the site today. The surrounding area is largely a United States wild life refuge. Except for a narrow paved road, some man-made duck ponds and a lighthouse, it remains much as Cabeza de Vaca saw it.

When they halted in Aute, the company had been on the trail for three months. When it left Old Tampa Bay, it consisted of two hundred and sixty men on foot and forty cavalrymen. At least a dozen horses had been killed en route. Eighteen men had died on the trek up to this point, one by drowning and seventeen in fights with Indians.

Now a new and terrible enemy struck—sickness in the forms of fever and dysentery.

Cabeza de Vaca wrote that after two days of rest in Aute, Governor Narvaez "begged" him to go in search of the sea. The use of the verb in this manner gives rise to interesting speculation. It implies that Narvaez had lost either his desire or his power to command. Under ordinary circumstances he had to "beg" no one to carry out his wishes. Had defiance of his authority reached an extent where he was unable to suppress it? Events of the next few days throw light on that question.

Accompanying Cabeza de Vaca on his mission to find the sea were two men, one white and one black, whom history was never to forget. Andrés Dorantes de Carranca was a native of Béjar del Castenar, in Estremadura. He had received a commission as a captain of infantry on the recommendation of Don Alvaro de Zuniga, Duke of Béjar. He was physically strong, a trained soldier, and by nature an adventurer. The other man was Dorantes' slave, an immense, towering Negro Moor named Estevan, more often called Estevanico, who came from Azamor on the western coast of Morocco. Estevanico, with great muscles rippling his shiny ebony skin, was wise in the ways of wild lands. He decorated himself with bangles, and displayed a never-ending interest in Indian girls.

They were two of the three men who were to share with Cabeza de Vaca the great adventure to come, loyal and stalwart to the end.

Also on the reconnoitering trip, commanding a company of seven horsemen and fifty foot soldiers, was the Captain Castillo who had gone with de Vaca to the mouth of the Withlacoochee in hope of finding the ships.

After traveling until the late afternoon through the low lands and coastal marshes, they reached an estuary of the Gulf of Mexico. There they came upon oysters in great abundance, and they sang God's praises as they gorged themselves on them.

In that unidentified place they camped for the night. The next morning Cabeza de Vaca dispatched a force of twenty men to explore the coast and ascertain the direction in which it ran. The patrol was gone overnight and until the next evening. Their report was discouraging. The bays and inlets they had seen appeared to run far inland, and in many directions, and they had not been able to reach the open sea on foot. It was obvious that this could be accomplished only by boat.

Cabeza de Vaca led the little company back to Aute, where he found conditions in a deplorable state. Many of the men were sick and lay helpless on the ground. An Indian attack had taken place during the previous night, and those who were able to fight had great difficulty repulsing it. One of the valuable horses had been killed, and a number of soldiers had been wounded.

I gave a report of the embarrassing nature of the country.*

However embarrassing it may have been, it did not prevent Narvaez from ordering an immediate evacuation from their precarious postion in Aute. The march seaward began the following morning.

It was piteous and painful to witness our perplexity and distress.

* This quotation comes from the 1555 edition of the *Relacion,* which was translated in 1851 by Buckingham Smith, as does all the following extract material.

There were not enough horses to carry the sick and wounded. Men staggered along blinded and babbling incomprehensibly under the scourge of their fever. Others retched and soiled themselves, being unable to control their bodily functions. Flies and mosquitoes swarming about them in great clouds maddened all. The terrible heat of the August day beat mercilessly upon them.

It was evening when somehow the tortured column, after following the route Cabeza de Vaca had taken toward the sea, reached the place on the oyster-strewn estuary where he had camped.

The realization that they had come to the end of their resources, that they could endure an advance no longer, hammered on their brains and felled them. And—

There was not anywhere to go . . .

Even if there had been some place to which they might have turned with faint hope, "the people were unable to move forward, the greater part being ill, and those were few who could be on duty."

They had reached the end of the trail.

The warped minds of desperate men understandably spawn despicableness and cowardice. Now some of the cavalrymen whispered together in the darkness beyond the campfires. A sinister conspiracy took shape.

There were perhaps twenty-five horses still alive. Men on foot had no chance of being saved. If they seized the horses and set out, taking what food they might surreptitiously, or even forcefully, obtain, they might escape a terrible death from hunger and disease. A small party of twenty-five riders could travel swiftly over the route on which they had come north. There was good reason to think they could reach the Bahia de la Cruz—the name by which Tampa Bay was known to them. God willing, a ship might be found there.

Who was to stop them from going? The governor was

prostrate and helpless. They need have no fear of him, for he was a dying man. Indeed, death would soon take all officers on foot.

There was no physical force that might have stopped them, but they had not reckoned with the moral courage, the decency and honor which lived in Cabeza de Vaca, Dorantes, Father Xuarez and other gentlemen or *hidalgos.*

We showed them the deformity of their purpose.

They shamed them for conspiring to desert their captain and those who were helplessly ill and suffering from wounds, and "they determined to remain, and that whatever might happen to one should be the lot of all, without any forsaking the rest."

The governor, in great misery, bid all who were able to do so to gather about his bed in council. The eagle eye of Narvaez no longer glared, but was glazed with sickness. The arrogance, the haughtiness, for which he was known the length and breadth of the New World, had vanished, and in their places were patience and tolerance and a piteous plea for advice born of weakness and disease.

What shall they do to save themselves?

Many spoke their minds, and all listened to each speaker with thoughtful attentiveness, and gradually out of the confusion of ideas, schemes and conceptions that were projected, a plan emerged that was agreeable to all those present.

But, even though they voted to support the plan, seeing no reasonable alternative which would bring their united acceptance, they admitted in the same breath that it was inconceivable, it was impossible to carry out.

Thereupon, in that unhappy state of mind, they set to work to carry it out.

They set to work to build vessels in which they would attempt to sail from the dreadful land to a haven of salvation.

PART THREE

Desperate Voyage

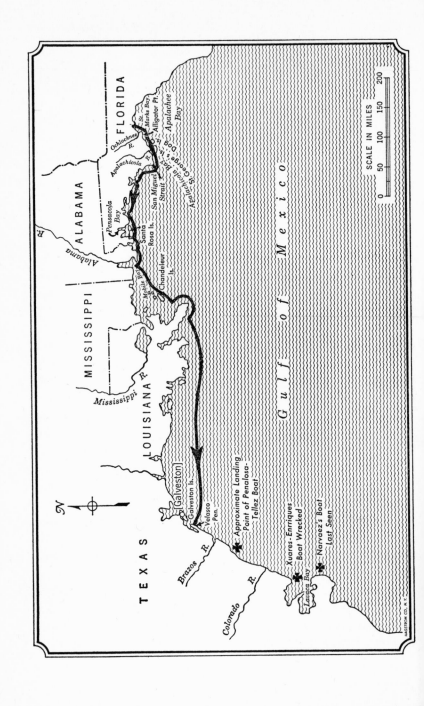

FLORIDA

ALABAMA

MISSISSIPPI

LOUISIANA

TEXAS

[Galveston]

Gulf of Mexico

Mississippi R.

Alabama R.

Brazos R.

Colorado R.

Ochlocknee R.

Apalachicola R.

Apalachicola Bay

St. Marks Bay

Alligator Pt.

Apalachee Bay

St. George Bay

St. George Is.

San Miguel Is.

Apalache Strait

Pensacola Bay

Santa Rosa Is.

Mobile Bay

Chandeleur Is.

Galveston Is.

Velasco Pen.

Lavaca Bay

Approximate Landing Point of Peñalosa-Tellez Boat

Xuares-Enrriques Boat Wrecked

Narvaez's Boat Last Seen

N

SCALE IN MILES

0   50   100   150   200

HAGSTROM CO., N.Y.

1

The little shipyard established on an arm of St. Marks Bay in August of 1528 was not only the first in the continental United States, but it was one of the strangest ever known in all the world.

There were workers, but no craftsmen. Only one man, Alonso Fernandez, a Portuguese, had received some training as a carpenter. When this was discovered, he became the recipient of great respect and was placed in charge of operations.

To begin with, there were no tools, no iron plates or bars, no forge, no tow, no resin, no rigging, and no one who knew how to make such things.

Neither was there sufficient food.

Each day sick men died. There was no cure for the mysterious maladies which had felled half the company.

The task of acquiring supplies was given priority. Men were assigned to catch fish. Others were sent out to hunt game. Others were dispatched to gather oysters and crustaceans in the surrounding creeks and inlets.

The most able-bodied men were organized into a raiding party. Within a few days they made four incursions into the corn and bean and pumpkin fields of Aute. Each was more or less a running fight with the Indians, who quite naturally objected to having their entire harvest stolen, but the raiders obtained more than six hundred bushels of maize and quantities of other vegetables.

Ingenuity combined with desperation created a formidable strength and an insuperable determination.

The celebrated carpenter devised a means of making bellows out of wooden pipes and deer skins. Armor, lances, guns, stirrups, conchos, belt buckles, crossbows—any piece of equipment and metal that could be spared without jeopardizing the company's safety—were melted and shaped into crude nails, hammers, chisels and axes. Even two or three saws somehow were manufactured.

Out of palmetto wood, a covering was woven for the boats. Seams were calked with the fiber of the same plant. Trees were split into planks with wedges and stone mallets.

The Greek soldier, Don Dorotheo Teodoro, became something of a hero when he discovered that pitch could be made from the resin of pine trees.

Ropes were made from the tails and manes of horses. Shirts, blankets, ponchos, coverlets, skins, expendable clothing of the living and all the garments of the dead were sewn together for sails. Oars were carved from savins. After long searching through the swamplands and forests flat stones were found that were suitable for anchors.

A party of ten men gathering shellfish became careless and walked into an Indian ambush. All were killed. Even though they wore armor, the arrows drove completely through their bodies.

Each third day a horse was slaughtered. The best of the meat went to the sick and to those who labored on the boats, but no part was wasted. Mixed with a little corn and some seafood, the entrails provided a thick, strength-giving broth. Skins from the legs were stripped off whole. After being scraped and dried they were sealed at the ends for use as water bottles.

The remaining hides were made into ship covering.

August passed, and forty men had died of fever, disease and wounds. Perhaps it should be said that their deaths prevented the occurrence of a dangerous and tragic situation. There would have been no room for them in the boats.

By the third week in September, only one horse and two hundred and forty-two men were still alive. The corn was almost gone, and they were being sustained mostly by opossum, raccoons, marsh rabbits, deer, ducks and seafood.

It was the general belief they were at least two hundred and eighty leagues from Bahia de la Cruz—a little more than seven hundred miles. Actually the distance overland would have been no more than that many miles! By sailing across Apalachee Bay and down the west coast of Florida on a fairly straight course, they could have reached their original landing place after traveling approximately one hundred and eighty miles!

The error is understandable. They were lost. They were sick and terrorized and hungry. They knew nothing whatever of the geographical outline of the immense Gulf of Mexico, nothing of the shape of the Florida coast.

False hopes were the fruit of their ignorance, and desperation blinded their senses and power of thought. Not one among them was a navigator. They knew nothing of the stars, nothing of the way of the sea, nothing of the habits of the winds. Natural signs told them nothing.

It can only be surmised, of course, what might have happened to them had they sailed toward the southeast. But it can be stated with certainty that if they had gone in that direction and had reached Bahia de la Cruz, less than two hundred miles away, they would have met one or more of their ships. For the ships were still waiting for them.

That was not in the cards of their fortune. Fate, or their lack of knowledge, caused them to reason that if they were two hundred and eighty leagues from Bahia de la Cruz, surely they must be closer to Pánuco.

Pánuco, the little Spanish slaving station on the central coast of Mexico, could not be that far away, not seven hundred and thirty-seven miles. Why not? Why, simply because they found hope and encouragement in the belief that it was nearer.

The truth was that Pánuco was at least six times farther away than Tampa Bay.*

On the morning of September 22, 1528, five of the strangest vessels ever seen afloat moved slowly under oar and pole through the shallow waters of the marshlands into St. Marks Bay.

Each was about thirty-three feet in length. Each was a weird conglomeration of rough pine planks, crudely hewn stays and ribs, horse hides, palm leaves, masts of debarked trees, fittings of silver, gold and brass, horse hair rigging, sails made of odd pieces of clothing, and stone anchors. Overloaded beyond the most remote degree of safety, their gunwales were not a foot above the water. So crowded together were the men that movement of any kind was almost impossible.

In the first boat was Governor Narvaez and forty-eight men. In the second was Alonso Enrriquez, Father Xuarez and forty-seven men. In the third was Captain Castillo, Andrés Dorantes and forty-six men. In the fourth were Captains Tellez and Penalosa and forty-five men. And in the

* In 1539, as Hernando de Soto was pushing northwestward through Florida, he was told by captured Indians about the Province of Apalachen and of how, years before, other Spaniards had reached it, and had been forced to build vessels to escape. No one knew where they had gone, or what had been their fate. The information struck fear in the hearts of many of de Soto's men, and they implored him to turn back before they, too, became trapped. De Soto pushed on, and in October some of his soldiers reached St. Marks Bay. They saw where a great tree had been felled and cut into stakes. Mangers had been built out of the tree's limbs. They also found the bleached skulls of horses.

fifth rode Cabeza de Vaca, Alonso de Solis and forty-seven men.

Two hundred and forty-two men crushed together in an almost helpless condition in five frail and unseaworthy craft. An experienced seaman would not willingly have set out in any one of them to cross a calm inland lake.

On through the waist-deep shallows they went, now rowing, now catching a bit of breeze that helped them along. They caught glimpses of the great Gulf, and at last they could hear the surf thundering against the outer banks.

In wide but protected water they turned southwestward. They saw the point on which the white shaft of the St. Marks Lighthouse rises today.

Then St. Marks Bay fell away behind them. They had named it Bahia de Caballos—The Bay of Horses.

2

The voyage of the little flotilla along the unknown northern coast of the Gulf of Mexico was not only one of the most remarkable in history, but was one of almost inconceivable privation and suffering. That the boats stayed afloat any time at all, low as they were and so heavily loaded that water sloshed continually over the gunwales, is almost too extraordinary to be believed.

The hand on the helm was the hand of death.

Seven days after departing they had gone only a few miles, having passed the mouth of the Ochlockonee River and Alligator Point, and entered the passage between Dog and St. George's Islands and the mainland of Franklin County, Florida. Greater progress might have been achieved had it not been necessary to land frequently for fresh water. The bottles made from the legs of the horses soon rotted and were useless.

In the strait, which they named San Miguel in honor of St. Michael's Day, September 29, 1528, they sighted some Indians in five canoes. As Cabeza de Vaca's boat, which was in the lead, approached them they abandoned the canoes and fled into the protective trees of St. George's Island, obviously terrorized by the strange craft which had suddenly appeared in their isolated little world.

Cabeza de Vaca took possession of the canoes. A landing was made on the island before a group of Indian dwellings in which a large store of dried mullet and several varieties of roe were found. The men enjoyed a hearty meal, and took the remainder of the food with them.

Passing farther along the strait, crossing the mouth of the Apalachicola River and the bay of the same name, they made another landing on the mainland. The five canoes Cabeza de Vaca had captured were put to good use. He had them secured along the sides of his boat in the manner of waist-boards, giving it both more steadiness and more protection from waves.

Their searches for water and food took them into numerous coves, creeks and inlets. The locations they reached on any particular day cannot be ascertained. Had Cabeza de Vaca been able to keep a written log, which, of course, he was not, it would have helped little in determining positions and distances traveled. None of the places they passed bore names known to them, and there were few natural features along that swampy coast upon which he might have remarked that would have permitted accurate charting of his course by later historians.

They apparently were near the western end of long Santa Rosa Island, outside Pensacola Bay, in the middle of October. Cabeza de Vaca states that they went ashore on a small island in search of water, but it is doubtful whether he knew it to be an island or a peninsula. This situation arises numerous times in his narrative. There are few Spanish documents recounting explorations in the New World more difficult to deal with because of a lack of directions, obviously inaccurate distances, and a dearth of details. This is quite understandable in view of the fact that he wrote his *Relacion* from memory years after events took place.

Nevertheless, it is known that while they were on shore in this place, they found no potable water, and before they could move on, a fierce storm swept in from the gulf.

For five days wind and water raged, making it impossible for them to escape. And for five days their thirst mounted until all were maddened by it. Four men, unable to endure the torture longer, drank salt water, became completely crazed, and died. What means others resorted to in an effort to relieve their suffering may be inferred from Cabeza de Vaca's words: "I do not believe there is any necessity for particularly relating the suffering and toils amidst which we found ourselves; since, considering the place where we were, and the little hope we had of relief, everyone may conceive much of what must have passed."

Perhaps, but it seems reasonable to suggest that even a person with a vivid imagination would find it difficult to "conceive" the truth of that terrible experience.

On the sixth day, although the storm had not ceased, they commended themselves to God and pushed into the angry seas. If death was to come upon them, the form in which it came did not matter; drowning would not be as painful as the unimaginable thirst, and it would be swifter.

But they did not drown. The boats, in which the men clung desperately to each other, withstood the battering of the waves. They were carried westward, and at sunset turned a point into the calm waters of Pensacola Bay.

During their meandering journey along the coast they had met few Indians, occasionally sighting some fishermen whom Cabeza de Vaca described as a "poor and miserable lot." That he could employ such a description in view of his own condition is somewhat surprising.

The situation was quite different in Pensacola Bay. Several canoes came out to meet them. The paddlers were large and well-formed men. They appeared to be unarmed, but they kept at a safe distance from the boats, calling out unintelligible words. At last they turned back to the land.

Following them, the Spaniards soon sighted a village and landed. The half-crazed men staggered ashore. A number of clay pots before the houses held fresh water, and they drank it madly, crying out for more while savagely consuming the cooked fish found about the campfires of the settlement.

A chief made the governor welcome, and invited him and others into his house. There they were given more fish to eat. In return for the food, the governor presented the Indian headmen with a few handfuls of maize and some trinkets.

It seems appropriate at this point to inject a footnote. On only a few occasions in the Florida section of his *Relacion* does Cabeza de Vaca remark that fish and seafood were caught. In the chapters telling of the voyage along the Florida coast he makes no mention of securing fish or crustaceans to assuage their constant hunger. This form of sustenance was obtained only from Indians. Yet, they had sailed through waters rich in seafood of many kinds. Sea trout, redfish, flounder, drum, grouper and mullet, to name only a few species, abound in the area. Porpoises must have played about the boats as they passed through the deeper sounds and across the mouths of the larger rivers. If not delectable, porpoise flesh would stave the craving of a starving man for a brief time. The shallow bays and inlets, especially in the vicinity of Apalachicola and East Point and

Carrabelle, provide three quarters of the large annual Florida oyster harvest.

As darkness fell over the Indian village on the shore of Pensacola Bay, the campfires revealed the forms of exhausted men sleeping on the ground, their thirst temporarily quenched, their bellies momentarily pacified. Many of them had been in a stupor, only half conscious when they arrived, and they slept in the crumpled positions in which they had fallen.

The hospitality and friendliness of the Indians had deceived them into dropping their guard. Narvaez, Cabeza de Vaca and some others willingly accepted an invitation to spend the night in the house of the chief.

The unexpected attack came sometime after midnight. Falling suddenly upon the sick men sleeping along the shore, the Indians killed three soldiers before any effective resistance could be accomplished.

A group assaulted the men in the chief's house. Narvaez was beaten in the face with a stone, and went down. Cabeza de Vaca and several companions quickly went to his assistance. It was their quick action which undoubtedly saved the governor's life. They seized the Indian chief, but in a wild struggle he was liberated by tribesmen. In the melee his royal robe of civet-marten was torn from his body.

The wounded governor was carried to his boat, and the Spaniards formed to make a stand at the water's edge. They were barely successful in repulsing three ensuing attacks. Cabeza de Vaca was wounded in the face. Rocks and arrows inflicted injuries on many others.

An encircling tactic, executed in darkness that was relieved only by the faint light of the campfires, prevented a disaster. Fifteen soldiers, led by Captains Dorantes, Penalosa and Tellez, went around the natives and attacked from the rear. Under this double pressure, they broke and fled.

At daylight a sharp north wind came up, churning **Pensa-cola** Bay to such an extent that the Spaniards dared not set out in the boats. Cabeza de Vaca ordered thirty Indian canoes, which were beached before the village, broken up for firewood. Throughout the day the men huddled about the fires, fully expecting the tribesmen to renew their attack.

No attack came, however, and in the late afternoon the wind subsided sufficiently for them to embark. They took the clay vessels from the village, filled them with water, and also took what food remained.

Up to this time they had made their way westward along the Gulf of Mexico coast approximately two hundred and fifty miles. Had they traveled in the opposite direction, they undoubtedly would have reached Tampa Bay in much less time. It is even more probable that they would have met a supply ship searching for them.

They went on westward. At the end of "three or four days," suffering once again grievously from hunger and thirst, they came into the entrance of another large body of water that reached far inland.

It was Mobile Bay. A lone canoe carrying several Indians came out to meet them. They requested water, and the natives readily agreed to supply it if they were given utensils in which it might be transported out to the boats. The precious clay pots were placed in the canoe.

It was in Mobile Bay that the first desertions since the expedition had landed in Florida took place. Dorotheo Teodoro, the clever Greek who had made pitch out of pine resin, clambered from his boat into the canoe of the Indians, announcing that he intended to go with them. He was joined by a Negro whose name is not known to history.

Despite pleas made by Narvaez and others, the two men remained determined to take their chances on shore with the savages. Life in the boats was no longer bearable for them, and they had abandoned all hope of reaching Pánuco.

Still believing that they might change their minds, Cabeza de Vaca ordered two of the Indians seized and held as hostages, and the struggling natives were dragged from the canoe. It departed without them.

Darkness already had settled when the canoe returned. The clay water vessels were still empty. The two hostages attempted to plunge overboard, but were held. Once more the canoe vanished into the night.

Daylight revealed the presence of twenty more canoes hovering near-by. At least three of them carried chiefs who wore robes of marten with ties of lion skin, "making a brave show."

A demand was made for the hostages, but Narvaez refused to surrender them until Teodoro and the Negro were safely returned. These terms would be met, a chief replied, and water and food would be given the Spaniards, if they would land.

The Spaniards, at last, seemed to have learned the danger of relying on the word of an Indian. An ultimatum was delivered: two Christians in exchange for the two hostages on the boats.

Almost at once the angry Indians attacked, and here for the first time Cabeza de Vaca tells of the use of slingshots. Many of the Indians were armed with them, and fired stones at the men in the boats.

It was a running fight. As the five boats made their way slowly away from the shore, the canoes, which were faster, encircled them, attempting to stop the flight. Clubs, stones and some arrows (strangely, the Indians had only a few bows) rained on the Spaniards. A freshening wind gave them an advantage. The water soon became too rough for the canoes, and the Indians were forced to turn back.

In 1540, men with the expedition of Hernando de Soto heard from some Alabama Indians how the vessels of Narvaez had arrived in Mobile Bay "in want of water." The explorers were told that a Christian named Teodoro and an "Indian" had left the Narvaez company and remained there. They were shown a dagger that had belonged to Teodoro. The possibility arises that the Negro who deserted with the Greek may have been part Carib or Arawak. Several half-breeds of this type were with Narvaez. The de Soto men received no information as to how Teodoro and his companion had died.

Cabeza de Vaca wrote that the Christians were "sorrowful and much dejected" by the loss of the two men. He did not disclose the fate of the two Indians carried away in the boat.

The rag-bag, water-logged flotilla, bearing its cargo of starving, thirsting men, sailed on southwestward from Dauphin Island. Perhaps they sighted the Chandeleur Islands off Louisiana. A favorable wind carried them steadily along for two days to an event of which American histories have never taken due notice.

In the afternoon of the second day at sea after leaving Mobile Bay, Cabeza de Vaca's boat was in the lead. It came around a point of land and passed a broad river. De Vaca dropped anchor to wait for the other boats to come up. Governor Narvaez did not choose to join him, however, and continued on to a bay in which there were several small islands.

All the boats came together there. The current was powerful. Tasting the water, they were delighted to find that it was fresh enough to drink.

They had entered one of the smaller mouths of the Mississippi River.

For the purpose of parching some of the small store of maize that was left, a landing was made on a low-lying island. Finding nothing there which might be used as fuel, the boats set out again in a search for wood.

Passing around a long point of land, they were caught suddenly in a violent current. Despite strenuous efforts to breast it, they were driven swiftly seaward. They soaked the maize and ate it raw.

Hernando de Soto did not discover the Mississippi River, as American schoolchildren have been taught.

Spanish navigators, exploring the coast between Florida and Pánuco—especially Pineda in 1519—knew that a great river entered into the Gulf of Mexico near its northern head. The charts they made to show it were extremely inaccurate.

Now white men, for the first time, had sailed on it, had felt the great strength of its current, and had seen its several mouths.

This was fourteen years before de Soto stood on the river's bank.

3

A strong offshore wind conspired with the currents of the Mississippi Delta to drive the boats seaward, but gradually they made progress in a semicircle, navigating generally west by north. At last the floods of the river fell astern.

For three days and nights they struggled on, hoping to reach land. As dawn rose on the fourth morning, they had drifted far apart and had lost sight of each other.

Cabeza de Vaca presently saw several columns of smoke rising on a distant shore, but fearing an Indian ambush he continued on westward. His men were in no condition to engage natives.

Late in the afternoon of the fourth day after leaving the Delta, he came in view of two of the boats. One was too far ahead to be identified. The other, toward which he turned, was Narvaez's boat.

The true nature of Narvaez, his incompetence, selfishness and cruelty, have been illustrated a number of times, but never were these qualities exemplified more graphically than in the occurrence which took place that afternoon off the coast of Louisiana. It was either the last day of October or the first day of November.

When Cabeza de Vaca had come up, Narvaez asked his advice. It was Cabeza de Vaca's opinion that they should join the boat ahead of them, and proceed together for their mutual protection.

This suggestion was quickly rejected. Narvaez felt that the other boat was too far away. He was anxious to reach land, and waiting until all boats could come together would mean unnecessary delay.

In this view Narvaez was supported by Captain Pantoja, who expressed the further belief that if they did not come to land that afternoon, "in six more days they would not reach it, and in that time they must inevitably perish." What foundation Pantoja had for his statement is not known. It would seem that he had none, unless it was that he saw a personal advantage in retaining the favor of Narvaez.

That speculation may be well founded. Narvaez's boat was not only the best of the five, but it carried the best equipment and the most able-bodied men. Narvaez had made certain of these things before leaving the Bay of Horses.

He ordered his boat to proceed in the direction that land was believed to lie. If Cabeza de Vaca wished to follow him, he could very well bend to the oars, for it was only by hard rowing that land could be gained. With that ultimatum, Narvaez moved off.

Discovering his will, I took my oar, and so did everyone his, in my boat. We rowed until near sunset.

Cabeza de Vaca's men had become exhausted. They fell over their oars. He called out to Narvaez that he could no longer keep up, and asked for a rope by which he might be helped along. Night would soon fall, and the boats would again become separated unless secured to each other by line.

The hollow voice came back over the water: Narvaez's men had all they could do to get themselves to shore. They had no time to help others.

Cabeza de Vaca cried out: The governor could see the feeble condition of his men. What would he have him do?

And the answer came: Do as you please. The time had gone by when one man should command another. It was now every man for himself. If Cabeza de Vaca could not keep up, that was his misfortune.

The boat of Narvaez moved away into the gathering dusk. Cabeza de Vaca never saw it or the governor again.

His men unable to row, Cabeza de Vaca gave his boat to the wind, attempting to steer toward the third boat. He was grateful to discover that it was waiting for him. It was the boat commanded by Captains Penalosa and Tellez.

The next four days and nights must have been like a terrible nightmare. They saw no land, and for a good reason, but one that was unknown to them. From Isle Dernière, off Louisiana, the Gulf Coast swings northward in a wide arc until reaching Sabine Pass, in Texas, where it turns toward the southwest. As strong winds blew them westward, the coast was receding from them. "Such was the weather," wrote de Vaca, "that only by God's favor we did not all go down."

It was gray and bitterly cold. The wind lashed at them, and they rolled and pitched. This constant punishment added to their unbearable thirst and hunger—once a day each man was apportioned a handful of raw maize—brought utter despair.

On the fourth day the weather degenerated into a severe storm. Once more the boats lost sight of each other, and they never came together again.

When darkness fell only Cabeza de Vaca and one other man were strong enough to hold the steering oar. Cabeza de Vaca speaks of that man as the "master." He was apparently an officer assigned as "captain" of the boat.

Only these two were on their feet. The others "were fallen one on another, so near to death that there were few among them in a state of sensibility." Two hours after dark, the master's strength failed him. He fell, convinced that his own death was near.

Until midnight Cabeza de Vaca alone fought the helm. Then securing it, he went forward to learn the master's condition. By some miracle he had regained enough strength to take a turn at steering.

Cabeza de Vaca lay down, but sleep would not come.

> I declare in that hour I would more willingly have died than seen so many people before me in such condition.

The new day was not far off when Cabeza de Vaca's ears caught a strange sound. It was a low rumbling far ahead, like the intermittent rolling of distant bass drums. He called out to the master. Together they listened.

The rumbling soon became louder, and they knew at last that they were hearing surf beating against a shore. They took a sounding, and found they were in forty feet of water. With the hope of holding the boat at sea until daylight, the master attempted to tack with the ragged sails, and Cabeza de Vaca took an oar, giving his swiftly diminishing strength to pulling on the land side.

When the first gray light rose, they gave the boat's stern to the sea, and resigned themselves to their destiny. A low shore soon became visible directly ahead. Behind it the dark line of some trees cut against the morning sky.

They were swept with increasing speed toward the land, and the noise of the surf resembled thunder. Suddenly they came into great combers. Their power was so great that they threw the boat completely out of the water. Then they drove it forward and it struck the beach with terrific impact. The dazed men were thrown violently out of it. Hardly conscious, they staggered and rolled and crawled through the boiling water onto a sand spit, and they lay there gasping like fish that were as much dead as alive.

The voyage had ended.

In forty-six days they had sailed nearly a thousand miles on their wandering course. Somehow their flimsy, battered, makeshift, leaking boat had held together. And somehow they had survived.

The day was the sixth of November, 1528.

PART FOUR

The Coast of Death

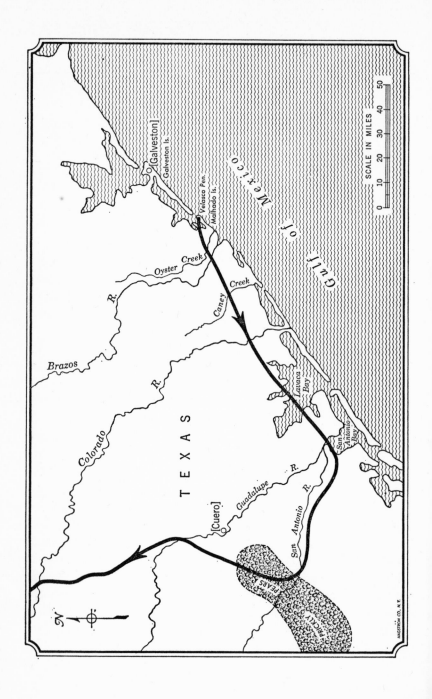

1

No stone monument or bronze plaque marks the place where Cabeza de Vaca landed on the bleak Texas coast. It would be a significant memorial, if it existed, but its erection is precluded by the circumstance that the exact site cannot be determined with unquestionable accuracy.

Yet, certain assertions, distances cited, fragmentary descriptions and other evidence to be found in his *Relacion* point convincingly toward two places very close to each other: Galveston Island and the Velasco Peninsula.

Cabeza de Vaca stated that he and his men landed on an island somewhat less than two miles in width and about thirteen miles in length, and inhabited by two distinct tribes speaking different tongues. In part, this information eliminates any other "islands" in the area.

The existence of two smaller islands off the northern shore of Velasco also conforms to the narrative. He speaks of a bay behind "his" island as being about five miles in width at its widest part, a dimension that could have been applicable to the present West Bay. The locations of certain streams to the south, as cited in the *Relacion*, also gives support to the belief that one of these sites was the landing place.

Hodge analyzed the question in this way:

"On general principles, Galveston Island would seem to supply the conditions, in that it more likely would have been inhabited by two distinct tribes, perhaps representing distinct linguistic families, as it is known to have been occupied by Indians [Karankawa] at a later period, besides having the smaller island or islands behind it. But its size and other conditions are not in favor of the identification, for its length is at least twice as great as that of Malhado [Cabeza de Vaca's island], as given in the narrative, and it is also more than two leagues from its nearest end to the first stream that the Spaniards crossed after departing from the island [as recounted by Oviedo]."

Hodge's deductions are sound, except for one fact. Apparently he was not aware that at the time Cabeza de Vaca landed, Galveston Island was *two islands*. A hurricane in the early nineteenth century closed the narrow pass between them.

Hodge continued:

"Mr. James Newton Baskett * suggests that the so-called Velasco Island, next south of Galveston Island, better fulfills the requirements, as indeed it does topographically, except for the fact that it is really a peninsula. Aside from this, it possesses all the physical features—length and width, distance from the first stream to the southward, and having the necessary island or islands [Mud and San Luis] off its northern shore."

Cabeza de Vaca wrote of four streams and two large bays which were crossed on a journey of sixty leagues to the south made by four men of his company. They could not, of course, have traveled in even a reasonably straight line in the coastal country.

The streams were described as being "very large and of rapid current." One of the largest and a smaller one flowed

* In his "Study of the Route of Cabeza de Vaca." *Texas State Historical Quarterly*, Vol. 10.

directly into the Gulf of Mexico. As the trip was made in the spring, they all undoubtedly were swollen with flood.

The distances between the streams and the bays, as given in the account, make it possible to identify them as Oyster Creek, the Brazos River, Caney Creek, the Colorado River, and La Vaca and San Antonio Bays.

The spotlight seems to fall on the Velasco Peninsula. That it was not a genuine island at the beginning of the twentieth century, when Hodge's observations were made, does not mean that it was not detached from the mainland early in the sixteenth century. Tropical storms both wear away and rebuild the Gulf of Mexico coastline. Hurricanes change it overnight. Galveston Island is a pertinent illustration of this erosion and construction. An estuary or inlet in existence one day may have vanished the next, and the reverse is equally true. There may well have been a pass at the south end of the Velasco Peninsula in the late fall of 1528.

Cabeza de Vaca called the place of the shipwreck Malhado Island, a name he might justifiably have given to a number of sites in which the expedition had met with misfortune during the previous year. He must have looked upon their situation as worse than any they had faced. He had no knowledge of the whereabouts of the other boats. Indeed, he had no knowledge of his own whereabouts. What land had they reached? How far away was Pánuco? Was it possible they had passed it?

There, without hope of salvation, wearied beyond description, starved, ragged, aching with cold, he might understandably have crossed himself and dropped to the ground to await the end. That he did not remains an unqualified tribute to his phenomenal courage.

The men crawled from the water into a small ravine that afforded some protection from the bitter sea wind, and there they found small pools of rain water to soothe their burning leathery throats. Some maize was salvaged from the wreckage, and they parched it over fires as they sought to warm their frigid bodies.

Stout Lupe de Oviedo * recovered his strength faster than the others. Seeing him on his feet and apparently in possession of his faculties, Cabeza de Vaca ordered him to climb a tree in a near-by grove for the purpose of gaining some knowledge of the country about them.

Returning from his mission, de Oviedo reported they were on an island. Cabeza de Vaca then sent him to reconnoiter on the ground. Looking around, de Oviedo came upon a footpath. He followed it some distance through the trees and scrub growth and salt flats until he saw ahead a group of Indian houses. Approaching cautiously he found them deserted, the only occupant of the village being a small dog.

Concerned about the length of de Oviedo's absence, Cabeza de Vaca dispatched two men to search for him. They met him a short distance away. He was returning to camp, bearing in his arms a quantity of dried mullet, an earthen cooking pot, and the dog. Trailing him were three natives armed with bows and arrows.

The Indians called to de Oviedo to stop, but he only beckoned to them to follow him, and continued on. The meat of the dog was soon dispensing savory odors from the cooking pot, and the men were enjoying the admirable taste of dried mullet.

Squatting some distance away on the shore, the three Indians curiously observed the scene. In a short time they were joined by a hundred other bowmen who came silently out of the trees.

If they were not large, our fears made giants of them.

The futility of attempting any kind of defense was obvious to Cabeza de Vaca. He would have had difficulty find-

* No relation to the historian, Fernández de Oviedo y Valdés.

ing six men with more than enough strength to stand on their feet.

Praying that an attack would not come, he secured several hawk-bells and some beads from the boat. Then he and Alonso de Solis went forward to face the Indians. The bells and beads were distributed with gestures signifying their desire for peace.

His relief must have been immeasurable when a number of the warriors presented him with arrows, an unmistakable pledge of friendship. Furthermore, he was deeply gratified when a spokesman informed him by signs that regrettably the Indians had nothing to eat with them, but he could depend upon them returning in the morning with food for the strange men who had come out of the sea.

The promise was kept. At sunrise a long file of red men entered the camp. They carried large quantities of roots dug from the shoal waters, and armfuls of fresh fish.

Wholesome roots, various kinds of fish and all the good water a man desired—the Indians provided it, too—was a diet which might strike a spark of new hope even in a man who was close to death. It did that, and it brought some new strength to their sick and abused bodies. After several days of feasting and rest most of them were revived enough to consider salvaging the boat and making another attempt to save themselves by sea.

The Indians brought their families to watch the spectacle of men digging the battered craft from the sand. The women and children were ecstatic over the trinkets, the useless buckles and glittering pieces of metal and scraps of leather given to them.

Slowly and painfully the weakened men freed the boat, patched it, and with satisfaction saw it once again in shape to be launched. All their clothes were stowed in dry places aboard, and naked they rolled it into the water. The exertion drained them of their limited strength, but all managed to clamber into it. They shoved off and bent to the oars.

Inching away from shore against a strong tide, they had progressed "the distance of two crossbow shots" when disaster struck. A large wave rolled down upon them. The boat was swamped. The cold water quickly numbed the naked men and the oars slipped from their hands.

The boat swung crazily, and the next wave capsized it. Alonso de Solis and two other men held on too long and were pulled underwater and drowned. The others fought their way toward shore. Without their clothes, their bodies horribly emaciated from months of malnutrition, they appeared like a band of skeletons staggering and crawling to safety on the beach.

Fortunately the fires of the camp were still burning, and they built them up, and huddled beside them against a rising north wind. Cabeza de Vaca saw them as "perfect figures of death. And thus were we asking mercy of Him and pardon for our transgressions, shedding many tears, and each regretting not his own fate alone, but that of his comrades about him."

The Indians, still mysteriously imbued with the spirit of kindness, brought more food to the camp at sunset. The tragic condition of the white men struck them with compassion and pity, and the sight of the bodies which had been washed ashore brought from them loud wails of sorrow. They sat down among the naked men and wept and howled out their anguish.

When at last the wild lamenting and the moaning had ceased, Cabeza de Vaca held a council, proposing that they ask the Indians for shelter in their houses. Some of the men feared to make such a move, believing it would place them in a position to be sacrificed to the pagan gods.

Cabeza de Vaca failed to see how any position could be more dangerous than their present one. As he saw the situation, the choice to be made was not between two ways of saving themselves but between two ways of dying. The boat, their clothing and what little equipment they had possessed had been carried away beyond recovery. Life could not long be sustained on that wintry, wind-swept shore. The houses proffered some shelter, be it only temporary. The men accepted his reasoning.

When the Indians were informed that the white men desired to be guests in their houses, they responded with cries of delight. Men were quickly dispatched to gather wood, and the Indians soon had fires blazing at intervals between the camp and the village.

Some of the Spaniards were so weak that they had to be carried from one fire to the next. This task the Indians undertook without complaint, and within a few hours all the strangers were together in a house in which several fires gave out a welcome heat.

Apparently in celebration of their hospitable accomplishment, the Indians started a dance which lasted through the night. At sunrise they brought fish and roots, and the few skins and grass coverings they could spare to make the Spaniards as comfortable as possible.

The fear of being sacrificed which had occupied some of the helpless Christians began to diminish.

Cabeza de Vaca did not record what kind of article he saw in the possession of an Indian that day, but he knew that it had not come from his boat or from any of his men. A discreet inquiry as to its origin brought the surprising reply that it had come from other white men who, like themselves, had been wrecked not far away.

The Indians readily agreed to guide him to the camp of the others. A party set out, but it had gone only a short distance before Captains Andrés Dorantes and Alonzo del Castillo appeared out of the brush, followed by the complete company from their boat. Indians had informed them of

Cabeza de Vaca's arrival, and they were in search of their companions.

> They were very much surprised at seeing us in the condition we were, and very much pained at having nothing to give us, as they had brought no other clothes than what they had on.

The reunion generated a feeling of greater safety, and revived spirits to the extent that plans were made to refit the Dorantes-Castillo boat and to make another attempt to escape.

The boat of Dorantes and Castillo had been driven ashore near the northern end of the island. Although the boat could not carry all of them, it was agreed, de Vaca noted, "that those of us might go in her who had vigor sufficient and disposition to do so, and the rest should remain until they became well enough to go, as they best might, along the coast until God our Lord should be pleased to conduct us alike to a land of Christians."

An infeasible plan, if there ever was one. It would be difficult to imagine that any of the men, sick or well, would volunteer to remain behind.

One man named Tavera died while the work of refitting the boat was in progress. In a sense, his demise may be looked upon as an inexplicable gesture of kindness by an otherwise cruel Fate. He was at least saved from the suffering and bitter disappointment that was to come.

The terrible problem of who was to go and who was to remain behind was settled in the end, however, by a power far greater than any possessed by the castaways. Immediately upon being launched the boat sank to a depth from which there was no possible chance of raising it.

With remarkable calmness and fortitude, Cabeza de Vaca states: "We yielded obedience to what necessity required."

It was one way of saying that with half the company naked, or nearly so, with cold weather upon them, without the means of carrying provisions, even if they could have obtained any food at all, they gave up all thoughts of traveling overland, a journey that would involve crossing the countless rivers and bays which the Indians informed them would be encountered.

They resigned themselves to remaining in the village until the winter had passed.

Yet, not all effort to find civilization was abandoned. They agreed that four of the most robust men, who were also good swimmers—surprisingly few of the Spaniards knew how to swim—should set out in an attempt to reach Pánuco, which some of them were convinced could not be far off.

> . . . and if, by Divine favor, they should reach there, they could give information of our remaining on that island, and of our sorrows and destitution.

But the Divine favor which Cabeza de Vaca so fervently had hoped for was not to come.

In keeping with their custom, the Spaniards on Misfortune Island did not count Indians or Negroes as men. In any enumeration only those who were Christians—that is, Roman Catholics—were listed. So the *Relacion* states that four men set out in November 1528, for Pánuco, and that "they took with them an Indian from the island of Cuba."

The name of the Cuban Indian was not recorded, but the four others who undertook the dangerous mission were Alvaro Fernandez, the Portuguese carpenter who had been so useful at the Bay of Horses; Figuroa, a native of Toledo; a man named Mendez; and Astudillo, a citizen of Cafra.

The quintet beat their way courageously southward, breaking trail through a country no white man had ever seen, nor any Cuban Indian, either, for that matter. They attempted to keep close to the coast, perhaps fearing they might miss Pánuco, living off what seafood, roots and animals they could secure.

It was an heroic, if short, march. They were the first Europeans to cross the Brazos and the Colorado Rivers that rushed into the sea from the totally unknown void of the west. They got across La Vaca Bay somehow, and made their way to the shore of San Antonio Bay.

There the trail ended.

No longer able to stand up under intolerable hunger, exhaustion and cold, Astudillo, Fernandez and the unnamed Cuban slipped into sleep from which they did not awaken.

Figuroa and Mendez tried to go on alone, but were soon captured by a coastal tribe and made slaves. Shortly afterward, Mendez escaped. He was pursued, retaken and put to death.

Figuroa alone was left alive.

2

After the departure of the ill-fated five, seventy Christians, one Negro Moor, and perhaps two hundred Indians remained crowded into the grass and pole huts on Malhado Island.

Recounting this period in his incomparable saga, Cabeza de Vaca sets down the first known accounts of the aborigines who inhabited the Texas coastal area and the adjacent territory. Indeed, in this respect his *Relacion* is a document of inestimable value to anthropologists and historians throughout its length. He was the first to describe the cultures, physiques, customs, mores and habitations of the many different native peoples he encountered in all the immense area of his wanderings.

Two tribes speaking different tongues lived on Malhado Island for at least several months of each year. They went there to trap fish in cane weirs and to gather the edible roots which grew in the shallows. He speaks of them as the Capoques and the Hans.

The Spaniards found shelter and hospitality in the villages of both families. The narrative indicates that Cabeza de Vaca and his men lived with the Capoques, while the men from Dorantes' boat remained among the Hans.

Although of different tribes, the two peoples lived largely in the same manner and had many customs in common. Cabeza de Vaca's statements must, of course, be viewed in the light of generalizations. In describing what he saw, he does not ascribe habits or peculiarities specifically to one tribe or the other.

He speaks of the Malhado Island natives as being large and well-formed, and relates: "They have no other arms than bows and arrows, in the use of which they are very dexterous. The men have one of their nipples bored from side to side, and some have both, wearing a cane in each, the length of two palms and a half, and the thickness of two fingers. They have the under lip also bored, and wear in it a piece of cane the breadth of half a finger. Their women are accustomed to great toil. The stay they make on the island is from October to the end of February. Their subsistence is the root I have spoken of, got from under the water in November and December. They have weirs of cane and take fish only in this season; afterwards they live on the roots. At the end of February they go into other parts to seek food; for then the root is beginning to grow and is not food.

"Those people love their offspring the most of any in the world, and treat them with the greatest mildness. When it occurs that a son dies, the parents and kindred weep as does everybody; the wailing continuing for him a whole year. They begin before dawn every day, the parents first and after them the whole town. They do the same at noon and at sunset. After a year of mourning has passed, the rites of the dead are performed; then they wash and purify themselves from the stain of smoke. They lament all the deceased in this manner, except the aged, for whom they show no regret, as they say that their season has passed, they having no enjoyment, and that living they would occupy the earth and take aliment from the young. Their custom is to bury the dead, unless it be those among them who have been physicians. These they burn. While the fire kindles they are all dancing and making high festivity, until the bones become powder. After the lapse of a year the funeral honors are celebrated, everyone taking part in them, when the dust is presented in water for the relatives to drink.

"Every man has an acknowledged wife. The physicians are allowed more freedom: they may have two or three wives, among whom exist the greatest friendship and harmony. From the time a daughter marries, all that he who takes her to wife kills in hunting or catches in fishing, the woman brings to the house of her father, without daring to eat or take any part of it, and thence victuals are taken to the husband. From that time neither her father nor mother enters his house, nor can he enter theirs, nor the houses of their children; and if by chance they are in the direction of meeting, they turn aside, and pass the distance of a cross-bow shot from each other, carrying the head low the while, the eyes cast on the ground; for they hold it improper to speak to each other. But the woman has liberty to converse and communicate with the parents and relatives of her husband. The custom exists from this island the distance of more than fifty leagues inland.

"There is another custom, which is, when a son or brother dies, at the house where the death takes place they do not go after food for three months, but sooner famish, their relatives and neighbors providing what they eat. As in the time we were there a great number of natives died, in most houses there was very great hunger, because of the keeping of this custom and observance; for although they who sought after food worked hard, yet from the severity of the season they could get but little; in consequence, the Indians who kept me, left the island, and passed over in canoes to the main, into some bays where are many oysters. For three months in the year they eat nothing besides these, and drink very bad water. There is great want of wood: mosquitoes are in great plenty. The houses are of mats, set up on masses of oyster shells, which they sleep upon, and in skins, should they accidentally possess them.

"The inhabitants of all this region go naked. The women alone have any part of their persons covered, and it with a wool that grows on trees. [Spanish moss.] The damsels dress themselves in deerskin. The people are generous to each other of what they possess. They have no chief. All that are of a lineage keep together. They have a custom when they meet, or from time to time when they visit, of remaining half an hour before they speak, weeping; and, this over, he that is visited first rises and gives the other all he has, which is received, and after a little while he carries it away, and often goes without saying a word."

Here is the first known written description of Indian giving, a practice that was looked upon with contempt by the white pioneers. In this form it brought about a constant exchange of goods and possessions. The recipient was soon visited by the donor, and their positions were reversed.

December came with cruel cold damp, and storms blew in from a raging gray gulf. No longer could the roots be obtained, for if a man could struggle against the roughness of the shallows, he could not endure the coldness of the water and the icy wind.

In the open mat houses, the starving white men began to die.

The lowest extremity was reached by five men who were quartered together in a shoreside hut. Their names were Sierra, Diego Lopez, Corral, Palacios and Goncalo Ruiz.

As each died his flesh was eaten by those still alive. Only the body of the last to die was found whole.

It is an interesting commentary on the character of the Indians that when they discovered that some of the Spaniards had become cannibals they were deeply disturbed and condemned them. Yet, both the Attacapan and Karankawan people of the Texas coast, to which the Capoques and the Hans probably belonged, were reputedly cannibals. If Cabeza de Vaca did not see them eat human flesh, he saw them drink water containing the ashes of cremated medicine men.

The Malhado Island natives must have understood that the white men generally respected each other. Also, they must have admired them and held them in high esteem. There seems to be merit, therefore, in the conclusion that their emotional distress came with the realization that the extraordinary strangers were, after all, not gods born of the sea, but were no more than ordinary mortals who could degenerate to the point of eating each other. Or perhaps their condemnation was a psychological reaction of some sort, or a reflection of some quirk or oddity in their religion. The truth cannot be known.

As the year 1529 began only fifteen Christians and the Moor were alive on the island.

They were : Cabeza de Vaca, Alonzo del Castillo, Andrés Dorantes, his two cousins, Diego Dorantes and Pedro de Valdivieso, Estrada, Tostado, Chaves, Gutierrez, Father Asturiano, Diego de Huelva, Benitez, Francisco de León, Heironymo de Alaniz the notary, Lupe de Oviedo and Estevanico the black.

What had happened to the men in the three other boats remained a complete mystery, but the little band clung desperately to the hope that they had reached safety and would send out a rescue expedition. In many a prayer they pitifully beseeched God to fulfill this request.

As if a sadistic Fate were not satisfied with the tortures and suffering already inflicted, the Indians were stricken with a disease of the bowels. The dreadful malady swept through them in an epidemic. Men, women and children dropped in agonizing death. Within a few days, half the natives on the island had perished.

Seeking desperately to discover a reason for the scourge, for a way in which they might appease the angry gods who had punished them so severely, the Indians turned on the white men. In a complete reversal of the tolerant attitude they had displayed toward the cannibalism, they accused the Spaniards of destroying them with some magic power.

Logically, the only way to halt such sorcery was to burn those who practiced it at the stake.

The Indian in whose house Cabeza de Vaca was quartered revealed himself as a man of compassion, and perhaps superior intelligence. He opposed the executions, advancing the contention that if the Spaniards possessed such a diabolical power, they would not have used it to kill their own kind. Reason told him they had no powers at all, for they had stood helplessly while their companions succumbed. In his eyes the white men still alive were no more than miserable wretches struggling to save themselves. He advised that they be left unharmed, for in their weakened condition they could hurt no one, and they would die soon enough.

"God our Lord," said Cabeza de Vaca, "willed that the others should heed this opinion, and be hindered in their design."

The winter dragged slowly on. Frequently as many as three days would pass during which neither Indians nor white men tasted a mouthful of food. Cabeza de Vaca wondered how life "could be so prolonged."

Time meant nothing. The nights and the days went their way unidentified one from the other, and each bringing nothing more than a continuation of the terrible ordeal.

Cabeza de Vaca carried a burden the others did not share. He had always held an intense dislike for seafood. In Florida he had not eaten fish ten times, living almost entirely on maize, other vegetables and wild meat. He had been unable to bring himself to eat the flesh of the horses. During the sea voyage and on Malhado Island he ate fish and oysters only as a last resort.

The vagaries of the Indian mind defied understanding. The Spaniards had not been sacrificed when the tribesmen became persuaded that they possessed no supernatural powers. Now they decreed that Cabeza de Vaca and several others, whose names are not known, must become medicine men.

There is a touch of humor in Cabeza de Vaca's statement that "they wished to make us physicians without examination or inquiring for diplomas."

The Indians, he wrote, "cure by blowing upon the sick, and with that breath and the imposing of hands they cast out infirmity." When he was commanded to become versed in this practice, Cabeza de Vaca ridiculed the idea, arguing that it was folly, and maintaining that he had no knowledge of the art of healing. How mistaken he was would soon be made clear to him.

Having lost a number of their best physicians in the diarrheal epidemic, the Indians were determined to replace them with a kind heretofore unknown, and which, they were convinced, would develop superior abilities. If the white men refused to co-operate in the program, they would receive no food at all and would soon die of starvation.

Endeavoring to induce Cabeza de Vaca to accept the assignment, an Indian criticized him for having no confidence in the medicine of the Capoques. Virtue dwelt in all things, even in the stones of the field. The Indian had seen pain driven from a body by merely passing a pebble over it. If such a simple thing could contain a beneficent influence, certainly a man as extraordinary as Cabeza de Vaca must possess greater powers. The Indian did not know the truth of his own words.

Cabeza de Vaca's hesitancy was not due to unwillingness to assume the role, but to the fear that his ministrations would fail, in which case he could expect to be burned alive as an imposter.

Hunger, however, made the decision. Without examination or diploma, he became Dr. Cabeza de Vaca. It was probably the most vital act of his life.

He quickly became proficient in his new career. When summoned to the bed of an ailing Indian, he would scarify the area of pain, suck blood from the incision, and then cauterize it. Then came the blowing on the wound which, according to Indian practice, completed the treatment.

Cabeza de Vaca, however, as well as the others who had been driven into the quackery, added to the basic ritual some ceremonies of their own which, although utterly mysterious and incomprehensible to the Indians, appeared to fascinate and delight them.

They blessed each sick person they attended, and kneeling beside him recited a Pater Noster and an Ave Maria, and they prayed to their own Heavenly Master that He would give him health, and they asked in all humbleness that He influence other Indians to treat lost Christians with kindness. Their prayers were answered.

In His clemency He willed that all those for whom we supplicated should tell the others that they were sound and in health, directly after we made the sign of the blessed cross over them.

The Indians rejoiced, and those they attended not only endowed them with all their worldly goods, but called on relatives for more possessions of value to be given the white physicians in payment for the miraculous cures they effected. Not only were they treated kindly, but Indians deprived themselves of food, if need be, so they might have sufficient, and they were given skins to wear.

God had, indeed, answered them.

3

More than four years were to pass before Cabeza de Vaca's hope of survival was to be kindled into an encouraging flame. They were to be dreadful years, years filled with unending labor, terrible sickness, hunger, tragedy and disappointment.

Early in the year 1529 the Hans left Malhado Island and crossed the bay to some oyster beds on the mainland shore. They took Castillo, Dorantes and several other Spaniards with them.

Soon afterward, Cabeza de Vaca and Francisco de León were obliged to accompany the Capoques to a mainland camp. There Cabeza de Vaca collapsed with a sickness he was unable to diagnose. He felt himself closer to death than he had ever been.

> If anything before had given me hopes of life, this were enough to have entirely bereft me of them.

Dorantes, Castillo and the others returned with the Hans to the island in April. The weather was warm and balmy. The time had come for them to make an attempt to reach Pánuco by land.

They put their heads together to work out a plan of escape, and here the illness of Cabeza de Vaca stood them in good stead.

They announced that they wished to visit the dying de Vaca on the mainland. One of them, by good fortune, still had the marten-skin cloak taken from the chief in the battle of Pensacola Bay, and it was given to an Indian to transport them across the bay in a canoe.

Heironymo Alaniz and Lupe de Oviedo were too weak to travel, and were left behind on the island. Those who departed, numbering twelve, were Castillo, Andrés Dorantes, Diego Dorantes, Valdivieso, Estrada, Tostado, Chaves, Gutierrez, Father Asturiano, de Huelva, Estevanico and Benitez. Reaching the mainland, they were joined by Francisco de León.

Cabeza de Vaca's condition was so serious that he was unable to rise from his bed. The thirteen men started on their journey without seeing him.

Although he recovered, Cabeza de Vaca's sickness destroyed the Indians' faith in him as a physician. If he could not cure himself, he assuredly retained no power to cure others. On the basis of this unfounded reasoning, they reduced him to the lowly position of a menial.

He was to spend a year in this painful subjection. He toiled without relief, responding to the beck and call of his masters. He dug roots from the water until his fingers were so worn that the touch of a straw would cause them to bleed. Broken canes in the root fields tore his flesh. He gathered wood and built fires and fished and performed other chores about the camp, living like a dog to which the savages would toss an occasional bone.

It was an almost insupportable life, but he carried on, never did his courage fail him. He gave no indication that he was thinking of escaping, but he never ceased to watch for an opportunity to flee his oppressors.

At last he found it.

He contrived an ingenious plan which would permit him to make his home among the Charrucos. These Indians lived in a forest region of the mainland, and during periodic trips from the island Cabeza de Vaca had been taken among them by the Capoques. He knew the Charrucos would welcome him and would treat him with favor.

Having become expert in the sign language, Cabeza de Vaca set himself up as a kind of commission merchant and traveling peddler.

His captors, finding him to be more useful to them in such a role than he was as a slave, let him go. With a pack on his back he traveled deep into the interior, and up and down the coast. Indians gave him orders for things they needed, and which they were unable to obtain themselves, chiefly because incessant hostilities made it unsafe for them to traverse the country.

He trafficked in cones and sea snails, conch shells which were used for cutting, other shells, reeds and canes. Such items were valued by the interior tribes, and for them they gave in exchange skins, ochre for painting the face, hard wood suitable for arrow shafts, sinews for bow strings, flint for arrowheads, and tassels of deer hair made red by dying. The most valuable of his wares was a small fruit with the appearance of a bean which was used as a stimulant and as a medicine.

The returns from his new occupation were highly satisfactory, the hours were his own, and there were numerous fringe benefits. Wherever he went he was treated with respect and fairness. The women liked him, and some presumably favored him with their charms. The men admired his shrewdness as a trader. He ate well, and rested as he desired. The most enjoyable feature of all, however, was the liberty.

There were drawbacks, of course, as there must be in any capacity a man enters. Often storms caught him alone in the wilderness, but he was fortunate enough to survive these harrowing experiences. "I came forth from them all by the great mercy of God our Lord. Because of them I avoided pursuing the business in winter, a season in which the natives themselves retire to their huts and ranches, torpid and incapable of exertion."

He was a free man. Why didn't he escape? The opportunity was constantly at hand. He knew the country. His reputation had grown to the point where he was a man of prominence, held in high esteem by the Indians of many tribes. Why did he stay there, peddling his homely commodities, for four years?

Heironymo de Alaniz had died on Malhado Island. Only Lupe de Oviedo was left there. Cabeza de Vaca stayed because he would not leave de Oviedo alone in that God-forsaken place among the savages.

Each spring Cabeza de Vaca made a special trip out to the island to entreat Lupe de Oviedo to escape with him. His pleas were in vain. Lupe de Oviedo, although having regained strength, was filled with fear. Each year Lupe de Oviedo promised that he would go with the arrival of the next spring, but it was not until the fifth spring of his stay on the island that he found the courage to leave.

Only the bones of three score men remained on Malhado Island to give witness to the tragedy that had taken place there. The last of the living had gone.

4

A glance backward at events which transpired after the land expedition set out from Tampa Bay, in May of 1528, seems appropriate at this point.

As the last of the soldiers disappeared into the Florida

bush, one of the ten women on the vessels anchored in the lagoon expressed the belief in a tearful farewell that the column was marching to its doom.

She was the wife of the gentleman adventurer who had on two previous occasions—during the voyage across the Atlantic and on the eve of his departure for the interior—repeated to Narvaez the sinister prognostication of the Moorish mystic of Hornachos.

Now she believed it would come true in all its predicted dreadfulness. Neither the governor, her husband nor any of the others would ever again be seen alive. She "knew" it. They were destined to perish in that forbidding land.

In view of the futility of harboring any hope that they would return, she thought it would be wise for the women to rearrange their lives at once. A widow had nothing to gain. She intended to remarry without further delay, and she admonished the others to do the same.

They did. Before many days had passed, all were settled in new nests, although some of them who were not quite so certain of what the future held, did not enter into a marriage ceremony. They simply became concubines.

Obeying Narvaez's orders, Captain Caravello, who had been left in command of the ships, sailed in quest of the elusive Bahia de la Cruz. Its entrance, of course, was only a few miles to the south of them. They went north.

One of the vessels soon struck a reef and was destroyed by breakers. How far the others proceeded along the coast is not a matter of record. They came upon no good harbor, and after some days abandoned the search and turned back.

Five leagues below the lagoon in which the expedition had landed, they found Tampa Bay. There they were joined by the brigantine which Narvaez had sent back to Cuba for supplies, and by the vessel commanded by Captain Alvara de la Cerda, which had been waiting in Havana for orders. There were good reasons for rejoicing. They had fresh provisions, and their protection was assured. The harbor was one of the largest and finest in all the New World. It ran for seven or eight leagues into the land. It had a bottom of fine white sand. No sea or storm could damage ships anchored there. Seafood was in great abundance. Havana was only a hundred leagues away.

For a year they waited, watchful for the appearance of the explorers from the green jungle. Occasionally they made short cruises along the coast with the hope of meeting them.

At last they gave up. Captain Caravello had been told by Narvaez to sail for Pánuco, but the location of that far-off place was as indefinite as that of Tampa Bay had been. With supplies exhausted and the season of the great storms approaching, it would be folly to go in search of a port which might be anywhere along that seemingly endless coast.

In the summer of 1529, Captain Caravello set a course for Mexico, and once more the Bahia de la Cruz was left to itself in emptiness and silence.

One of the gentlemen who had remained with the ships was Juan Ortiz. He was a native of Seville and a member of a prominent family. After reaching Mexico, he made his way back to Cuba. For the purpose of personally expressing his condolences, he called on the widow of Narvaez.

It was the greatest mistake of his life. The wily woman induced him to return to Florida to make another search for her husband.

The best Ortiz could secure in the way of a boat was a pinnace, hardly adequate for the voyage, but with twenty men hired for the venture, he bravely set sail in it.

Skirting the southwestern coast of Florida, he turned into Charlotte Harbor, the scene of the Ponce de León disaster.

Almost ten years later, a party of men led by Baltazar de

Gallegos, a lieutenant of Hernando de Soto, came upon him.

In his famous narrative of the de Soto Expedition, The Gentleman of Elvas * gives a vivid account of the experiences of the generous Ortiz, who had attempted to perform a favor for a distraught lady.

Wrote the Gentleman of Elvas: "Coming to the port in sight of the town, they saw a cane sticking upright in the ground, with a split in the top, holding a letter, which they supposed the governor [Narvaez] had left there, to give information of himself . . . They asked it to be given to them, of four or five Indians walking along the beach, who, by signs, bade them come to land for it, which Ortiz and another did, though contrary to the wishes of the others. No sooner had they got on shore, when many natives came out of the houses, and, drawing near, held them in such a way that they could not escape. One, who would have defended himself, they slew on the spot; the other [Ortiz] they seized by the hands, and took him to Ucita, their chief. The people in the pinnace, unwilling to land, kept along the coast and returned to Cuba.

"By command of Ucita, Juan Ortiz was bound hand and foot to four stakes, and laid upon scaffolding, beneath which a fire was kindled, that he might be burned; but a daughter of the chief entreated that he might be spared."

I interrupt here to remark that this is the first known appearance of the story, which was to become universally popular, about a white man being saved by an Indian prin-

* The Gentleman of Elvas, a member of the de Soto Expedition, was a native of Elvas, Portugal. His name is thought to have been Alvaro Fernández. He wrote his narrative of the memorable and tragic adventure after his return, drawing it from memory. So far as is known, he kept neither a diary nor notes. Some of his descriptions are vague, distances are sometimes incorrect, and he made other unquestionable errors. Yet, his account remains the best and most complete preserved for us. It was first published at Evora, Portugal, in 1557. An authentic English translation was made by Buckingham Smith in 1866.

cess. The narrative of The Gentleman of Elvas was first published in Portugal in 1557. This was thirty-eight years before Pocahontas, who allegedly saved the English colonist, John Smith, was born.

The Gentleman of Elvas continued: "Though one Christian, she said, might do no good, certainly he could do no harm, and it would be an honor to have one for a captive; to which the father acceded, directing the injuries to be healed. When Ortiz got well, he was put to watching a temple, that the wolves, in the nighttime, might not carry off the dead there, which charge he took in hand, having commended himself to God. One night they [the wolves] snatched away from him the body of a little child, son of a principal man; and, going after them, he threw a dart at the wolf that was escaping, which, feeling itself wounded, let go its hold, and went off to die; and he returned, without knowing what he had done in the dark. In the morning, finding the body of the little boy gone, he became very sober; and Ucita, when he heard what had happened, determined he should be killed; but having set on the trail which Ortiz pointed out as that the wolves had made, the body of the child was found, and a little farther on a dead wolf; at which circumstance the chief became well pleased with the Christian, and satisfied with the guard he had kept, ever after taking much notice of him."

At the end of three years, Ortiz lost his job as guardian of the Indian morgue. The disruption came as a result of an attack on Ucita's domain by a rival chief named Mococo. Ucita and his followers fled while their town, and presumably the burial ground, was destroyed by the raiders.

Ucita established new headquarters on the coast, and for some unexplained reason turned once more on the unlucky Spaniard. But once again Ortiz was saved from the sacrificial altar by the angry chief's daughter, who warned him that he was to burn at the stake the following day. She urged him to flee to the victorious Mococo, "who she knew would receive him with regard," and she even went half a league out of town with him after dark, to be certain that he took the right road.

"Ortiz," wrote the Gentleman of Elvas, traveled all night, and in the morning came "to a river, the boundary of the territory of Mococo, where he discovered two men fishing. As this people were at war with those of Ucita, and their languages different, he did not know how he should be able to tell them who he was, and why he came . . . that they might not kill him. It was not, however, until he come up to where their arms were placed that he was discovered, when they fled toward the town. . . . As they arrived, shouting, many Indians came out of the town, and began surrounding, in order to shoot him with their arrows, when he, finding himself pressed, took shelter behind trees. . . . At the moment, it pleased God that an Indian should come up, who, speaking the language [of Ucita], understood him and quieted the others. . . . Three or four ran to carry the news, when the *cacique,* much gratified, came a quarter of a league on the way to receive him. He caused the Christian immediately to swear to him . . . that he would not leave him for any other master; and in return, he promised to show him much honor, and if at any time Christians should come to that land, he would let him go freely."

Ortiz was glad to swear allegiance to Mococo. He spent another six years in comparative comfort. Mococo was as good as his word, bestowed kindness and hospitality on his curious guest, and not once threatened to burn him alive.

By the time nine years had passed, Ortiz's hope of being rescued had almost vanished. Then suddenly the ships of de Soto appeared on the blue horizon, and his men landed on the shore near the residence of Ucita, Ortiz's old enemy.

It was Mococo himself who told Ortiz of the arrival of the

Christians. Ortiz, thoroughly disheartened, did not believe the chief. Recounted the Gentleman of Elvas: "The captive, thinking himself jested with . . . said that his thoughts no longer dwelt on his people, and that his only wish now was to serve him. Still the *cacique* assured him that it was even as he stated, and gave him leave to go, telling him that if he did not, and the Christians should depart, he must not blame him, for he had fulfilled his promise.

"Great was the joy of Ortiz at this news, though still doubtful of its truth; however, he thanked Mococo, and went his way. A dozen principal Indians were sent to accompany him; and on their way to the port, they met Baltazar de Gallegos. . . . Arrived at the camp, the governor [de Soto] ordered that apparel be given to him, good armor, and a fine horse. When asked if he knew of any country where there was gold or silver, he said that he had not been ten leagues in any direction from where he lived; but that thirty leagues distant was a chief named Paracoxi, to whom Mococo, Ucita, and all they that dwelt along the coast paid tribute, and that he perhaps had knowledge of some good country, as his land was better than theirs, being more fertile, abounding in maize. Hearing this, the governor was well pleased."

Ortiz apparently had become well versed in the Indian sign language, and he was engaged by de Soto as an interpreter and scout.

He was with de Soto in the Province of Apalachen when Indians told them of Narvaez and his men having been there, and how they had built boats and sailed away westward, because they were starving and helpless to escape by land.

Wrote the Gentleman of Elvas: "Every mind was depressed at this information, and all counseled the governor to go back to the port, that they might not be lost, as Narvaez had been, and to leave the land of Florida; that, should they go further, they might not be able to get back, as the little maize that was yet left the Indians would secure: to which de Soto replied, that he would never return until he had seen with his own eyes what was asserted, things that to him appeared incredible."

Ortiz was in Alabama with de Soto when Indians recounted how the Narvaez boats had arrived in Mobile Bay "in want of water," and how Teodoro and another man had deserted. They saw the dagger that had belonged to the Greek.

So Ortiz came to visit these sites on the long journey into darkness taken by his former companions.

A veteran of more than a dozen years in the wilderness, having never had a taste of civilization all that time, Juan Ortiz died in Autiamque, an Indian town thirty miles east of Fort Smith, on the south bank of the Arkansas River.

It was a loss, wrote the Gentleman of Elvas, that Hernando de Soto greatly regretted.

5

The party led by Captain Andrés Dorantes, which set out from Malhado Island in the spring of 1529 for Pánuco, followed a course that kept it close to the coast. Reaching the Brazos River, the men constructed several small rafts. The stream was in flood, and the current was stronger than they had judged it to be.

One of the rafts was swept out to sea, and the four men clinging to it were drowned. By the time the others had reached San Antonio Bay, another member of the group had died, unable to endure longer the diet of crabs and boiled kelp.

The narrative is not clear as to which men were lost at sea and which one succumbed on the trail, but the identities of the five can be established through events which transpired later and in which the names of the surviving seven are mentioned.

Those who were lost were Estrada, Tostado, Chaves, Gutierrez and Benitez.

Somewhere along the coast, probably in the vicinity of La Vaca Bay, they came upon the wrecked boat which had been in the command of Father Xuarez and Alonso Enrriquez, the comptroller. They found no evidence to indicate what had happened to its complement, and they pressed on with another weight of sadness added to their many burdens.

On the shore of the bay they came upon some Indians gathering berries. At sight of them the natives leaped into canoes and paddled away. Feasting on the berries, the men debated as to the best means of crossing the wide barrier of water before them. Presently they saw that a canoe carrying two men was approaching them.

They presumed the men to be Indians, but were astonished to see, as the canoe came to shore, that one of them was Figuroa. It was both a sad and happy reunion. Glad to find Figuroa alive, they were deeply discouraged by the news that none of the five "strong swimmers" who had left Malhado Island during the winter had broken through to Pánuco.

Figuroa had a tragic story to tell. He related how Fernandez, Astudillo and the Cuban Indian had died of cold and hunger, and how Mendez, making a brave attempt to escape from some Indians, had been slain.

Figuroa had been made a slave. He learned after a time that another white man was held by a neighboring tribe, the Quevenes, and when the opportunity came he went in search of him.

The prisoner of the Quevenes was Hernando de Esquivel, a native of Badajoz. He was the last known survivor of the men who had sailed in the Xuarez-Enrriquez boat. Esquivel also had been a witness to the catastrophe of Governor Narvaez.

This was the story Esquivel told Figuroa, and which Figuroa repeated to Dorantes and his men:

Narvaez was near-by when the Xuarez-Enrriquez boat was capsized and destroyed. He sailed on across the bay, landed his men, and returned for those who had been shipwrecked. After ferrying them to the south side of the bay, Narvaez performed the last official act of his life.

Enrriquez, as comptroller, served in the capacity of a lieutenant to the governor. Narvaez, without explanation, revoked his commission, and replaced him with the favored Captain Pantoja. Under the circumstances, it was a senseless exercise of his power.

That night, Narvaez, a very sick man, remained in bed on his boat. Only two aides were with him, he having ordered all others to camp on the shore. The boat was anchored with a stone. During the night a strong wind rose.

In the darkness no one on shore could see the boat break its mooring and disappear. Obviously it was carried out to sea by the wind and tide. Neither it nor Narvaez and his two aides were seen again.

With the sycophantic Pantoja in command, the company advanced along the coast until they were halted by another wide reach of water, presumably San Antonio Bay. They got across it with great difficulty on some pole rafts, landing on a wooded point. A few Indians who were camping near-by put their mat huts into canoes and disappeared.

The trees afforded some shelter, and there was fuel for fires. A few crabs and shellfish were found in the surrounding waters. It was not enough food to sustain them, and the protection was inadequate against the November cold.

One by one they slipped away into death.

Esquivel related how Pantoja had abused his subjects. His inherited authority had gone to his head. He had command of a company of dying men, men helpless and trapped and without hope of salvation, a company of skeletons and ghosts, and he appeared to find some kind of sadistic satisfaction in mistreating them. Perhaps Pantoja, Lord of Ixtlahuaca, the close friend of Narvaez who had accompanied him on the ill-fated mission to Mexico, had gone mad.

Perhaps Soto-Mayor also was mad. Soto-Mayor, who held the post of camp master and had the manners of a gentleman, was a brother of Vasco Porcallo de Figuroa, the wealthy *encomiendero* who had offered Narvaez a quantity of supplies in Trinidad. It was in that Cuban port that one of the ships had been lost in a hurricane.

In a wild outburst, Soto-Mayor struck Pantoja on the head with a club, instantly killing him.

Each day and each night others died, if by less violent means and less suddenness, with far greater suffering. The living dried the flesh of the corpses and sought to survive on it, but they, each in his turn, also perished.

The last to die was Soto-Mayor, and Esquivel fed upon him, and upon seafood and kelp, miraculously sustaining himself until March. Then an Indian found him and took him to a village, and gave him shelter and food.

When Figuroa met Esquivel in the camp of the Quevenes, he proposed that they escape together and make another attempt to reach Pánuco, but Esquivel refused.

Esquivel was convinced they had passed Pánuco. It was far behind them, only God knew where, and they were lost somewhere on the coast of central Mexico.

Figuroa left the poor wretch in the Indian village. They never saw each other again.

At last Figuroa met Dorantes and his little band.

Now they were able to account for four of the boats. Including those who had been in the fifth boat, only fifty-eight of the three hundred men who had started from Tampa Bay more than a year before could be counted, but only tentatively, among the living.

The Indian who had come in the canoe with Figuroa to meet Dorantes and the six others offered to give them some fish if two men would go back with him across the bay. Father Asturiano and probably de Huelva, both of whom could swim, volunteered for the mission.

The four men left in the canoe, but when they reached the Indian's village on the opposite shore of the bay, the Spaniards were made prisoners and were not permitted to return.

It was not long before Andrés Dorantes, Diego Dorantes, Castillo, Estevanico and Valdivieso also were taken as captives. They soon learned how Figuroa, Father Asturiano and de Huelva had fared.

The padre and Figuroa had made an attempt to flee, but had been quickly overtaken. Both were severely beaten, and the clergyman had been stripped of his ragged vestments and had suffered an arrow wound in the arm. Undaunted, they made another attempt to escape, and this time had met with success, vanishing into the wilderness.

De Huelva had made the mistake of moving from the Indian house in which he was quartered to another without permission. For this violation he was put to death.

Fifty-seven might be presumed to be still alive.

Dorantes and his four companions entered into a miserable, brutal life of slavery. De Vaca noted later that they were "forced with more cruelty to serve than the Moor would have used. Besides going stark naked and barefooted over the coast burning in summer like fire, their continual occupation was bringing wood and water on the back, or whatever the Indians needed, and dragging canoes over inundated grounds in hot weather.

"The natives eat nothing the year round but fish, and of that not much. They experience far less hunger, however, than the inhabitants inland. . . . They have fingernails that for any ordinary purpose are knives."

When they had nothing else to occupy their minds, the Indians amused themselves by pulling out the facial hairs of the Spaniards, or beating them with sticks.

Andrés Dorantes one day come upon the mutilated body of his cousin, Diego. Valdivieso met a similar death.

Now the last chapters of the personal stories of fifty-five men remained unwritten.

For fourteen months, until the late summer of 1530, Dorantes, Castillo and Estevanico the Moor endured the cruel treatment and ceaseless labor.

At the end of this period, Dorantes escaped. He made his way some distance inland in a northerly direction, finally reaching a village of the Yguazes tribe. Their brutality surpassed even that he had suffered before, and once again he fled into the wild.

He found haven the next time among some Mariames, and it was there he learned of the fate of Esquivel.

Fifty-four left to be accounted for.

Castillo and Estevanico remained prisoners of the Indians from whom Dorantes had escaped for a year and a half before they, too, found an opportunity to slip away.

Dorantes had reached the Mariames late in 1530. Now the *Relacion* accounts unsatisfactorily for the passage of time, but it indicates that the three men came together again among the Mariames early in the year 1532.

One day in the spring of the following year, an Indian appeared at the hut in which Dorantes was living. He brought word that another white man had been seen with a group of Quevenes not far away.

6

Cabeza de Vaca could swim well, but Lupe de Oviedo could not swim at all. As they made their way southward from Malhado Island in the spring of 1533, it was necessary for Cabeza de Vaca to support de Oviedo while crossing a body of water, and if a stream were wide or swift, as the Brazos and the Colorado were, they were obliged to build rafts or float across while clinging to a log. De Oviedo was constantly in fear of the water, as well as numerous other things.

When they neared La Vaca Bay they fell in with some Doguenes Indians who were traveling southward to eat walnuts. Cabeza de Vaca was well known to them as a trader and peddler, and they readily accepted him and de Oviedo as traveling companions.

After they had crossed the bay, however, Cabeza de Vaca entered a country in which he had never been on his trading journeys. A party of Quevenes, on a similar quest for nuts, soon appeared. They were a tribe Cabeza de Vaca had never encountered, but probably because of the attitude of the Doguenes, they displayed no unfriendliness toward him.

The Quevenes told him that some distance toward the south, serving as slaves with the Mariames, were two white men and a black, the latter being of great stature, and a wonder to behold.

Eagerly Cabeza de Vaca inquired of the condition of his old companions. He received a discouraging reply. They were badly used by their captors, frequently beaten, and were forced to work hard each day.

The Quevenes had more sad news to relate. All other white men who had come into the area of the two bays had long since died of starvation or had been killed. However, it was believed that the three men still alive would soon arrive near-by with the Mariames to eat nuts, and Cabeza de Vaca might see them if he wished to go to their camp.

To demonstrate the manner in which Dorantes, Castillo and Estevanico were treated, the Quevenes set upon Cabeza de Vaca and Lupe de Oviedo, slapping them, beating them with sticks, throwing mud on them, and holding arrows against their hearts.

De Oviedo was struck with terror. When the women of the Doguenes were sent back across the bay, he announced his intention to go with them. He would make no more attempts to leave the country. There he would live and die.

Cabeza de Vaca pleaded in vain with him to remain. Lupe de Oviedo went back with the women, and he was never heard of again.

Once more Cabeza de Vaca was alone.

The walnut trees were large and numerous in the area. The nuts were the size of those which grew in Galicia. The Indians ground the meats, and for two months existed chiefly on this food.

Arrangements to travel to the place in which the Mariames were encamped were not easily completed. The Quevenes now became suspicious of Cabeza de Vaca, and their respect for him faded. At last a friendly Doguenes agreed to guide him, if he would flee to a certain place in the woods and wait. Cabeza de Vaca slipped away, and the following morning his friend and several other Doguenes met him and took him with them.

Dorantes and Cabeza de Vaca cried with joy at the sight of each other. Four years had passed since Dorantes had left Malhado Island. Each had long before presumed the other to be dead.

We gave many thanks at seeing ourselves together, and this was a day to us of the greatest pleasure we had enjoyed in life.

They were soon joined by Estevanico and Castillo in a reunion for which each was profoundly grateful.

Thus the Almighty had been pleased to preserve me through many trials and diseases, conducting me in the end to the fellowship of those who had abandoned me, that I might lead them over the bays and rivers that obstructed our progress.

Now Cabeza de Vaca heard the tragic stories told by Figuroa and Esquivel, of how Narvaez had been carried off in the night, and of the terrible deaths of the men from the two boats.

Still nothing was heard of the boat which had been commanded by Captains Penalosa and Tellez. Even the mysterious Indian telegraph, by which news travels swiftly and far in the wilderness, brought no word of its forty-seven men.

When Dorantes, Castillo and Estevanico heard Cabeza de Vaca's plan for going on southward, they quickly cautioned him against moving hastily or letting the Mariames know of his intentions. They held the opinion that if they were to make a successful escape together, they would have to wait for at least another six months. At that time the Mariames journeyed north and west to an area in which prickly pears were abundant. A number of other tribes, some of which would come great distances, would arrive at the pear fields in the same season. It would then be possible to leave with other Indians, perhaps with a tribe that lived to the west where the Mariames would not venture in an attempt to retake them.

Cabeza de Vaca sadly accepted the advice. The three men were wise in the ways of the Mariames, and although he was bitterly disappointed by the prospect of facing another long delay, he was constrained to heed their counsel.

Castillo was sent away to live with the Yguazes, probably

having been traded to them. Cabeza de Vaca and Dorantes became slaves of a family, all the members of which were blind in one eye.

So they labored and waited with inconceivable patience for the time of the prickly pears.

7

Cabeza de Vaca wrote of people who soon after his time vanished from the earth. They left few traces by which anthropologists, who came in the wake of the pioneers and settlers, could judge and classify them.

When Cabeza de Vaca was among them, they had moved only a few steps beyond the shadows of the Stone Age. They cultivated no fields or orchards on the Texas coastal plain, domesticated no animals. Their weaving reached its apex in the mats of reeds of which their portable houses were constructed. They wove no cloth in this area of wilderness America. Their garments were of animal skins and clumps of Spanish moss, but generally they wore none at all. Their tools were stone hammers, and knives, needles and fishhooks of bone. The furthest advance of their culture was marked by the bow and arrow.

In the humid, disagreeable country between Malhado Island and San Antonio Bay, and for some distance inland between the Guadalupe and Colorado Rivers, dwelt perhaps a score of tribes, speaking several languages, and following greatly varying customs. Cabeza de Vaca recorded their names, but, as Hodge points out, it is not known whether a name he used was one applied to a tribe by its own members or was one used by another tribe speaking a different language. By the time civilization in its crudest form reached Texas, no remnant of this large aboriginal population existed.

Cabeza de Vaca set down the names as they had sounded to his Spanish ear, and he gave two or more spellings to some of them. A few are close enough to known names to provide a clue which suggests a positive identification, but not many, and the majority of these peoples must remain unknown, forever wrapped in primeval mystery.

The Capoques and the Hans shared dreary Malhado Island, and on the near-by mainland lived the Chorruco, who allegedly took their name from the forests. Moving southward along the coast, Cabeza de Vaca located the Doguenes, the Mendica, the Quevenes, the Guaycones, the Quitoks, the Camoles, and a tribe he identifies only as the People of the Figs.

Some of the other mainland Indians named were the Mariames, the Yguazes, the Atayos, the Acubadoes, the Chavavares, the Maliacones, the Cultalchulchas, the Susolas and the Comos.

Although all differed in their tribal mores, they did have some habits in common.

A pregnant wife was abandoned by her husband for two years. Some children were suckled until they had almost reached the age of puberty, a custom that had its roots in stark reality. Time of want, as Cabeza de Vaca knew well, came frequently. Often a village would be without food for several days. The children, some of them twelve years of age, were breastfed to save them from famishing and growing into weaklings.

Nocturnal assassinations were commonplace occurrences. The infliction of "gross barbarities" was the rule, not the exception. A man might expect to be waylaid and robbed, beaten, stabbed or otherwise mutilated at any time.

It was not Cabeza de Vaca's destiny, nor that of his three companions, to meet death through such violence, although they were close to it innumerable times. One example taken from the narrative is sufficient to illustrate the peril in which they lived: "While I was among the Doguenes, their enemies, coming suddenly at midnight, fell upon them, killed three and wounded many, so that they ran from their houses to the fields before them. As soon as these ascertained that their assailants had withdrawn, they returned to pick up all the arrows the others had shot, and following after them in the most stealthy manner possible, came that night to their dwellings without their presence being suspected. At four o'clock in the morning the Doguenes attacked them, killed five, and wounded numerous others, and made them flee from their houses, leaving their bows with all they possessed. In a little while came the wives of the Quevenes to them and formed a treaty whereby the parties became friends. The women, however, are sometimes the cause of war."

An Indian who became sick on a trek usually was left to perish alone, unless a relative chose to assist him.

Childless men changed wives as they pleased, but those who were fathers generally remained with the mother of their children. Connubial loyalty, however, was not a requirement, nor was it a common practice.

Men settled quarrels with their fists, the members of the same tribe rarely resorting to weapons. Sometimes fights were halted by the women, but men never interfered. He noted, "After they have fought . . . they take to their dwellings and go into the woods, living apart from each other until their heat has subsided. When no longer offended and their anger is gone, they return. From that time they are friends as if nothing had happened. If those that quarrel are single, they go to some neighboring people, and although they should be enemies, they receive them well and welcome them warmly, giving them so largely of what they have, that when their animosity cools, and they return to their town, they go rich."

There were numerous homosexuals among these Indians. Cabeza de Vaca mentions encountering them especially among the Yguazes and in the villages of another tribe which he does not identify.

He was astounded to see eunuchs, and wrote: "I witnessed a diabolical practice; a man living with another, one of those who are emasculate and impotent. They go habited like women, and perform their duties, use the bow and carry heavy loads. Among them we saw many mutilated in the way I describe. They are more muscular than other men, and taller: they bear very weighty burthens."

Both the Mariames and the Yguazes seemed to be more influenced by dreams than the other peoples. They sometimes sacrificed male children in the hope of appeasing an angry god who had appeared before them as they slept.

They cast away females at birth, leaving them to die of starvation or be eaten by dogs and wild animals. This practice had its foundation in their eternal struggle to survive. They were constantly at war with other tribes, and if their daughters lived and were taken captives, the progeny would only increase the number of their enemies, and in the end they would be overcome and made slaves.

It was unthinkable to them that they might permit their daughters to survive and marry among their own people. The idea of a Mariames or a Yguazes girl as the wife of a man of her own tribe filled them with disgust. It was far better to kill them than to give them to their own kind to be bred.

Cabeza de Vaca remarks that he found no other tribes on the coastal plain which followed this savage custom. Most of the natives, he said, "love their offspring the most of any in the world, and treat them with the greatest mildness." This is a characteristic of most American Indians.

The Mariames and the Yguazes evidently were rare exceptions to the rule.

They bought their wives from their enemies. The cost of an average woman was a bow. If she were gifted in some respect, two arrows were added to the purchase price. The marriage continued only so long as the sex act was mutually satisfactory. Should one or the other become displeased, it was promptly dissolved.

The stature of the Yguazes was not as great as that of the Mariames, but they were no less well proportioned. They were fine archers. The men wore pieces of cane inserted in their nipples and lips.

Roots were their main staple. They traveled considerable distances to secure them, for they were vital to their existence. Occasionally they killed deer and caught fish, but their country was exceedingly poor, and the quantities obtained of these wholesome foods were small.

They supplemented their fare in times of scarcity with spiders, the eggs of ants, worms, lizards, salamanders, rattlesnakes, other poisonous vipers, and deer dung. The bones of animals and fish were beaten into powder. Nothing that could possibly be digested was wasted.

"The women work very hard," de Vaca remarked, "and do a great deal; of the twenty-four hours they have only six of repose; the rest of the night they pass in heating the ovens to bake those roots they eat. At daybreak they begin to dig them, to bring wood and water to their houses and get in readiness other things that may be necessary."

The Yguazes were notorious thieves. They stole not only from enemies, but from each other. They were equally distinguished as liars, and they were drunkards without peers. Their liquor was brewed from the mescal button.

Cabeza de Vaca tells of seeing Indians run down deer, pursuing them from dawn until dark, if necessary, to kill them. Most of the natives along the coast lived in houses made of mats placed over hoops. These were easily disassembled, and could be transported in canoes.

Generally these coastal natives were merry people, "considering the hunger they suffer; for they never cease, notwithstanding, to observe their festivities and *areytos.*"

The happiest time of the year was the season when the prickly pears were ripe. Then hunger could be easily appeased, and they danced as they gorged themselves.

The prickly pear, of which there were numerous varieties, was the fruit of the Opuntia cactus. It was the size of a hen's egg, and vermilion and black in color. Cabeza de Vaca found its flavor agreeable. After squeezing out the juice, which was drunk, the pears were split and laid out to dry. The dried fruit was taken back to the village and held in reserve for times when other food was scarce. The peel was beaten to a powder.

De Vaca observed: "It occurred to us many times while we were among this people, and there was no food, to be three or four days without eating, when they, to revive our spirits, would tell us not to be sad, that soon there would be the prickly pears when we should eat a plenty and drink of the juice, when our bellies would be very big and we should be content and joyful."

Cabeza de Vaca made no attempt to record the various tongues he heard. His only allusion to the subject is the brief statement which Buckingham Smith translated as follows: "There is a language in which calling to a person, for 'look here' they say 'Arre aca,' and to a dog 'Xo.'"

Fanny Bandelier, translating the 1542 edition of the *Relacion,* gave a different version: "Among them is a language wherein they call men 'mirra acca, arraca,' and dogs 'xo.'"

Hodge remarks that the Karankawas used the word "haka" for "sit down." Cabeza de Vaca heard several Karankawan dialects. The word *mira* is Spanish, and Hodge wonders if

Mrs. Bandelier regarded it as a part of the Indian exclamation.

Everywhere he went, Cabeza de Vaca found Indians stupefying themselves with some sort of a smoke. So treasured and sought after was this unidentified opiate that a native addicted to it would give all he possessed to acquire it.

The Indians also stimulated themselves with "a tea made from leaves of a tree like those of an oak."

The drink was prepared with great care and ceremony. First the leaves were toasted in a vessel, and when thoroughly parched were covered with water.

De Vaca described the making of this drink in detail. "When the liquor has twice boiled, they pour it into a jar, and in cooling it use the half of a gourd. So soon as it is covered thickly with froth, it is drunk as warm as can be supported; and from the time it is taken out of the pot until it is used they are crying aloud: 'Who wishes to drink?' When the women hear these cries, they instantly stop, fearing to move. . . . Should one of them move, they dishonor her, beating her with sticks, and greatly vexed, throw away the liquor they have prepared; while those who have drunk eject it, which they do readily and without pain. The reason they give for this usage is, that when they are about to drink, if the women move from where they hear the cry, something pernicious enters the body in that liquid, shortly producing death. . . . They are three days drinking it, eating nothing in the time.

"When the women have their indisposition, they seek food only for themselves, as no one else will eat of what they bring."

The drink was made from the leaves of the ilex, and it was the same potion as that prepared by tribes throughout the southern United States. Generally it was known as the "black drink." The Indians believed that in order to gain spiritual power they must induce a nervous state and a disordered imagination in themselves. The "black drink" actually contained caffein, and taken in strong doses it was purgative, vomitive, and diuretic.

Cabeza de Vaca reported there were three kinds of mosquitoes in great abundance in the coastal country. He did not describe the different species, but they had at least one common quality. Each tortured natives and white men without racial bias.

> From my own experience, I can state there is no torment known in this world that can equal it.

As a protection they made great fires around their camps and villages, burning rotten or wet wood in order to create dense smoke. De Vaca remembered that "the night long we did little else than shed tears from the smoke that came into our eyes, besides feeling intense heat from the many fires."

The Indians who lived farther in the interior, where the marshes ended and the drier plains began, had a different method of combating the mosquitoes. They fired the grass and the forests to drive them away.

The destruction served another purpose as well. It was a method of hunting. Deer, lizards, rabbits and other game were trapped by the fires and killed.

A line here in the *Relacion* is historically significant:

> The pasturage is taken from the cattle by burning.

This is the first printed reference to the American bison, and in the next paragraph Cabeza de Vaca sets down the first description ever written of this celebrated and most valuable animal. "Inland are many deer, birds, and beasts than those I have spoken of. Cattle come as far as here."

He was speaking of the plains which rise gently toward the west from the swamplands of the Texas Gulf Shore, and which in his mind were a part of the vast coastal province called Florida. De Vaca enjoyed the change in diet these "cattle" offered. "Three times I have seen them and eaten of their meat. I think they are the size of those in Spain. They have small horns like the cows of Morocco; the hair is very long and flocky like the merino's. Some are tawny, others black. To my judgment the flesh is finer and fatter than that of this country."

Whether he meant "finer and fatter" than Morocco's cows, or than any flesh to be obtained in the coastal lowlands remains a matter of conjecture. "Of the skins of those not full grown the Indians make blankets, and of the larger they make shoes and bucklers."

Now Cabeza de Vaca makes another important statement which may have influenced his thinking greatly, and may well have had a bearing upon the vital decision he was obliged to make—which direction he would take when the time and the opportunity came to put the coastal country behind him.

Still writing of the cattle, he said: "They come as far as the seacoast of Florida [Texas] from a northerly direction, ranging through a tract of more than four hundred leagues; and throughout the whole region over which they had run, the people who inhabit near, descend and live upon them, distributing a vast many hides into the interior country."

Four hundred leagues was more than a thousand miles. The buffalo ranged over that distance. Therefore, this was evidence which must be accepted as showing that the land ran at least that far "in a northerly direction."

It was a great distance, a disheartening distance. Yet, somewhere to the west was the great sea which Balboa and others had seen. It formed the western coast of New Spain. Then what lay at the end of four hundred leagues to the north or the northwest? Another undiscovered ocean? A strait to India and Japan? An unknown country richer than Mexico and the lands of the Caribbean?

He must have asked himself many questions. The information about the four hundred leagues must have been given to him by the Indians, and it must have come to them over the long trails of war and trade. Who knew how far? Why not a thousand leagues?

Perhaps Cabeza de Vaca misread the signs used by the Indians to denote great distances. The length of a journey from one designated place to another was measured by the number of suns that must pass in order to complete it. Walking or running were the only yardsticks of travel. These Indians had never heard of a horse.

There are reasons to believe, founded on statements of his narrative, that, despite the ordeals he had gone through, despite the years beyond the farthest outpost of civilization, the desire to look into the unknown had not been killed in Cabeza de Vaca.

It need hardly be said that if he was anything—and he was many fine things—he was a true explorer, one of the greatest who ever lived.

Perhaps the dream of riches which had carried him and all the others westward across the sea, and into a wilderness no white man had ever seen, had not died. Now, with the prospect of escaping from the degraded, brutish people who had for so long held him captive and made him a slave, perhaps that dream had been kindled into a new flame.

If these things were true, they did not alone bring about his final decision. He had been too long in the wild, he had suffered too much, to be rash or to be carried away by illusions of uncountable fortunes awaiting him in the unknown country ahead.

Practical considerations guided him as much, or more, than anything else.

The people of the coast were "all evil disposed." That was enough reason to get away from them. Traveling southward among the coastal tribes would be inviting more hardships and delays. Pánuco was obviously the closest Spanish settlement, and it was to the south, but that asset was destroyed by the dangers and trials involved in an attempt to reach it.

He listened, he thought, he sought more information, he weighed advantage against advantage, drawback against drawback, and he weighed them against each other. At last, out of innumerable conclusions, his decision was made.

It would be wise to travel inland, he felt, for the people of the interior were "of a better condition." In the interior he and the three others could expect more favorable treatment, and from all he could ascertain the interior would be "more populous and better provisioned."

There were other pregnant reasons for going inland. This one, for instance: "Thus much I have wished to say, beyond the gratification of that desire men have to learn the customs and manners of each other, that those who hereafter at some time find themselves among these people, may have knowledge of their usages and artifices, the value of which they will not find inconsiderable in such an event."

He thought of being of service to men who might follow him.

Then there is this note: "Moreover, we chose this course because in traversing the country we should learn many particulars of it, so that should God our Lord be pleased to take any of us thence, and lead us to the land of Christians, we might carry that information and news of it."

His body was naked, worn and bleeding, but neither his ideals, his intelligence, nor his courage had failed him.

Their course would be north and west.

8

The Twenty-ninth Parallel, North Latitude, marks the approximate northern limit of the prickly pear belt in southeastern Texas. It passes through Brazoria, Matagorda, Wharton, Jackson, De Witt Counties, and near the town of Cuero.

Customarily the Mariames, who held Cabeza de Vaca, Dorantes and Estevanico, trekked some seventy or eighty miles inland from their homes in the vicinity of San Antonio Bay for the annual pear harvest. This would place them in the general vicinity of the western part of Goliad County, or perhaps in Karnes County. Most likely they traveled, at least for a part of the journey, up the San Antonio River.

The Yguazes, who held Castillo captive, were accustomed to camp in the same area during this season.

There in the fall of 1533, the four men were reunited. They quickly formulated a plan of escape.

They selected a meeting place and set the night for their break, but shortly before the appointed time arrived an event occurred which once more thwarted them.

Some Mariames and Yguazes warriors got in a fight over a woman. Fists flew and heads were cracked. When the melee ended, both tribes departed from the scene in brooding anger, taking their white slaves with them.

Men of lesser courage, like Lupe de Oviedo and Esquivel, would have resigned themselves to living out their last days on earth in drudgery and debasement, their only comfort in the thought that death would bring relief.

Cabeza de Vaca, Dorantes, Castillo and Estevanico, quite

to the contrary, resigned themselves only to waiting another year, until the time of the prickly pears once more had arrived.

In this time I passed a hard life, caused as much by hunger as ill usage. Three times I was obliged to run from my masters . . .

Three times Cabeza de Vaca was overtaken and threatened with death, but "God our Lord in his mercy chose to protect and preserve me."

It was the fall of 1534. Once again the tribes trekked inland to the pear fields. Once again the four men were together, and once again they made their plans to escape.

They agreed to meet at a designated place in the brush on the night of the full September moon.

Cabeza de Vaca's opportunity to get away came on the thirteenth day of the moon. So we know that on the night of September 21, he escaped from the Mariames and went to the rendezvous.

Dorantes and Estevanico came quietly out of the shadows to meet him. They brought the distressing news that Castillo had been sent to live with some Indians called the Lanegados.

However, the situation might prove to be advantageous. The Lanegados were not unfriendly, and they would be in the vicinity of the hiding place the next day. There was a chance that Castillo could be recovered at that time.

They waited, moving cautiously toward the path over which Dorantes believed the Lanegados would travel. The prediction turned out to be well founded.

They found haven for the next night with the Lanegados, and it was from these Indians that they received the first news of the boat of Captains Penalosa and Tellez.

On the coast north of the Lanegados' homeland were the villages of a warlike tribe of Camoles. It was in this area

that the boat had been thrown ashore. The men were so en-
feebled by hunger and thirst that they could offer no resistance when the Camoles attacked. Many of them were slain
as they lay helpless on the beach, and all were killed.

In substantiation of the report, the Lanegados displayed
several crossbows, lances and articles of Spanish raiment
which they had secured in trade from the Camoles. If the
four men cared to go the place of the massacre, they would
find the wrecked boat and the skulls of their friends.

The four men had other plans, and going again among
the Indians of the coast was not one of them.

PART FIVE

The Medicine Trail

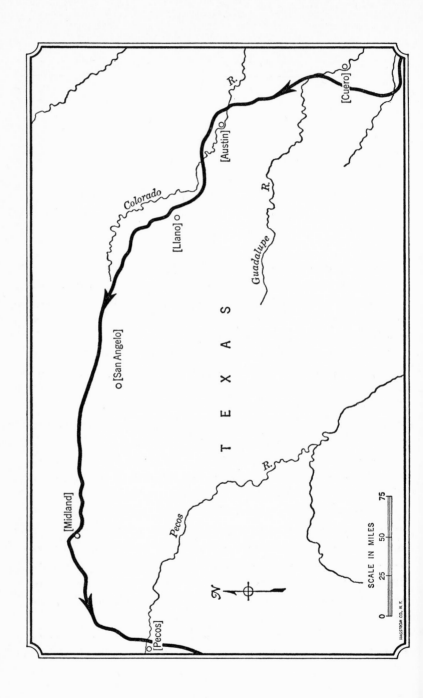

TEXAS

[Cuero]

[Austin]

Colorado

[Llano]

Guadalupe R.

R.

[San Angelo]

R.

[Midland]

Pecos

[Pecos]

N

SCALE IN MILES

0   25   50   75

HAGSTROM CO., N.Y.

1

It was September 23, 1534.

That day, wrote de Vaca, "we commended ourselves to God and set forth with speed, trusting, for all the lateness of the season . . . we might still be enabled to travel over a large territory."

The most remarkable overland journey in the history of American exploration had begun. It was a journey of suffering and privation without equal. It was a journey that at times had the colorful aspect of a triumphal march, and at other times it was no more than a flight of four haunted men running like hunted animals.

It is to be regretted that Cabeza de Vaca did not choose to set down detailed physical descriptions of himself and his companions. Occasional remarks in his *Relacion,* and sparse comments of contemporaries who wrote of that time, are all that remain to provide a picture of the three Spaniards and the Moor. Yet, quite a bit can be determined from these brief passages. Combined with logical conclusions, they not only reveal something of the appearances of the men but they throw light on their characters and their natures.

Castillo had many of the manners of a gentleman, even though he had not always adhered to the code of one. A doctor's son, he was educated and sophisticated. He acted and spoke with the assurance of an aristocrat, but there was nothing soft about him. He was attracted by the life of a gambler and adventurer, and he had won his spurs, and his captain's bars, as a soldier in battle.

Dorantes was also an infantry captain. Although not a large man, he possessed remarkable strength. He was more serious in his attitude toward life than was Castillo, less of a gambler but no less of an adventurer, and his courage was not to be questioned.

More is known of Estevanico than either Castillo or Dorantes. An extremely large and powerful black, he had the cunning of a panther and the heart of a lion. His un-tutored mind was shrewd and quick and dangerous. In several respects, his inherent wildness was no less than that of the warriors he met. If he accepted his lot as a slave, it was not because he did not understand freedom, but because he was wise enough to realize that he had no alternative. He became in a short time a master of the sign language, and he displayed a diplomatic ability and a friendliness that gave him great value as an emissary. The Indians, while standing somewhat in awe of him, generally liked and trusted him. He marched on through the wilderness defying the elements, cursing the dangers, a pillar of brute strength, and a monument to the brave of the world.

In stature, Cabeza de Vaca was the smallest of the four. Handsome, dignified, gentlemanly, he represented the finest type of Spanish officer. Paying tribute to his courage would be anticlimactic. It was unlimited and unqualified. He was kindly and considerate, but these characteristics in no way cast a shadow on his qualifications as a leader. He was highly intelligent, determined and resolute. His religious faith was as genuine as the sun which had burned his body a deep shade of mahogany. Never did he abandon his code of honesty and justice, never did he forsake his God, and never did he lose heart in the face of ordeals that would have destroyed most men. Because Castillo and Dorantes and Estevanico recognized his superior intellect, because they understood that they could trust him in any situation and under any conditions, because they admired him for his unwavering adherence to his ideals, and because they knew he was unafraid of the vast darkness which lay before them, they made him their captain and they dutifully obeyed him.

Driving themselves on through the cactus and brush with all possible speed, glancing back frequently in dread of being pursued, the four men saw in the late afternoon the smoke of some distant fires and headed toward them.

Presently they caught sight of a lone hunter, but despite their friendly shouts and gestures he refused to wait for them to come up to him. At last the three white men stopped and Estevanico went on alone. The Moor succeeded in getting close enough to the frightened Indian to talk with him.

Estevanico obtained the information that the smoke came from a camp established only that day by a band of traveling Chavavares. The hunter had at first offered to guide him to it, then had changed his mind and vanished into the bush.

In his travels as a trader and peddler, Cabeza de Vaca had encountered Chavavares on several occasions when they had come down from the inland plains to trade with coastal Indians. They were fine archers and makers of excellent bows which were highly prized by the tribes of the swampy lowlands.

With night approaching, weary from their fast trek of the day, and having no food, the four men decided to seek haven in the camp ahead. As they came up to it, they found that the Chavavares not only had been apprised of their approach by the hunter they had met, but that their identities were known.

They were enthusiastically received as famed medicine men. Cabeza de Vaca's diplomatic announcement that they had traveled far with the single hope of finding the Chavavares did nothing to lessen the fervor of their welcome.

They were quickly given a meal of prickly pears, then shown to lodgings in the houses of the band's physicians, quarters befitting their rank as celebrated shamans.

Inasmuch as none of the four had practiced since their days on Malhado Island, it was apparent that news of their descent from the high plane to which their quackery had lifted them at that time had not yet reached these inland Indians. They understood that this could be an advantage, or it could be extremely perilous, if not completely disastrous. The natives hailed success with great joy and admiration, but failure was neither understood nor countenanced.

Cabeza de Vaca was disposed to view their situation with rare optimism and faith that, considering the nature of events which had transpired, was nothing less than extraordinary. He voiced the conviction that the Lord, having once endowed them with powers to work wonders among the Capoques and the Hans would not now forsake them in a time of even greater need for His favors.

Moreover, there were other reasons for holding such a belief. When there were no paths for them, the Lord had been pleased to "open ways for us through a country poor like this, to afford us people where oftentimes there are none, and to lead us through immediate dangers, not permitting us to be killed, sustaining us under great want, and putting into those nations the heart of kindness."

The faith of Castillo was perhaps no less pronounced, but he had grounds for avoiding patients who were seriously afflicted with internal or mental disorders. The conduct of his own life had not always been commendable, and looking back on it he saw his earthly path marked periodically by irremovable shadows. This oppressive retrospection gave rise to a profound fear. It was that the Lord's favor might not continue to be given with the necessary fullness. Perhaps this time the Lord would do no more than permit him to be successful in treating persons troubled by nothing more serious than evil visions. He decided that it would be wise not to stretch his luck too far until he had received a sign that he was not to be punished at the moment for his transgressions.

The first patients to appear were several men with a common complaint. Each suffered from a severe headache. As payment for the relief they requested, they brought pieces of venison.

This was a matter Castillo felt he could handle in safety. Over each man he made the sign of the cross, commending him to God.

The results of this ministration were instantaneous. Proclaiming themselves completely cured, the men departed with cries of praise for the great physicians who had come among them.

Cabeza de Vaca and the others fell to wolfing the venison, which was a delicacy they seldom had been privileged to enjoy during the years of their captivity.

Word of the miracle spread with prairie fire swiftness. Runners carried it away to other camps. More patients quickly arrived at the door of the clinic. They continued to come out of the shadows beyond the campfires with all manner of afflictions, with boils and cramps, with diarrhea and ague, with blisters and hemorrhoids, with indigestion and mental depression, with constipation and wens. The halt, the lame, the demented, the healthy and the sane crowded together about the lodge, all pleading for attention, and all proffering generous pieces of venison, the compensation for which the miracle men had shown such great esteem.

Which ailments were real and which imaginary, the harried Drs. Castillo and Cabeza de Vaca had no way of knowing, but it did not matter. Their pharmacology was not chemical. It was spiritual, and it contained only two remedies—a blessing and a sign of the cross.

Taking each person in turn, they applied their ministrations with unprofessional brevity, while the stacks of venison mounted beside them.

. . . the quantity became so great we knew not where to dispose of it.

When the last Indian patient had been dismissed in ecstacy, crying out his gratefulness, they fell upon their knees and made the sign for their own benefit.

We gave many thanks to God, for every day went on increasing His compassion and His gifts.

Castillo could be doubly thankful. Once more, at least for the time being, he had been spared. Once more God had seen fit to permit him to participate in the performance of a miracle. It was no less than that. Almost the entire village had come to them in sickness, and all had been sent away whole and in good spirit.

The Indians gave further demonstration of their gratefulness in their own way, addressing their own gods. They painted their faces, decorated their bodies, which were now magically filled with glowing health, then launched into a dance that continued for three days and three nights.

The exhausted travelers slept in warm deerskins, stirring themselves during the festivities only long enough to refill their bellies with venison and the satisfying juice of prickly pears.

It is doubtful that a more unstable mind than that of the American aborigine ever existed. From ocean to ocean, capriciousness and inconstancy were qualities as inherent in him as the skin pigmentation and the physiognomic characteristics with which nature distinguished his race.

On the contrary, the cultural and intellectual levels of different tribes were at great variance. Cabeza de Vaca would come to understand this; he would recognize and note the contrasts.

In his terrible years in Texas, however, he was coping with people hardly more than qualified for inclusion in the species of Homo sapiens. It was an unfair contest, deadly in every aspect, and one in which even an undistinguished mentality could not hope to combat successfully the forces of brute strength and animal cunning. Only a paleolithic man could have done that.

The savages who inhabited the miserable land and endured the abominable climate of southern and eastern Texas could be depended upon to do only one thing with unfailing regularity—change. Degenerate, verminous, dwelling in utter degradation, they had no conception of the meaning of integrity or responsibility. Their promises were worthless. Their declarations were meaningless. They knew as much about what the next moment would bring as they knew what they would do when it arrived. They lived more by instinct than by thought, uncomprehending in their responses to the dominant urges to feed and fornicate.

Cabeza de Vaca believed that he survived only because God willed that he should, and not because of his courage and ingenuity.

He had become wise in the ways of the wilderness and in the ways of the low form of mankind who dwelt in it. Probably because history knows a little more about him, because his legacy reveals something of his thoughts and a great deal about his character, there is a tendency to think of him as being wiser and more accomplished than his companions. He did not claim to be either of those things.

The assumption seems to be without foundation. Certainly he was no more experienced, and he suffered no more than they.

During their first days in the village of the Chavavares they had been honored, feasted and treated with respect, and in that situation all of them found a basis for profound concern. It was not in the nature of the Indians to follow a pattern, and even if they desired to follow one, life in the Godforsaken country would not permit it. That was one good reason why the four men could expect an unfavorable development to occur at any time. They had another: the circumstances were not without precedent. Once before they had achieved reputations as extraordinary medicine men, only to be cast down without warning into the roles of menials and slaves.

Cabeza de Vaca possessed a casualness that the others did not, and he was assigned to make discreet inquiries about the country ahead. The sum total of the responses made to him created a bleak and discouraging prospect.

He learned that while prickly pears abounded in the region toward the northwest, the season in which the fruit was edible was drawing to a close. The tribes were leaving the fields and trekking back to their homes. With their departure, the land would be empty, for there were no other people in it. Winter was approaching. Skins would be unobtainable, for a large proportion of the wild game also departed with the arrival of cold weather. There would be no food.

If the Spaniards were thinking of going on into that forbidding land, the Chavavares declared, they would be wise to reconsider their plans. They would be better off where they were, where they had robes and houses to shelter them, where they were welcome, and where a certain amount of food, if not always adequate to fill them, could be obtained.

In the view of the Chavavares, consideration should be

given to the thought that if the spirits were disposed to be kind, game would be found about them, at least some rabbits and birds, and an occasional deer. Sleeping ground squirrels, mice, snakes and lizards could be dug from their burrows. Perhaps they might even have the extreme good fortune of killing some cattle, but admittedly that opportunity could not be depended upon to present itself every year. The cattle were animals of strange habits, and no one could predict when or if they would come. Sometimes several years passed in succession during which they did not appear.

In a drafty, smoky hut the four men held a huddled council. The flickering light of the small fire revealed the gravity of their faces, the bearded, emaciated faces of the white men, and the broad ebony face of the powerful Moor. Once again they had reached a crossroads at which life or death might hinge upon the turn they took. Yet, the decision had to be made.

In their deliberations it was not so much the apparent factors which concerned them as it was the unknown elements with which they were confronted. Certain things that were indisputable might prove in the end to be of no consequence.

Indians were pathological liars, dwelt among ghosts, possessed childlike imaginations, uttered statements that were founded upon nothing more tangible than an illusion, committed acts that were born of unfathomable impulses. Yet, if the Chavavares' power to reason was minimal, it was sufficient to permit them to conceal a motive behind the advice they proffered. They looked upon their guests as more than performers of miracles. They saw them as entertainers, fascinating and incomprehensible hairy men, not born of woman but of the sky. If they lied about the country ahead, if they exaggerated in relating the adverse conditions to be found there, it was because they wanted to retain the strange quartet whose powers inspired their awe, whose ways and actions were amusing, and whose mysterious incantations brought great mental and physical comfort.

Other weights on the scale were discernible to the four lonely men about the little fire. Their only garments were a few animal skins, gifts of the Chavavares, and if they departed their former owners might elect to repossess them. They were dependent upon the savages not only for sustenance but for guidance. In every region they had known there had been countless animal and Indian trails, and without natives to lead them they might wander aimlessly until they perished of thirst, starvation or exposure. If the Chavavares had told them the truth, they would be entering an empty, cold, barren land. If the Chavavares had given them false information, they would still be entering another strange land in the face of oncoming winter. Who could say what they would find there? What could they believe?

The scale tipped before them, and they saw that the invisible weights of the unknown were the greater. The decision was made for them. They were forced to stay.

2

In their eternal quest for food, the Chavavares wandered over a large area along the Guadalupe River, forty to seventy miles east of what is now the city of San Antonio.

The physical features of the three Spaniards and the Negro Moor were different from those of the Indians, but their way of life was not. It was an existence of the Dark Ages, a naked, savage, animalistic existence for white, red and black alike. They were completely dependent upon the poor bounties of that forlorn land. There were no drones, and the visitors grubbed and hunted as the others, cooked their meat over campfires or ate it raw, gathered roots and seeds and nuts, snared lizards and rabbits and squirrels. The aged and the incapacitated, the unproductive, were turned out to die. The only law was the law of the jungle, the survival of the fittest.

If they were given women to take to their deerskin beds, Cabeza de Vaca did not mention them. It would be illogical to presume that sex had no place in their lives at the time. The circumstances were unfavorable for such abstention. They were constantly in close association with naked females. No moral code precluded them from seeking to satisfy their desires. Women were bought, sold and traded like bows and pelts and shells. The strangers were obviously men, and men possessed of magic powers, distinguished men, and their rejection of women offered to them might well have stirred resentment in the Chavavares. Certainly it would not have been understood.

Frequently on the long treks in search of food, they met traveling groups from other tribes. On such occasions the sick were brought before them to be cured. Cabeza de Vaca mentions numerous incidents of this kind. For instance, five men suffering from severe cramps came, offering their bows and arrows in payment for treatment. They were blessed, commended to God, and told to go to bed. In the morning all arose well and sound, "as strong as though they never had a disorder. It caused great admiration, and caused us to render many thanks to God our Lord, whose goodness we now clearly beheld, giving us firm hopes that He would liberate and bring us to where we might serve Him."

Giving of their own thanks to God was as much a part of each treatment as was making the sign of the cross over the patient. It would be fallacious to assert that spiritual strength gave less sustenance to their bodies than the raw meat of a lizard or a handful of roasted nuts. It gave more.

It was their salvation. They gorged themselves on food as the opportunities came, but without their faith they would not have survived.

> For myself I can say that I ever had trust in His providence and that He would lead me out of that captivity, and thus I always spoke of it to my companions.

In the beginning, Dorantes and Estevanico acted mainly in the role of assistants, practicing little on their own, but always giving moral and spiritual support to Castillo and Cabeza de Vaca. Dorantes' reticence to act with boldness was not due to a lack of faith, but to a lack of confidence in his own ability. As for Estevanico, he was restrained by the others. The Moor was not a Christian. It was feared that the Lord might look with disfavor on the idea of a heathen performing the rites of a denomination into which he could not be received.

So many Indians sought relief, however, that the three Catholics were forced to readjust their thinking on this situation. Inasmuch as Castillo was timid and Dorantes had little faith in himself, the greater part of the burden fell upon Cabeza de Vaca. It was more than he could handle. In the end they concluded the Lord might be kind enough to instill more confidence in Dorantes and liberal enough to overlook Estevanico's paganism, at least long enough to let him carry a full share of the case load until they could be on their way once more.

They took the chance that the Lord would withhold His objections. All four became full-fledged shamans, and great was their relief when no chastisements were inflicted upon them from above.

As they wandered through the bush, the sick, continually crowding about them, came from the Cultalchulches, the Maliacones, the Coayos and Susolas and Atayos. All through the vast empty country, de Vaca later wrote, the Indians, "talked only of the wonders which God our Lord worked through us, persons came from many parts to seek us that we might cure them."

It was a supreme demonstration of positive thinking; a moving testament to the power of faith.

No one whom we treated but told us he was left well; and so great was the confidence that they would become healed if we administered to them, they even believed that whilst we remained none of them could die.

Although all four were successful, Cabeza de Vaca enjoyed the greatest fame, and, "in being venturous and bold to attempt the performance of any cure, I was the most remarkable."

One winter day runners from the Susolas came to entreat Cabeza de Vaca to journey to their camp to save a man who was near death. The seriousness of the case frightened Castillo, and he excused himself from participating, but Dorantes and Estevanico agreed to accompany Cabeza de Vaca.

They saw at once upon reaching the Susolas' camp that they had come too late. Their prospective patient needed only to be buried. The Indians were gathered about his corpse, weeping and crying out their sorrow. His hut and all his worldly possessions, in keeping with custom, had been destroyed.

Cabeza de Vaca knelt beside the dead man, finding "his eyes rolled up, and the pulse gone, he having all the appearances of death, as they seemed to me and as Dorantes said."

Removing the mat with which the body was covered, Cabeza de Vaca crossed himself and supplicated the Lord to restore life. He prayed fervently, bestowed a blessing, then resorted to the Indian ritual of breathing living breath upon the stricken.

As compensation for his efforts, he received the dead man's bow and a basket of pounded prickly pears. After tarrying to minister to several other Susolas who were affected by a "stupor," he returned to his own camp.

During the night Indians came to tell him that soon after his departure the "dead" man had "got up whole and walked, had eaten and spoken."

> This caused great wonder and fear, and throughout the land the people talked of nothing else. All to whom the fame of it reached, came to seek us that we should cure them and bless their children.

The miracles were not confined to the Indians. When the four men were personally in dire need of heavenly assistance, it was not denied to them. An occasion on which Cabeza de Vaca was as close to perishing as he had been during all his years in the unknown land serves as a dramatic illustration of this divine protection.

On one of their journeys in search of food, the Chavavares and their guests trekked for five days up the Guadalupe River in great hunger. Cabeza de Vaca became separated from the others. Naked and alone, he was lost in the interminable thickets. He staggered on, his weakness increasing as the cold of the night settled.

Muttering a prayer, he gave himself to God and resigned himself to death. Suddenly before him a tree was ablaze with fire. He crouched in its protective heat and light, and it burned steadily throughout the night.

When the sun rose, he gathered sticks, and taking two brands from the burning tree, started again in search of the Indian camp. For four more days and nights he traveled through the low woods along the river, "ever with my fire and my load; for if the wood had failed me where none should be found, as many parts are without any, though I might have sought sticks elsewhere, there would have been no fire to kindle them."

Each day as the sun set he dug a hole in the ground, and he lighted four fires in the shape of a cross about it. The supply of dry wood was abundant wherever he was obliged by the hour to stop. Several times each night he got up to replenish the fires. He gathered reeds and tall grass that was like straw, and covered himself in the hole. One night sparks ignited the straw, and he was burned before he could escape. "All this while I tasted not a mouthful, nor did I find anything I could eat. My feet were bare and bled a good deal. Through the mercy of God, the wind did not blow from the north in all this time, otherwise I should have died."

Near the end of the fifth day, he reached the riverbank camp of the Chavavares. His companions had given up hope of ever seeing him again, presuming he had been bitten by a viper, and great was their rejoicing at his return. His terrible craving was soon halted by a meal of the invaluable prickly pears.

They trekked on, moved by whim and by fancy and by necessity, often falling in with other people on the trail. Somewhere during these winter peregrinations they heard news that greatly saddened them.

Some traveling Indians, whom Cabeza de Vaca does not identify, brought word that Father Asturiano and Figuroa were slaves of the People of the Figs, who lived far eastward on the coast.

That was the last they ever heard of them. History does not know how long they lived, or how or where they died.

The Indians opened their minds to Cabeza de Vaca, recounting their dreams, revealing their superstitions, their visions, their most private thoughts. It was another manner in which they demonstrated the supreme confidence they placed in him, another way of showing their unqualified respect and their absolute belief in both his mental and spiritual powers.

There was a rather pitiful hope behind their relation of

the gruesome experiences they had with a monster they called Badthing, and it did not escape him. He proved his shrewdness, and illustrated his perspicacity, by making the response they wanted to hear.

As near as he could determine, Badthing had appeared among the Chavavares some fifteen years before he arrived. The story of Badthing is best told in de Vaca's own words.

"He was small of body and wore beard, and they never distinctly saw his features. When he came to the house where they lived, their hair stood up and they trembled. Presently a blazing torch shone at the door, when he entered and seized whom he chose, and giving him three great gashes in the side with a very sharp flint, the width of the hand and two palms in length, he put his hand through them, drawing forth the entrails, from one of which he would cut off a portion more or less, the length of a palm, and throw it on the embers. Then he would give three gashes to an arm, the second cut on the inside of an elbow, and would sever the limb. A little after this, he would begin to unite it, and putting his hands on the wounds, these would instantly become healed. They said that frequently in the dance he appeared among them, sometimes in the dress of a woman, at others in that of a man; that when it pleased him he would take a *buhio*, or house, and lifting it high, after a little he would come down with it in a heavy fall. They also stated that many times they offered him victual, but that he never ate: they asked him whence he came and where was his abiding place, and he showed them a fissure in the earth and said that his house was there below. These things they told us of, we much laughed at and ridiculed; and they seeing our incredulity, brought to us many of those they said he had seized; and we saw the marks of the gashes made in the places according to the manner they had described. We told them he was an evil one, and in the best way we could, gave them to understand, that if they would believe in God our Lord, and become Christians like us, they need have no fear of him, nor would he dare to come and inflict those injuries, and they might be certain he would not venture to appear while we remained in the land. At this they were delighted and lost much of their dread."

There were no regal chieftains among either the Chavavares or the other Indians with whom the Spaniards and the Moor lived during the winter of 1534-1535. There were none of exalted position whom the others served, or to whom obeisance was paid. Not even a physician as powerful as Cabeza de Vaca was excused from the daily labors which of necessity had to be performed. If a medicine man wanted to eat, he worked, he helped to provide.

So Cabeza de Vaca and his companions struggled constantly against starvation. They considered themselves well treated. "We dug our own food and brought our loads of wood and water. . . . The country is so broken and thickset, that often after getting our wood in the forests, the blood flowed from us in many places, caused by the obstruction of thorns and shrubs that tore our flesh wherever we went."

As they were naked most of the time, the sun and dry air caused great sores on their bodies, and they were never without pain. Periodically they shed their skins like serpents. "At times," de Vaca noted "when my turn came to get wood, after it had cost me much blood, I could not bring it out either on my back or by dragging. In these labors my only solace and relief were in thinking of the sufferings of our Redeemer, Jesus Christ, and in the blood He shed for me, in considering how much greater must have been the torment He sustained from the thorns."

Cabeza de Vaca did not overlook the opportunities that came to engage in trade, his other profession in the wilderness. He made combs, and exchanged them for bows and arrows and nets. One great service he and his companions rendered was in weaving mats. They became adept at it, and their products were in great demand.

Most of the time, and especially in the winter, the Indians were forced to apply themselves to securing food. Reserves were virtually unknown, for the country was too poor to permit them to be established. They were always in need of new mats for their shelters, and if they gave time to making them, they soon became "pinched with hunger." They gladly traded pieces of meat for them.

Cabeza de Vaca and his companions usually ate the meat they received raw, for, he remarked, "if we had put it to roast, the first native that should come along would have taken it off and devoured it; and it appeared to us not well to expose it to this risk; besides . . . we could not have digested it so well as raw. Such was the life we spent there; and the meager subsistence we earned by the matters of traffic which were the work of our hands."

Cabeza de Vaca was always grateful when he had a chance to scrape and soften skins which some hunter brought into the camp. These were the days of his greatest prosperity, and he scraped with all the vigor and thoroughness he could command, for he could eat whatever scraps of meat he removed. At times he lived two or three days on these scrapings alone.

The moons came and went, and after seven had passed while the men were with the Chavavares, the forests and thickets wore dresses of new green growth, and the air was balmy, and the prickly pears once more began to ripen.

It was the spring of 1535, and it was time to think about setting out once more on the trail into the unknown.

3

Leaving was not a mere matter of saying farewell and marching off. The Chavavares had known good health during the stay of the four men, they had been protected from such evil spirits as Badthing, and they had received favors from a great new God called the Lord.

Cabeza de Vaca and Estevanico set the stage for their departure by scouting the countryside. Slipping away from the Chavavares camp, they journeyed northward for a day and reached a village of the Maliacones.

The Maliacones were preparing to trek to an area in which, "on certain trees," a small fruit was to be found, and on which they planned to sustain themselves while waiting for the prickly pears to become ripe. The situation appeared to Cabeza de Vaca to be auspicious, and he dispatched Estevanico to tell Dorantes and Castillo to join him as soon as possible.

The three men vanished at night from the Chavavares camp, and the Moor led the way to the Maliacones village in which Cabeza de Vaca was waiting for them. They were soon on their way to the fruit trees with these Indians.

The Maliacones welcomed their visitors and treated them with respect, but for some reason Cabeza de Vaca does not explain, he deemed it advisable to leave them after a march of a few days. This maneuver was accomplished within sight of a village inhabited by Arbadaos.

The Maliacones registered keen disappointment at losing their distinguished guests, but gave no indication they might resort to violence to hold them. It was for a time, however, a delicate situation, and Cabeza de Vaca was greatly relieved when he understood that his wishes were to be granted.

The Maliacones departed in peace, and the four men remained camped on a plain outside the Arbadaos village, awaiting an invitation to enter. They could see that the Arbadaos were discussing the matter about a council fire. The powwow finally broke up, and several emissaries came out, took each visitor by the hand and escorted him into the village with the proper ceremony.

Progress had been made, but it brought privation greater than that they had known with either the Chavavares or the Maliacones. The Arbadaos evidently were suffering from extreme malnutrition, for they were "weak, lank and swollen, so much so as to cause us great astonishment."

Each day they were with these Arbadaos the travelers were able to secure no more than two handfuls of green prickly pears each, the milk of which burned their mouths. Water was as scarce as food in the area, and they knew maddening thirst.

After long and exasperating negotiations they managed to purchase two mangy dogs. Unsavory as it was, the meat seemed to give them enough strength to go forward.

The Arbadaos supplied directions for reaching another village of the same tribe, but they soon lost their way. Rain swept over the dry cactus plains. At day's end they took refuge in a thicket. They gathered prickly pear leaves and constructed an earthen oven in which they baked them overnight.

Their course was still toward the north. Various statements in the *Relacion* indicate a route passing through the present Caldwell County.

It is an interesting commentary that Cabeza de Vaca's account up to this point contains the first written descriptions—meager as some of them are—of Indians belonging to nine linguistic families dwelling in the territory that is now the United States. In Florida, Alabama and Mississippi he had heard the Timuquanan and the Muskhogean tongues. In Louisiana and Texas he had heard the Chitimacan, Attacapan, Karankawan, Tonkawan, Coahuilecan, Athapascan and Caddoan languages.

Traveling northward from the Guadalupe River, he was entering the easternmost part of the enormous region in which the Shoshonean language, was spoken, the tenth he had heard.

Although two or more tribes he encountered might belong to the same linguistic family, he undoubtedly was confused by dialects and led to believe that in each instance he was listening to a different language. It seems likely that this was the basis for his frequent remark: "they spoke a different tongue."

After a morning meal of baked prickly pear leaves, they set out and in time came upon landmarks mentioned in the directions given them by the Arbadaos. They met two women and several boys in a thick wood during the afternoon who fled at sight of them. Going on, they soon found themselves surrounded by natives who peered timidly at them from behind trees.

These were the Arbadaos they had hoped to find. Considerable conversation by signs was needed before they were persuaded to approach the strangers, but at last their confidence was won and they agreed to lead the way to their camp.

The village contained some fifty huts. It was apparent that although these people had heard of the celebrated medicine men, they had never seen them. This was a situation, however, which presented no difficult aspects. The men soon quelled the fears of the villagers by methods well tested on previous occasions. The boldest came forward cautiously, touched the hands and faces of the three white men and the Moor, then rubbed their hands over their own bodies. When it was realized they were to suffer no ill effects from this performance, a familiar scene took place.

> . . . the Indians brought us their sick, beseeching us that we would bless them. They gave us of what they had to eat . . . with kindness and good will, and were happy to be without anything to eat, that they might have food to give us.

This generosity comprised an inducement difficult to reject, and the hungry four remained several days, conducting their rituals while regaining their strength.

Cabeza de Vaca does not identify the natives who arrived "from beyond" during their stay in this village. They must have been traveling in a northerly direction, however, for he announced that he and his companions would leave with them.

The Arbadaos were keenly disappointed and advanced strong arguments in an effort to persuade the doctors to remain for a longer time. Cabeza de Vaca had good reasons for his firm rejection of the invitation. There were few good trails through the broken country and its great thickets and endless reaches of cactus. Traveling without a guide only increased the number of hazards they were obliged to face. Indians knew the country as well as the wild animals, indeed they shared the paths and water holes with them, and Indians knew the locations of prickly pear fields, nut groves and the haunts of game. There was every advantage to be gained in accompanying a moving band, and there was no danger at all of becoming lost.

The men took their departure with the unnamed Indians, and the Arbadaos wept copiously as they watched them go.

In the next few chapters the *Relacion* is tragically vague about the many different tribes they met and with which they traveled. Not only does Cabeza de Vaca make no attempt to identify them, but his fragmentary remarks about their customs and appearances provide few clues by which their tribal affiliations might be even tentatively established. The omissions are especially regrettable in view of the fact that after their departure from the Arbadaos the four men were never again alone. From this point forward, as they traveled from village to village, and tribe to tribe, they were never without a contingent of natives, sometimes numbering in the hundreds.

He speaks of them with an aggravating casualness:

Leaving these Indians, we went to the dwellings of numerous others.

So we parted from these Indians, and went to others by whom we were welcomed.

. . . we reached a hundred Indian habitations.

Many of these people were aborigines who were destroyed by disease or absorbed by stronger tribes before the first settlers invaded the Texas wilderness, and their names and their cultures are forever lost.

The dividing line between the Athapascan and the Shoshonean linguistic families, as delineated by the American Bureau of Ethnology, runs closely for a long distance to the northwesterly route Cabeza de Vaca followed in Texas.

He was, therefore, in a land inhabited by two great peoples, the Comanche and the Apache. They were composed of numerous divisions, tribes and clans, but which of these Cabeza de Vaca encountered can never be accurately established. It can be stated with certainty, however, that they were not the powerful, fierce fighters in 1535 that they were to become in later years.

Cabeza de Vaca met them before the arrival of the horse, and it was the horse which provided the mobility that gave them equality with their white antagonists. It was the horse that made it possible for them to stand against the onslaughts of the traders, the cattlemen, the settlers and the

United States Cavalry for two centuries. It was the horse—
and, of course, the gun when in time it supplanted the bow—
that gave them a high position among the greatest raiders
and fighters western America ever knew.

The Arbadaos had wept, but that was as much a custom
as an expression of true emotion with some Indians. They
wept as easily as they laughed. The four men pressed forward with their unidentified new guides, giving their
thoughts and their regards only to the moment, the people
and the circumstances at hand. They did not look back.

The country was ablaze with ragged patchwork quilts of
wild flowers, the tiny lilies that bloomed quickly after a
shower, the retama that was the juniper of the Old Testament, and the buffalo clover, or wolf flower, which the Spanish christened *el conejo* because of the white tip's resem-
blance to a rabbit's tail, but to which pioneer women gave
the name of bluebonnet. The thickets of chaparral and post
oak and blackjack rolled in waves toward each horizon,
washing against distant ridges and hills that shimmered
under a blue haze.

For the first time, in some unknown village lost in the
immensity of that land, they were given a strange flour to
eat. Cabeza de Vaca speaks of it as the "flour of mezqui-
quez."

It was mesquite flour. From time immemorial the plant
with its pulpy fruit has been a main article of diet of the
natives of the Southwest. The beans are used as food by
Indians of southern Arizona and northern Mexico today.

Cabeza de Vaca was the first to describe the method and
the ceremony with which it was prepared for consumption:
"The fruit while hanging on the tree is very bitter and like
unto the carob; * when eaten with earth it is sweet and

---

* An evergreen tree of the senna family, found in the Mediterranean
region, bearing red racemose flowers. The pod and its pulp were used as
fodder.

wholesome . . . they make a hole of requisite depth in the
ground, and throwing in the fruit, pound it with a club the
size of the leg, a fathom and a half in length,* until it is
well mashed. Besides the earth that comes from the hole,
they bring and add some handfuls, then returning to beat
it a little while longer. Afterward it is thrown into a jar,
like a basket, upon which water is poured until it rises
above and covers the mixture. He that beats it tastes it,
and if it appears to him not sweet, he asks for earth to stir in,
which is added until he finds it sweet. Then all sit around,
and each putting in a hand, takes out as much as he can. The
pits and hulls are thrown upon a skin, whence they are
taken by him who does the pounding, and put into the jar
whereon water is poured as at first, whence having expressed the froth and juice, again the pits and husks are
thrown upon the skin. This they do three or four times to
each pounding. Those present, for whom this is a great banquet, have their stomachs greatly distended by the earth
and water they swallow. The Indians made a protracted
festival of this sort on our account." Here then is the first
printed American recipe.

Late on an early summer afternoon, they came to a river
and crossed over, the water reaching to their breasts.

It might be as wide as that at Seville; its current was very
rapid.

He was comparing the stream with the Guadalquivir. It
was the Colorado, the same river which Dorantes, Castillo
and Estevanico and their ten companions had crossed near
its delta on the Gulf of Mexico coast in the spring of 1529,
seven years before, and the same river over which Cabeza
de Vaca had helped the fear-filled Lupe de Oviedo after
they had fled from Malhado Island.

On the trail they had picked up several women as guides,

* Obviously an error either in printing or translation.

and they led them up the left bank of the river. At sunset a large village containing "a hundred habitations" was seen ahead.

The reception they received as they approached the town was tumultuous. The people poured out of their huts, dancing, leaping in the air "with such yells as were terrific," striking the palms of their hands violently against their thighs.

Obviously western America had never seen a demonstration like it, for neither white man nor black had ever set foot in that country before, but neither did western America ever know a spectacle—the wild, unrestrained and uncontrollable pageantry—like that which began this summer evening on the bank of the Colorado River in south central Texas.

It was the beginning of the stark drama which has no counterpart in the annals of western history, and makes the *Relacion* of Cabeza de Vaca an incomparable saga. It was the start of a savage, colorful parade without equal, a riotous, weird march that was to traverse plains, mountains and deserts, a march of triumph and of death, of starvation and abundance, that would continue almost across the width of a continent that was then a void on the maps of the world.

The four men were swept from their feet by the howling mob and carried into the village. Indian men, women and children fought madly to get close enough to touch them.

They pressed so closely that they lacked little of killing us.

The gods in human form were borne to a house that had been prepared for them when word of their approach had been received. There, besides ample food, they were awarded the highest honor the Indians could bestow. They were presented with gourds which had small holes bored in them and which contained pebbles.

These were the famous medicine rattles of the Southwest.

The American Museum of Natural History prizes a fine collection of them today. At the time of Cabeza de Vaca's journey, and for many years thereafter, they were the holiest of all Indian religious instruments. So sacred were they that they were used only on the most momentous occasions, in the most important ceremonies. No one dared to touch a medicine rattle, except its owner. "They say there is virtue in them, and because they do not grow in that country, they come from heaven; nor do they know where they are to be found, only that the rivers bring them in their floods."

It is a statement which might well be thoughtfully weighed. For countless centuries the Pueblo Indians cultivated gourds, making medicine rattles of them and using them as utensils. The four men had crossed the Colorado River in the vicinity of the present Austin, a very long way from the nearest pueblo known to have been occupied at that time. Presumably the Indians who gave them such a royal reception had no direct contact with the sedentary tribes of New Mexico, for they did not know where the magic gourds were to be found. The gourds came to them in the floods of rivers. They were Indians of the plains, and even though they might not have wandered as far northwest as New Mexico, their hunting and trading expeditions took them great distances from their homeland. It seems to be clearly indicated that they journeyed westward to the Pecos and the Rio Grande. There were the pueblos from which the gourds could have come on the northern reaches of both of these streams.

After filling themselves with wild meat and mesquite beans, the four men refused to bestow more blessings, and demanded quiet and privacy. The ecstatic villagers were shut out, but their joy and enthusiasm did not abate. Moving some distance away, they began a dance that lasted through the night.

On no account would we consent that they should rejoice over us any more that night.

For years the four men had adapted themselves to the ways of the savages with whom they were forced to live. When the opportunity came which permitted them to invoke their powers as medicine men, they had accepted the challenge, and they had known an incredible success. Now they had learned how to command. With a few words they drove the entire population of a village away so that they might have the comfort of a quiet night's rest.

All through the following day Indians came to touch the physicians and to be touched by them. They had no peace, until night again fell.

4

The next day we left, and all the people of the place went with us.

There was to be no peace. Runners sped ahead of the wild throng, and the riotous receptions continued in each village the amazing shamans reached. If they were celebrated men before this, now they were elevated to the stature of living gods.

. . . when we came to the other Indians we were as well received as we had been by the last. They gave us of what they had to eat, and the deer they had killed that day.

So the *Relacion* is tediously repetitious. In each place the same mad scene took place.

Then suddenly a new element enters into the account.

Perhaps it was inevitable, under such circumstances, that what had become a crusade conducted under the banners of Christian faith, and in the name of God Almighty, should degenerate into a vandalic invasion.

A frenzied horde of naked savages was howling its way through the wilderness, driven by religious fervor that produced madness, impelled by superstition that overshadowed sanity. Zeal, passion, blind idolatry drove the disciples to violence, thievery, wanton destruction in their frantic efforts to serve and to please the supreme beings who had come to anoint and cure and protect them.

Minds that had lost all stability created senseless new tenets. Out of dreams and visions came inane new rules of conduct. Childish imaginations devised stupid schemes and pointless ceremonies. Blood flowed as men fought to force their ideas and devices on others.

Not even the powers of the miracle men were strong enough to establish any form of order. They were helpless to enforce any sort of discipline. As a result, a great new fear arose in them, and they asked themselves if God was no longer watching over them, if His favor was at last to be withdrawn.

Out of fanaticism came the ritual that the sick who asked to be cured must first be deprived of their worldly possessions. The notion prevailed that treatments would be ineffective, except for paupers. As a consequence, upon entering a village the marchers stripped those waiting to be cured of their bows, arrows, beads, pelts—anything and everything they owned. Only after these depredations were the afflicted permitted to go before the physicians.

The patients accepted the decree without complaint, believing it was invoked by the Spaniards themselves. After receiving treatment, they invariably departed "highly pleased," and believing themselves to be well. Then, as converts, they set out to boast of their good health, and they joined the parading throngs, racing ahead to other villages to proclaim that with only the touch of a hand, the sign of the mysterious cross, their ailing bodies had been made whole.

They made great rejoicing and dancing so that they left us no sleep.

The crusade was out of control. The inhabitants along the trail up the Colorado River began to suffer from the invasion as much as they benefited from it.

Those who accompanied us began to use them so ill as to take their goods and ransack their houses, without leaving anything.

Thievery was not only a highly developed practice among the Indians, but was looked upon as fully justified from every aspect. A successful thief was greatly admired. Here, with the traveling physicians, therefore, was a paradise on earth in which pillaging could be carried on without danger and in the name of religion.

To witness this unjust procedure gave us great concern, inflicted too on those who received us hospitably.

As much as they regretted seeing the trusting, hospitable people plundered by the mob, the travelers were actually troubled more by another grave concern. It was that retaliation by the victims might come at any time. In such event, fighting would occur, and general warfare could very well follow. This would place them in an extremely perilous situation.

They understood the instability of the Indian mind. Inhabitants of villages which had been raided might be very likely to turn first on the men whom they thought to be responsible for causing the disasters.

Cabeza de Vaca asked God not to let them be dealt such an unfortunate blow. There was nothing he and his companions could do to halt the thievery. "As we were in no condition to make it better," wrote de Vaca, "or to dare chastise such conduct, for the present we had to bear with it, until a time when we might have greater authority."

Their displeasure and dejection was apparent, and in one place, at least, some Indians who had been robbed sought to console them with the philosophical assertion that the state of affairs, deplorable as it was, was not completely without benefit. These victims counseled the physicians not to grieve for them, for they were happy and gratified, and they considered the loss of their property an insignificant price to pay for the privilege of being visited by men who surely must have come from beyond the earth. Anyway, when the next village was reached, they themselves would have their turn, they would be among the raiders, and they would get back as much or more than they had lost.

On the parade moved across the rising plains, over the ranges of hills, through the valleys, day after day, and the hundreds of followers steadily increased until at times they "were accompanied by three or four thousand persons."

They caught sight of mountains, of which de Vaca noted, "they appeared to come in succession from the North Sea, and, according to the information the Indians gave us, we believe they rise fifteen leagues from the sea."

Hodge suggests that Cabeza de Vaca was speaking of the escarpment that extends from Austin to Eagle Pass, but in view of the time that had passed and the large number of tribes encountered, it seems likely that they had traveled beyond that point. Undoubtedly the range they saw ahead of them was the Blue Mountains.

Cabeza de Vaca's statement about the proximity of the sea is confusing. What did he mean by the "North Sea"? Certainly he was fully cognizant that they had been traveling away from the Gulf of Mexico. That had been their purpose from the beginning. The remark suggests that he believed another sea lay to the north of them.

If that were the case, however, he chose not to seek it.

This decision was probably unanimous, and based on good reasons. The four men had had all they wanted of Indians who lived along the coast. Even if this was a different coast to the north, they had nothing to show them that the Indians who lived there would be any less diabolical than those at whose hands they had long suffered.

They set a course directly toward the mountains, and on the parade went. An indication of their approximate location is found in several passages at this point in the narrative. As the long column crawled ahead over the rough lands of the Edwards Plateau, the Indians in the lead, de Vaca wrote, "guided us by the way of some kindred of theirs; for they wished to take us only where were their relations, and were not willing that their enemies should come to such great good, as they thought it was to see us. After we arrived they that went with us plundered the others [their own relatives]; but as the people there knew the fashion, they had hidden some things before we came; and having welcomed us with great festivity and rejoicing, they brought out and presented to us what they had concealed. These were beads, ochre and some little bags of silver."

It was not silver. The historian Oviedo discovered that the word "silver" was a printer's error. It should have been "mica."

> We . . . traversed a ridge seven leagues in extent. The stones of it are scoria of iron.

The Indians, de Vaca said, gave them "many little bags of margarite and pulverized galena."

They were somewhere in the rough mineral region of which the present Mason County is a part.

On the wild, chanting, singing, dancing mob moved along the Indian and game trails, up the long hills, down into the green depths of canyons, through the great thickets and the dark woods of oaks, cottonwoods, sumacs, cedars. Granite outcroppings marked the slopes, and formed cliffs between which the streams rushed in white foam. Metals and sharp rocks cut their feet.

So great was the crush about the four men each day that no escape was possible for them. When a tribe decided to turn back, each member demanded to be touched and blessed in turn. It sometimes took three hours to complete the ordeal.

They came to a village in which many of the people were blind. De Vaca was surprised. This "caused us great astonishment. They are a people of fine figure, agreeable features, and whiter than any of the many nations we had seen until then."

Gifts were constantly showered on them, the larger part stolen goods—beads and pieces of galena, colored stones, arrows, feathers, buffalo robes, deerskins, furs. Once again they came upon flour made of maize, a food they had long desired, and they learned that farther to the northwest, along the upper Colorado River and its tributaries, they would find tribes which grew it and used it in trade.

An argument arose over which direction they would take, the four men wishing to keep on westward, and the Indians urging them to turn more to the north. It was the first time their wishes had been openly defied. A stalemate ensued, and the four went on alone. They soon arrived at a town of some twenty houses "where we were received in weeping and great sorrow; for they already knew that wheresoever we should come, all would be pillaged and spoiled by those who accompanied us. When they saw that we were alone, they lost their fear, and gave us prickly pears with nothing more. We remained there that night."

The stubborn Indians who had been left behind soon changed their attitude. Good opportunities to plunder were being wasted. They hastened to catch up. Arriving at the village in which the men were quartered at dawn, they raided the houses with wild screams. "As they came upon the occupants unprepared and in supposed safety, having no place in which to conceal anything, all they possessed was taken from them, for which they wept much."

As if contrite for their disobedience, the raiders told their victims that the four men were children of the sun, and not only could they cure the sick but they had the power to destroy those whom they did not like.

This was the highest accolade the Indians could bestow upon the four strange men. It gave them status in the spirit world. It placed them in the rank of gods. For it was to the sun and the moon and the stars that the Indian paid the greatest homage. These were the natural phenomena which he understood were the controlling forces of the universe—all the life in the sea and the land and the air—the forces that gave him life and closed his eyes in death. He could show no greater respect, no greater adulation, no greater reverence, than by adorning the three white men and the immense black with the title of "Children of the Sun."

The raiders traveling with Cabeza de Vaca, he recalled, told their victims "other lies even greater than these, which none knew how to tell better than they when they find it convenient. They bade them conduct us with great respect, advised that they should be careful to offend us in nothing . . . and that wheresoever they arrived with us, they should rob and pillage the people of what they have, since this was customary."

Tribes came and went, but always the four men pushed steadily west by north, always runners went ahead to spread the news of their coming, and always they were received with wild joy and dancing, gifts and food, and always, in keeping with custom, those accompanying them looted each village reached.

Also in keeping with custom, the women carried water for the marchers, but so great had the authority of the four men become, and so feared were they, that no one would drink without their consent.

Indian medicine men quailed before them, proclaiming their own inadequacies, the frailty of their own powers in comparison with the potions of the Children of the Sun. They gave the travelers their sacred gourds, and Andrés Dorantes was astonished to receive in one place a hawk-bell of copper.

It was, he recalled, "thick and large, figured with a face. They told him they had received it from others, their neighbors; we asked them whence the others had obtained it, and they said it had been brought from the northern direction, where there was much copper, which was highly esteemed. We concluded that whencesoever it came there was a foundry, and that work was done in hollow form."

It was a moment of great excitement. Although they were not to be easily deceived—they were too wise in the ways of the wilderness peoples for that—new hopes stirred in them.

Indians did not have foundries. They knew nothing of smelting or molding metals.

As they went on, they showed the bell to others, and in time they learned that the Indians either had lied about its origin or had been misinformed. The bell had not come from the north, but from the south.

> They told us that in the place whence that had come, were buried many plates of the same material; it was a thing they greatly esteemed, and where it came from were fixed habitations.

That would be Mexico, a land of fixed habitations! Mexico on the South Sea!

5

At night we arrived at many houses seated on the banks of a very beautiful river.

Cabeza de Vaca had long before this time lost track of the days. If he counted the moons, he would have been able to record the passage of time, at least by months. He says nothing of the matter.

However, it was sometime in the fall of 1535 that they came to the "beautiful river." It was the Colorado, but Cabeza de Vaca evidently did not know that. As the four men had traveled generally west by north, it had swung away from them. Now it had swung back to meet their path. They continued on northwestward along its right bank. It seems reasonable to assume that they were in the San Angelo area.

The inhabitants of the houses along the river rushed out on the trail to meet them. On this occasion the villagers did not wait to be robbed but at once bestowed everything they owned on the marchers.

Here the four men were given a food that was new to them, and it is a clue as to their whereabouts. De Vaca noted, "In that country are small pine trees, the cones like little eggs; but the seed is better than that of Castile, as its husk is very thin, and while green is beaten and made into balls, to be thus eaten. If the seed be dry, it is pounded in the husk, and consumed in the form of flour."

This was the nut pine. It would not have been found in quantity very far east of the Pecos River. Perhaps Cabeza de Vaca had not seen the tree at the point he writes about it in his narrative. More likely his description reflects responses to inquiries he made about it at the time he first ate its fruit. It grows prolifically in the valley of the Pecos, which was not beyond the reach of the Indian commerce of this area.

In the village of the pine nut flour, Cabeza de Vaca's skill as a medicine man was given one of its severest tests. "They fetched a man to me," he said, "and stated that a long time since he had been wounded by an arrow in the right shoulder, and that the point of the shaft was lodged above his heart, which, he said, gave him much pain, and in consequence he was always sick. Probing the wound I felt the arrow head, and found it had passed through the cartilage. With a knife I carried, I opened the breast to the place, and saw the point was aslant and troublesome to take out. I continued to cut, and, putting in the point of the knife, at last with great difficulty I drew the head forth. It was very large. With the bone of a deer, and by virtue of my calling, I made two stitches that threw the blood over me, and with hair from a skin I stanched the flow. They asked me for the arrowhead after I had taken it out, which I gave, when the whole town came to look at it. They sent it into the back country that the people there might view it. In consequence of this operation they had many of their customary dances and festivities. The next day I cut the two stitches and the Indian was well. The wound I had made appeared only like a seam in the palm of the hand. He said he felt no pain or sensitiveness in it whatsoever."

His power had reached its zenith. In the eyes of the awed Indians he was the supreme being on earth. They would not eat at any time after this until he, or one of his assistants, had breathed upon the food and made the sign of the cross over it. There could be no doubt now about his ability to perform miracles.

. . . it may be seen how great was the annoyance.

A hundred years later, Cabeza de Vaca was still being criticized by fanatical Roman Catholics for daring to usurp the clerical privilege of achieving miracles. He was just as strongly defended by historians who expressed the belief that under the circumstances he was entitled to do anything to help himself and his companions, and besides he hadn't really performed any miracles, but had simply acted in the role of a physician and surgeon, using what knowledge and skill he possessed to aid the afflicted.

The celebrated English clergyman and compiler of travel books, Samuel Purchas, writing in 1623-1626, took a somewhat more cynical view of the issue: "Cures very wonderful, yet true. Benzo (which traveled fourteene yeeres in the Indies with the Spaniards) saith that of six hundred of Narvaez his company scarsly ten returned, which at Mexico reported that they had by breathing on them cured the sicke, raised to life three dead men, etc. But, saith hee, Let their holines pardon me, I will easier beleeve that they killed foure living men then that they raised halfe one dead man to life.

"I permit some of these relations, more for knowledge of the Countrey, than for credit of Spanish cures in the Indies. . . . These here challenge no Divine end to convert people to God, and therefore are not like to have any divine beginning, but are either falsely told, or falsely done, or falsely intended by the Father of falsehood.

"And why may not they be ascribed to the Devil, either as lies, if never done; or if done, as devillish Arts to maintaine rapine and superstition? . . . This Cowes-Head the Author is also by Schmidel before, recorded for a bad man in his acts at the River of Plate."

Going on, they passed through so many different peoples, and heard so many different dialects, that Cabeza de Vaca was unable to recall them. He makes a statement at this point, however, which goes far toward clearing the clouds which obscure the course of his journey. Speaking of the crowds of Indians following him, he says: "They ever plundered each other, and those that lost, like those that gained, were fully content."

A massive exchange of gifts was continually under way. Indians plundered Indians and presented the plunder to Cabeza de Vaca. After blessing it, he gave it all back. Then Indians robbed Indians of the sanctified articles, and were robbed in turn by the first losers. In the end, while the Indians continued to steal from each other in a crazy routine, Cabeza de Vaca and his companions took nothing they did not need for their own welfare and comfort.

Additional color can be given to this picture by turning the spotlight of history ahead six years to the year 1541. Then Coronado and his army, under the guidance of the Turk, were marching on their futile and tragic search for the supposedly rich land of Quivira. While they were in the ravines of western Texas, Captain Rodrigo Maldonado was sent forward with his company to explore the countryside.

Pedro de Castañeda, the narrator of the Coronado Expedition, tells of Maldonado's experience this way: "He traveled four days and reached a large ravine like those of Colima, in the bottom of which he found a large settlement of people. Cabeza de Vaca and Dorantes had passed through this place, so that they presented Don Rodrigo with a pile of tanned skins and other things, and a tent as big as a house, which he directed them to keep until the army came up.

"He sent some of his companions to guide the army to that place, so that they should not get lost, although he had been making piles of stones and cowdung for the army to follow. This was the way in which the army was guided to the advance guard.

"When the general came up with the army and saw the

great quantity of skins, he thought he would divide them among the men, and placed guards so that they could look at them. But when the men arrived and saw that the general was sending some of his companions with orders for the guards to give them some of the skins, and that these were going to select the best, they were angry because they were not going to be divided evenly, and made a rush, and in less than a quarter of an hour nothing was left but the empty ground.

"The natives who happened to see this also took a hand in it. The women and some others were left crying, because they thought that the strangers were not going to take anything, but would bless them as Cabeza de Vaca and Dorantes had done when they passed through here.

"They found an Indian girl here who was as white as a Castilian lady, except that she had her chin painted like a Moorish woman. In general they all paint themselves in this way here, and they decorate their eyes."

The hides over which the men fought were the valuable and beautiful buffalo robes. The girl was obviously an albino. The relevant part of the quotation is the statement that the Indians expected the white men to bless their possessions, and not carry them off, as Cabeza de Vaca and Dorantes had done.

Captain Juan Jaramillo was also an officer under Coronado. In his invaluable account of the expedition, he tells of reaching a settlement of Indians "among whom there was an old blind man with a beard, who gave us to understand by signs which he made, that he had seen four others like us many days before, whom he had seen near there and rather more toward New Spain, and we so understood him, and presumed that it was Dorantes and Cabeza de Vaca and those whom I have mentioned."

This is substantial evidence showing that Cabeza de Vaca traveled through this area of Texas, and that his route was not far below the Colorado River.

They came into a country in which rabbits were abundant. The Indians armed themselves with clubs, drove the hares into a circle, and slaughtered them. "They surround it directly and throw numerous clubs at it with astonishing precision . . . according to my thinking, it is the most pleasant sport which can be imagined, as oftentimes the animal runs into the hand. So many did they give us that at night when we stopped we had eight or ten back-loads apiece."

Deer also were plentiful in this region. At dark the hunters would come in with five or six for each of the four men. They also brought large quantities of quail and other game. "Indeed, whatever they either killed or found, was put before us, without themselves daring to take anything until we had blessed it, though they should be expiring of hunger, they having so established the rule, since marching with us."

It was a time of plenty, a time of feasting, and compared to previous days it was a time of comfort. The women carried loads of mats on their backs throughout the long march of the day, and at night men set up a house for each one of the Children of the Sun.

Ovens were constructed and the hares and deer and quail were roasted. The men ate their fill, then ordered the remaining food that had been given to them to be divided among those who cared for it.

No one tasted meat until it had been breathed upon and blessed by the great shamans.

We crossed a great river coming from the north, and passing over some plains thirty leagues in extent, we found many persons coming a long distance to receive us.

The river was the Pecos, which rises far up in New Mexico, flows through the land of the Pueblos, and enters the Rio Grande in Val Verde County, far down in Texas.

PART SIX

A Buckle and a Nail

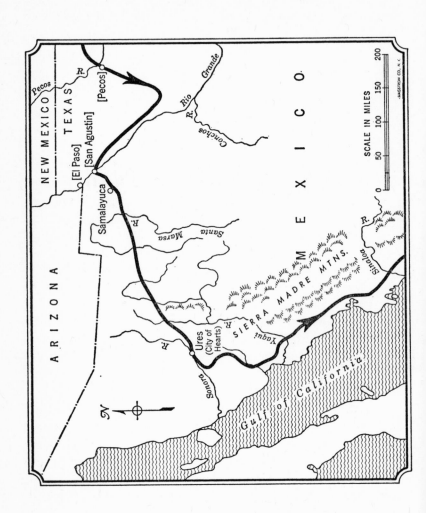

1

They had entered the mountainous country of west
Texas. It was a land of vast and magnificent distances.
Rugged peaks, wreathed in purple haze, edged sweeping
plains and tilted plateaus. Sagebrush and greasewood, cat-
claw, yucca and prickly pear blanketed the ranges. Seas
of gray and white sand washed in immense waves against
red and ochre mesas, and the wind flung smokelike plumes
from their crests.

The coyotes and the lobos barked and howled dismally
at night, and along the cliffs they heard the scream of the
mountain lion. They passed towns of prairie dogs, burrowing rodents quite palatable when fat and complemented
with toasted spiders and worms.

They listened to talk and tales about things of which they
had never heard. To the north were endless plains, plains
so unchanging, so flat and treeless, that not a mound, nor a
stick or bush rose to disfigure their smooth flow to the
horizons. Where they ended, no one could say. They ended
in the sky. On them the herds of cattle roamed in countless
numbers, herds so immense that they took several suns to
pass, herds that covered the earth like dark ragged blankets
as far as a man could see and crawled like the shadows of
the clouds that journeyed to nowhere.

To the northwest were great rivers that had cut deep canyons in the deserts, and in them were cities built high on the cliffs, empty, crumbling cities from which the people had mysteriously vanished. Other people had come there, and they had built houses on the ground, and they grew maize and gourds and beans and pumpkins and melons. These people were fabulously rich with blue stones that had glittering gold in them. They shut themselves up at night in their houses, which in some places were entered only through the roofs. They pulled ladders up from the ground, and their enemies could not reach them. Some of these cities were so large that no one could count the houses or the number of people who lived in them, and their wealth was beyond all comprehension. They ate from golden plates, and they wore silver pieces in their ears.

To the south and west was a river that flowed from one end of the world to the other, and along it were more people who also built permanent houses beside their fields. The river cut through deep gorges, and it swept through white plains which pained the eyes and on which nothing could live, and it flowed through fine green groves, and it made a gleaming highway through mountains that touched the sky. Beyond it was nothing but a desert, impassable and endless.

If Cabeza de Vaca asked himself—and undoubtedly he did—what part, if any, of this information might be believed, he could have found no answer. There was no way to distinguish truth from fancy in the talk of Indians. Yet, it was mandatory for him to set a course.

It seems logical to assume that his decision to turn toward the southwest was based on the assertion that the long river lay in that direction, and that people supposedly lived along it in permanent dwellings.

The capricious mind of the Indian took another unexpected turn. Now the marchers held that pillaging their friends, relatives and neighbors was improper. It stopped, and in its place a new custom was inaugurated. Instead of being robbed, the Indians who were visited along the trail were requested to present all they possessed to the four medicine gods. They, in turn, then gave everything they received to the "chief personages" accompanying them. The latter were supposed to distribute the loot among their own followers.

In keeping with this new procedure, de Vaca later recalled, upon entering a village the marchers would command the inhabitants "to retain everything and make no concealment, as nothing could be done without our knowledge, and we might cause them to die, as the sun revealed everything to us. So great was their fear that during the first days they were with us, they continually trembled, without daring even to speak, or raise their eyes to the heavens."

The crossing of the Pecos cannot be pinpointed on a map. From the accounts of other Spaniards who passed through west Texas a few years later, and who were told by the Indians that Cabeza de Vaca had traveled in that area, as well as from Cabeza de Vaca's own descriptions of the people and the terrain, it may be deduced that they crossed in the vicinity of the present town of Pecos, somewhere in Reeves or Ward Counties.

Writing later from memory, Cabeza de Vaca states: "They guided us through more than fifty leagues of desert, over rough mountains, which being dry were without game, and, in consequence we suffered much from hunger."

The distance could have been seventy or eighty leagues. His estimates were at best a guess. Specific days were lost beyond recall in the mist of his recollection. He held an indestructible mind picture of the wild column trudging on through the desert wastes, he recalled the peaks and the great mesas and the burning alkali flats, and the hunger, but associating these with the passage of time, or with the miles traversed, could not be done with accuracy.

Whatever the distance, this phase of the journey was an ordeal that seemed to be harder on the Indians than on the Spaniards. "Many . . . began to sicken from the great privation and labor they had undergone in the passage of those ridges, which are sterile and difficult in the extreme."

Beyond the ridges they came down into the valley of the Rio Grande, and they were conducted across a plain at the base of the mountains, and fording the river the water came up to their breasts.

People came to meet them "from a great distance," and "gave so many goods to those who came with us, that the half were left because they could not be carried."

This waste concerned Cabeza de Vaca, and he told "those who gave, to resume the goods that they might not lie there and be lost; but they answered that they could in no wise do so, as it was not their custom after they had bestowed a thing to take it back; so considering the articles no longer of value, they were left to perish."

It was an unusual attitude, to say the least, and quite contrary to the habit of "Indian giving," which prevailed throughout the length and breadth of the West.

As far as Cabeza de Vaca knew, all the rivers of the world flowed into the sea. The Indians had no idea where the Rio Grande went, or rather where its course ended, but Cabeza de Vaca had only to stand beside it, and note the position of the sun, to see that it was flowing toward the southeast. Going in that direction it could not reach the sea that allegedly lay somewhere to the north, nor could it reach the so-called South Sea that washed the western shores of New Spain, which was Mexico. Therefore, it must go to the sea from which they had come.

That understanding was enough to make him look westward.

We told these people that we desired to go where the sun sets.

When he was informed that the country in that direction was empty, and that the next people were far away, he became stern and ordered that runners be sent out to locate the natives and make known their coming. It was then revealed that the people to the west were enemies of the tribes living east of the Rio Grande.

Cabeza de Vaca was insistent that, despite this situation, they march toward the setting sun, and the Indians, "not daring to disobey," capitulated, but decreased the chances for the occurrence of inter-tribal warfare by sending only two women forward.

The international rules of armed conflict permitted the safe passage of women emissaries through enemy territory. One of the women dispatched was a member of a tribe in the march, but the other was a captive and belonged to the people whom they were sent to meet. It was thought that the kindly act of letting her go home would have a beneficial influence on the negotiations.

The main body followed the women for a time at a discreet distance, but at last it was deemed inadvisable to penetrate farther into the dangerous area. The parade stopped, a meeting place was agreed upon, and the women went on alone.

At the end of five days, the women not having returned, the Indians told Cabeza de Vaca it was useless to wait longer. Either the women had perished on the trail, or they had failed in their mission and were being held as hostages.

Well aware of the dangers of entering a country in which warfare might break out, Cabeza de Vaca elected to move northward. Once again he met a flood of objections. In the north, said the Indians, there were no people at all, not even enemies, and there was nothing to eat and no water to be found. Only death awaited them in that direction.

Convinced now that he was being deceived by natives who simply wanted to keep him to themselves as long as possible, Cabeza de Vaca unleashed his anger. Stalking off in fury, he forbade anyone to approach him. He made his bed in the brush, and there he was joined by his companions.

The display had the desired effect. The Indians soon approached his camp, and began to plead with him not to abandon them. De Vaca remembers that they "remained all night without sleep, talking to me in great fear, telling me how terrified they were, beseeching us to be no longer angry, and said they would lead us in the direction it was our wish to go, though they knew they should die on the way."

That Fate, Good Fortune, or the Lord—whichever you prefer—was still favoring the men soon became manifest.

> Whilst we still feigned to be displeased lest their fear should leave them, a remarkable circumstance happened.

A number of the Indians suddenly became seriously ill, and on the following day eight of them died.

The extent of the dread which occupied them after this demonstration of the Spaniards' demonic power can easily be imagined. De Vaca says that the terrified Indians "besought us not to . . . require that more of them should die. They believed we caused their death only by willing it, when in truth it gave us so much pain that it could not be greater; for, beyond their loss, we feared they might all die, or abandon us of fright, and that other people thenceforward would do the same, seeing what had come to these."

Not only the Indians were filled with fear. The four men looked in great alarm on the prospect of traveling by themselves in a forbidding country in which the Indians fled from them at sight.

The relatives of the ailing displayed great sympathy for them in their suffering, and cared for them as tenderly as

possible, but when death came these emotions halted with
the heart beats. After that they showed no feeling whatsoever, and "neither did they weep nor speak among themselves, make any signs, nor dare approach the bodies until
we commanded these to be taken to burial."

Two more days were spent in ministering to the ill.

We prayed to God, our Lord, to relieve them; and from that
time the sick began to get better.

Suddenly the two women who had been sent into the
west reappeared. They reported they had found few people, that it was the season for hunting the cattle, and nearly
all the Indians they had sought had gone far to the north for
that purpose.

They were lying, of course. This was made apparent by
the reappearance of the captive woman, who had been
given an opportunity to escape to her own people. Probably
they had gone no farther west than a short distance into
the bush.

Cabeza de Vaca said nothing about the matter, and ordered the trek to the north to start. The convalescents were
to remain behind, and catch up when they felt strong
enough to travel.

It was a silent, sober-faced column that set out. When an
infant cried, it was quickly taken to one side and scratched
with the sharp teeth of a rat from its shoulders to its feet.
Cabeza de Vaca protested to such cruelty, and demanded
to know the reason it had been inflicted. He was told that
the child was punished for daring to weep in his presence.
"These terrors were imparted to all those who had lately
come to know us," de Vaca noted, "that they might give us
whatever they had; for they knew we kept nothing, and
would relinquish all to them. This people were the most
obedient we had found in all the land, the best conditioned,
and, in general, comely."

At the end of three days of strenuous travel, no villages having been found, the procession was halted. The following morning, Castillo and Estevanico were sent to scout the country ahead. They took with them the two women who had previously been sent as emissaries into the west.

It proved to be a good maneuver. The captive woman knew the country, and she led the two men directly back toward the Rio Grande, where, she told them, there was a large town in which her father lived.

As the men gazed down from a high ridge on the river, a new chapter in the history of North America was begun. Castillo and Estevanico saw far below them a settlement which appeared to be composed of permanent structures.

They were the first to look upon the adobe houses of a pueblo in the southwestern United States, the first to meet a great people never before seen by the eyes of Europeans, a people not known to exist, yet who had lived from time immemorial in the vast silences of that unknown land.

The event was important in another way, as well. It provided posterity with evidence which, beyond a shadow of doubt, marked a point on the route of Cabeza de Vaca.

The Southwest is called a timeless land, meaning a land where time stands still. It is a romantic way of saying that things endure there longer than in other places, other climates. Its antiquities go back far beyond the beginning of recorded history.

Since the days of Cabeza de Vaca, and of Coronado who followed him, the locations of the pueblos and the permanent towns have been an indisputable matter. The pageant of life since those years has passed their walls. Many of them are still inhabited, and if the people are gone from others and walls have vanished into dust, the sites upon which they stood will always be known.

Cabeza de Vaca came to the Rio Grande the first time a short distance below the mouth of the Conchos River. Crossing over, he set out westward, but after several days turned toward the north and sent Castillo and Estevanico ahead to reconnoiter.

The women led them to the river in the vicinity of the Conchos, and there they saw the houses. The two men and two women were well received in the town, the inhabitants of which were Jumanos. Estevanico and the women remained there while Castillo, in the company of six townsmen, hurried back to inform Cabeza de Vaca that he had found "fixed dwellings of civilization, that the Jumanos lived on beans and pumpkins, and that he had seen maize. This news the most of anything delighted us, and for it we gave infinite thanks to our Lord. Castillo told us the Negro was coming with all the population to wait for us in the road not far off. Accordingly we left."

A dangerous situation arose. The Indians traveling with Cabeza de Vaca were avowed enemies of the Jumanos. Now once more Cabeza de Vaca's ability as a leader and his skill as a diplomat were given a severe test, and found to be not wanting.

Presenting the Indians with what little he possessed, he blessed them, made the sign of the cross over them, and persuaded them to turn back toward their homelands. Fighting and bloodshed had been averted, and the trail was clear before him.

The meeting with Estevanico soon took place, and the Spaniards were escorted into the town with great ceremony and festivity.

They gave us beans, many pumpkins, calabashes, gourds to carry water in, blankets of cowhide and other things.

Forty-seven years later, in the fall of 1582, Antonio de Espejo and a company of men were on their way northward in an attempt to rescue several Franciscan padres who were lost in the wilderness of what is now New Mexico.

Espejo descended the Conchos to the Rio Grande. Near the confluence of the rivers he came upon a pueblo, and journeying up the Rio Grande in the next twelve days he reached four others. He estimated the number of people in the five towns at more than ten thousand, but Espejo's estimates were always wildly exaggerated.

The matter of population is unimportant. What is important is the following excerpt from Espejo's account: "These people are all clothed and seemed to have some light of our holy faith; for they made signes of God, looking up towards heaven, and call him in their language *Apalito,* and acknowledge him for their Lord, from whose bountiful hand and mercy they confesse that they have received their life and being, and these worldly goods. Many of them with their wives and children came unto the friar that he might crosse and blesse them. Who demanding of them, from whom they had received that knowledge of God, they answered, from three Christians, & one Negro which passed that way, and remained certaine days among them, who by the signes which they made, were Alvaro Nuñez Cabeza de Vaca, and Dorantes, and Castillo Maldonado, and a Negro; all of which escaped of the company which Panfilo de Narvaez landed in Florida; who after they had been many days captives and slaves, escaped and came to these townes, by whom God shewed many miracles, and healed only by the touching of their hands many sicke persons, by reason thereof they became very famous in all that countrey."

Cabeza de Vaca and his three companions had been there, and although forty-seven years had passed between their visit and the arrival of Espejo, they were remembered. Moreover, and even more amazing, some of their teachings were remembered. The sign of the cross, the doctrines of a Christian God, from whom came all life and all the blessings of the earth, were not forgotten.

2

The colorful parade continued on up the valley of the Rio Grande, which ran toward the northwest. In the lead were the scouts or guides. Next came four of the strangest men ever found in all the pageant of North American history. Three of them were heavily bearded. Their long hair was held by thongs of deer hide. Except for skin breechclouts, they were naked. Their bodies were lean, hard, lithe, and deeply burned by years of exposure to the sun. About their necks crudely carved wooden crosses were suspended on cords of woven animal hair.

The fourth man was even more startling to behold. He was the color of ebony, and he towered above the Indians that swarmed about him. He had a great head of kinky black hair adorned with bright red feathers. His powerful muscles rippled, his white teeth gleamed, and he strode in a regal manner.

He laughed, and he sang, and he danced, reacting to the drums in the way of an Indian brave to whom the throaty rhythms were the sweetest and most inspiring music man was capable of producing. He ordered that women—and he saw to it they were the most comely—be assigned to attend him, and he had an appreciative eye for the supple limbs and full breasts of Indian girls.

He was circumspect under protest. At times in the past his brashness with women had brought objections from their spouses, and Cabeza de Vaca had been obliged to command Estevanico to be more cautious and to show more respect. On several occasions serious trouble was narrowly averted.

In the mind of Estevanico the privileges of godhood were not restricted by moral considerations, and he was no longer a slave subject to the orders of a master. He was a shaman, a famed medicine man, a Child of the Sun, and he saw no reason to restrain or conceal the natural urges he possessed.

There was a self-imposed limit, however, to his defiance of Cabeza de Vaca. This was not because he felt himself to be in a lower station. He did not. No man was superior to him. He was the equal of all men. He obeyed Cabeza de Vaca because he recognized in him an extraordinary intelligence. He understood that Cabeza de Vaca had capacities for leadership far greater than his own or those of Castillo and Dorantes.

Estevanico was wild and uninhibited, but he was not a fool. He wanted to live as much as the others, and he knew that without the companionship and guidance and the mind of Cabeza de Vaca he would not have survived. In addition, he saw in Cabeza de Vaca a courage, an honesty, and compassion that stirred his admiration and for which he held an unqualified respect.

They were a good team, each loyal to himself, and all loyal to each other.

In a physical sense they were nothing less than supermen. They no longer feared suffering, they no longer cringed at the prospect of hunger. They were afraid of nothing but God. Cabeza de Vaca wrote: "We never felt exhaustion, neither were we in fact at all weary, so inured were we to hardship."

It had always been Cabeza de Vaca's conviction that unnecessary talk was dangerous. The role of a god was better played in discreet silence. All four of them possessed immeasurable influence and authority, and in his estimation these advantages were best preserved through reservation and detachment. Familiarity and sociability, he believed, would tend to lower them to the level of ordinary men, and would weaken the Indians' awe and fear of them.

This attitude was shared by Castillo and Dorantes. The three white men stood aloof, never cold or unfriendly or disdainful, but never patronizing or purposefully amiable or engaging in small talk.

Estevanico's view of things was somewhat contrary. He saw no advantage to be gained by silence, and he entered with spirit into the native life as he found it, restraining himself no more than good sense demanded. De Vaca remarked, "The Negro was in constant conversation."

Perhaps because he was black, a child more of the moon and the night than of the sun, the Indians expected him to be different from his companions. Who knows? The fact remains that he was welcomed and respected and even revered as much as the others. The Indian women appeared to be more interested in him in some ways than they were in the other peculiar specimens of men who had come among them. If that were true, the curiosity was mutual.

Rather than follow the northwestward course of the Rio Grande, Cabeza de Vaca would have preferred to strike directly westward, but he had already had one unprofitable experience in attempting to travel that way after the first crossing of the river, and now the Jumanos strongly advised him to continue on up the valley. Only that way would he reach more settlements.

As he pushed on, he was breaking the trail that was to be a part of the long road from Mexico City to the Spanish missions and towns of New Mexico in the years to come. It was the road that ran through El Paso del Norte—the pass to the north—where the city of that name stands today.

Cabeza de Vaca's admiration for the Jumanos continued to increase.

They have the finest persons of any people we saw, of the greatest activity and strength, who best understood us and intelligently answered our inquiries.

He called them the Cow Nation, because each year they journeyed northward, east of the Pecos, to the great plains over which the buffalo herds wandered. The Jumanos' manner of receiving the medicine men differed from that of tribes they had previously visited. When they entered a town, they would find the Jumanos waiting indoors for them. In each house men, women and children would be seated on the floor facing the wall, their heads down. Their possessions had been gathered and placed on the floor in the center of the room. In this way everything they owned was presented to the visitors, who, after accepting the gifts with signs of gratefulness, returned them.

The Spaniards were puzzled at not seeing maize growing, yet they found the grain stored in clay pots and baskets, and it was cooked and served to them. When they inquired about the matter they were told that for more than two years no rain had fallen. Seed that had been planted had failed to grow and had been eaten by ground squirrels and other rodents. The maize in storage had been obtained in trade with more prosperous Indians who lived far up the river, and who spoke the Jumano language. If the Sun Men traveled that way they would find the country well populated, they would be well received, and would be given mantles of cotton, cattle robes, and other valuable things.

The Jumanos were talking about their relatives, the Pueblos, in the land of the supposedly fabulously rich Seven Cities of Cibola which Coronado was to set out to find a few years later.

Cabeza de Vaca's statement that the Jumanos and some of the Pueblos spoke the same tongue is significant. Hodge thought it accounts, in a measure, for the affiliation of the Jumanos and the Piros when missions were established by the Franciscans among these tribes east of the Rio Grande, in New Mexico, in 1629. The Piros were one of the principal Pueblo tribes. Their towns were scattered along the Rio Grande in New Mexico northward to within fifty miles of the city of Albuquerque. Others were east of the river.

The Jumanos beseeched Cabeza de Vaca to tell the sky to rain. He complied by saying a prayer. The results are not known. He was gone from the valley before the advent of the usual rainy season.

The Jumanos apparently began to leave the Rio Grande valley below El Paso at the end of the sixteenth century. In 1598, Juan de Oñate came upon four of their villages near the Salinas, east of the Rio Grande, in New Mexico. By 1629, the main body of the tribe lived on the Arkansas River, within the present state of Kansas. About 1672, the Salinas pueblos were abandoned.

Two factors seem to be largely responsible for the migrations. The Jumanos were not a warlike people. In the course of years they were badly decimated by the Apaches. The other influence which caused them to shift eastward from the desert was the horse. Even in the early days when Cabeza de Vaca saw them, and they lived somewhat sedentary lives, they made periodic journeys from the arid country through which the Rio Grande passed up the Pecos and northeastward to the buffalo ranges. Espejo knew of this custom, and it was he who called the Pecos Rio de las Vacas. As late as 1850, Jumanos were mentioned in connection with the wide-ranging Kiowas. Widely scattered, they eventually lost their identity, becoming absorbed by other peoples. The only place their name is preserved now is in the Mesa Jumanes in New Mexico.

The Jumanos' characteristics were more those of the plains Indians than of the Pueblos. Perhaps, in centuries long past before Cabeza de Vaca found them, they had dwelt in the country of the cows to which they eventually returned, and in which they vanished. He reached their villages in a period of prolonged drought, yet, even though they resided beside a river, they apparently did not attempt to grow maize by irrigation. This system of agriculture was practiced in the southwestern United States in prehistoric times, and it was practiced in Cabeza de Vaca's time by the Pueblos, just as it still is today.

The Jumanos' method of cooking was entirely new to Cabeza de Vaca, and greatly impressed him.

"How curious and diversified are the contrivances and ingenuity of the human family," he wrote. "Not having discovered the use of pipkins, to boil meat they would eat, they fill the half of a large calabash with water, and throw on the fire many stones of such as are most convenient and readily take the heat. When hot, they are taken up with tongs of sticks and dropped into the calabash until the water in it boils from the fervor of the stones. Then whatever is to be cooked is put in, and until it is done they continue taking out cooled stones and throwing in hot ones. Thus they boil their food."

It is another custom that supports the suggestion that the Jumanos were originally plains Indians. The manner of cooking may have been strange to Cabeza de Vaca, but it wasn't new among non-sedentary tribes who followed the buffalo herds, and who had difficulty transporting utensils. Hodge points out in this connection that the name *Assiniboin*, meaning "Stone Sioux," and usually abbreviated to "Stonies," is derived from this custom. If the Jumanos did not use pipkins, or pots, it was not because they had not discovered them. They saw them among the Pueblos.

Cabeza de Vaca interrupted the chronology of the *Relacion* to remark: "We passed through many and dissimilar tongues. Our Lord granted us favor with the people who spoke them, for they always understood us, and we them. We questioned them, and received their answers by signs, just as if they spoke our language and we theirs; for, although we knew six [Indian] languages, we could not everywhere avail ourselves of them, there being a thousand differences."

He breaks his story again to make another general comment. It is revealing and significant. Speaking of the vast territory through which they had passed, he said, "Throughout all these countries the people who were at war immediately made friends, that they might come to meet us, and bring what they possessed."

It might be asked what other Spaniards advancing into unknown lands, or what other Europeans of any nationality, indeed, what Americans, possessed such influence or left behind them such a commendable record. The answer would be: very few. De Vaca says, "In this way we left all the land at peace, and we taught all the inhabitants by signs, which they understood, that in Heaven was a man we called God, who had created the sky and the earth; Him we worshipped and had for our master; that we did what He commanded and from His hand came all good; and would they do as we did, all would be well with them."

Espejo could testify forty-seven years later that the teachings of Cabeza de Vaca had not fallen on deaf ears and had not been misunderstood. The sign words were never forgotten. They were handed down from father to son. A hundred years later, Indians of the Southwest repeated the story of three bearded white men and a black who passed through the land extolling the Supreme God whose powers were insuperable.

As he looked back on the years of his journey, Cabeza de Vaca wrote with regret, "Could we have had the use of language by which to make ourselves perfectly understood, we should have left them all Christians. Thus much we gave them to understand the best we could.

"When the sun rose, they opened their hands together with loud shouting toward the heavens, and then drew them down all over their bodies. They did the same again when the sun went down.

"They are a people of good condition and substance, capable in any pursuit.

"All came to us that we should touch and bless them, they being very urgent, which we could accomplish only with great labor, for sick and well all wished to go with a benediction.

"Many times it occurred that some of the women who accompanied us gave birth; and so soon as the children were born the mothers would bring them to us that we should touch and bless them.

"Indians ever accompanied us until they delivered us to others; and all held full faith in our coming from Heaven."

The Indians long remembered Cabeza de Vaca and his teachings, but the white men who came after him soon forgot both him and the words he had spoken. They ignored his counsel and his message. They tortured and killed and robbed and desecrated until at last the whole land was swept by the flames of war.

Cabeza de Vaca especially admired the Indians he met in the valley of the Rio Grande and in northern Mexico. He left them in peace, gave them a greater God to worship than any they had ever known, and inspired them with a belief in the honesty and kindness of the Spaniard. Few padres of the wilderness accomplished that.

In the middle of the seventeenth century, Spanish civil officials and missionaries bitterly opposed each other in administrative matters. The Pueblos became pawns, suffering even more grievously than they had previously under the cruel laws and policies of the dishonest colonial government. At last the Pueblos revolted.

In August, 1680, 21 of the 33 missionaries, and 375 of the 2,350 colonists, in the territory were slain. The missions, and all their records and furnishings, were destroyed.

The governor and the surviving colonists took refuge in the government buildings in Santa Fe, some of which are still standing and are occupied today. For ten days they withstood a siege by three thousand Pueblos. Finally, in a desperate counterattack, the Indians were driven off with three hundred killed and forty-seven of them captured.

The prisoners were promptly tortured and hanged. The government and about a thousand colonists fled to El Paso.

Fearing that the Spaniards would return with a stronger force, many Pueblos abandoned their settlements and built new ones on less pregnable sites. The former villages crumbled into dust.

Not until twelve years later were the Spaniards able to reconquer the country. Then Diego de Vargas smashed the revolt, and the torturing and hanging were resumed. The spirit of the Pueblos was finally broken.

The Jumanos did not take part in the rebellion, but several years after it had started, two hundred of them visited the Spanish government-in-exile in El Paso, and requested that missionaries be sent to live with them.

They wanted peace, and they wanted to hear the word of God, as their forefathers had heard it from three white men and a black, nearly a century and a half before.

The missionaries were too frightened to venture forth, and the Jumanos left without them.

3

The four men traveled for nearly three weeks up the valley of the Rio Grande. Then the place was reached where another vital decision had to be made. They were probably within thirty miles of the present site of El Paso at the time.

Several factors influenced their thinking. It was December—if they were not certain of the month, they knew it was winter—and while the cold had not yet become severe in the valley, they knew from information the Jumanos gave them that snow could be expected to fall at any time. It had already fallen on the peaks and in the north on the Pueblo settlements along the upper river. Blizzards already might have swept across the plains to the northeast over which the cattle roamed.

Westward was only a forbidding land in which there was little water and few people. It was an endless desert, and the Jumanos counseled them against entering it. They were urged to remain where they were until spring had returned. Then it would be possible to travel with safety in any direction they desired.

Cabeza de Vaca had no intention of passing another winter in idleness. He weighed the factors thoughtfully: the Rio Grande ran far to the north, but the Indians knew of no sea in that direction. The only sea of which they knew, but which they had never seen, lay an incalculable distance to the west. Going farther north would be a circuitous route to it, even though in that direction they could be assured of adequate food and protection.

Cabeza de Vaca advocated striking directly westward, and after due consideration the others agreed. It was a bold decision, the dangers involved were recognized, but once they had made up their minds, they did not hesitate.

They left the river near a village known today as San Augustine. It is about twenty miles south of Ciudad Juárez. From it a trail ran toward the southwest. With a number of Jumanos accompanying them, they set out on it across the vast desert reaches of Chihuahua.

Desert trails change only after the water holes along them change. The trail they took from San Augustine is still there, still followed. It took them to the green oasis of Samalayuca.

For seventeen days they pressed steadily on, passing through soft, blowing white sand hills, and passing the salt lake of the Salado, where there were a few sweet water pools. Thirsty, dirty, burned by blowing sand, and bone-weary, they reached the Santa Maria, a trickle called a river that flows two hundred miles to its death in the desert.

This was bigger country than any they had ever seen, bigger because there was always an infinity of distance on every side of them, bigger because there was always another range of mountains ahead of them—bigger because it had no end.

From the time of its creation it had waited for them, wrapped in a silence that no civilized voice had ever broken. Now it heard the sounds of words of a kind the wind never before had carried.

Time changed, and the days and nights, the suns and the moons came and went in their inexorable ways, but the silence and the emptiness and the immensity of the land did not change. Only the contours sketched on the sky, the colors, were different as the hours passed.

Now the land was flat and brown. As far as the eye could reach there was no ripple to break the levelness. Now it was cut in myriad gashes, yellow coulees, umber washes, serrated ridges, marshy salt bottoms, treacherous sands, and stained little creeks that ran away into nothingness. Now it was aglow under a penetrating sun, rising and falling in a monotonous succession of powerful swells. Now it was a violently heaving world of gray and green and amber hills, and the bright streamers, dancing from crest to crest, striking on broken ridge and bluff, made it a complicated network of contrasts.

The wind was playful, gentle, and came with a whispered message for the dry grass, indolent in the warmth of sun, leaving its languor in things crawling upon the earth. It came fresh, in stiff garb, brisk in its business of going about, whipping clothes and blankets and feathers, as if demanding more action, as if urging the men to move faster, to display vigor like itself. It came with sorrow, crying its woe, moaning in the cedars and the cottonwood groves along the little creeks. It came to snoop into the intentions of the invaders, turning up here and there suddenly and getting off quickly again. It came to scold like an old hag, whining and berating and snapping and complaining, harsh, and sending down epithets and ridicule. It went away with the evening, as if to think about what it had done, and returned in the morning as if remorseful and penitent. It came like a Pied Piper bringing a host of tiny clouds, as if mocking the invasion of the new country by the marchers with a parade of its own across the sky. It created great thunderheads which seemed in their sheerness, their angularity, to be modeled after rough canyon country, buttes and mesas tumbled against each other. It spread the clouds in a thick blanket, sullenly refusing to allow a rent to be made and the sun to shine through. It became furious, roared and tore at the earth, throwing dust over itself like an angry buffalo bull, biting and striking, as if it had no other desire but a vicious one to destroy everything in its path. It came hot, and made the people pant in the closeness, and it sickened them. It came cold, stinging through skin clothes, making the people bend shivering against it. It was friend and foe. With its whimsical nature it turned back grass fires and storms, and then came to hurtle destruction on all that lived before it.

"Always the wind tells us what we must do," the Indians said.

They came to the land which had been eaten by fire, a fantastic land of great red and golden cones, holed rocks, black reaches, pumice walls, cinder hills. The mesas were the color of dried blood. They trudged through saffron, topaz and slate scars, over rusted ridges, and the distant benches were bathed in violet mists, and the valleys were covered with olive blankets of sage and yellow cactus and gray-green cedars.

There were days without water, when alkali whitened their faces and seared their eyes and mouths, days when the sun ran in red fire over the buttes, and always overhead the buzzards circled on motionless wings waiting for them to drop and lie still.

Seventeen days to the Santa Maria, and then seventeen more they went on westward, until one day as the sun went down they saw ahead of them the walls of mountains higher than any they had ever seen.

They had come in sight of the great Sierra Madre.

In the eastern reaches of the mountains they "found a people who for the third part of a year eat nothing but the powder of straw, and, that being the season we passed, we also had to eat of it."

The country grew greener as they climbed, and the streams were faster and stronger, and there were birds and trees and meadows, and far above them the snows of the peaks glistened against the sky.

Then they started down a long valley, and the Jumanos and the people of the straw flour trekked devoutly along with them, and they came once more upon villages of permanent habitations, and there were storage bins filled with maize.

These were the Opata, and they "gave us a large quantity in grain and flour, pumpkins, beans, and shawls of cotton. With all these we loaded our guides, who went back the happiest creatures on earth. We gave thanks to God, our Lord, for having brought us where we had found so much food."

Then the Jumanos and the people of the straw flour turned homeward. They had shown the men the way over the great backbone of the North American continent, into a country occupied by a friendly people of advanced culture in the valley of the Yaqui, a river flowing toward the setting sun and the great South Sea.

4

The Opata belonged to the immense Piman linguistic family. The four men were the first Europeans to see them and hear their tongue.

As they went on they would pass through other tribes of the same family, the Nevome, Tarahumare, Tepecano, Tepehuane, Tepahue, Nio, Zoe, Eudeve, Jova, Cahita, Cora, Huichol, and others. Although many of these tribes are now extinct, or nearly so, in the time of Cabeza de Vaca they lived in the mountainous and canyon country of northwestern Mexico.

In general they held a high regard for honesty and morality; when driven to war they fought with exceptional bravery. The Opata especially were known for their humaneness and sense of justice, and they displayed these qualities in times of peace and toward enemies captured in conflict.

The women of most of the Piman tribes painted their faces like the Moorish women of Barbary. Castañeda wrote that both men and women drank a wine made of the "pitahayam which is the fruit of a great thistle which opens like the pomegranate. The wine makes them stupid."

A bread was made from the mesquite which, like cheese, might be preserved for a year. Melons were so large that a man could carry only one at a time. These were cut into slices and dried in the sun, after which they could be stored for months. Hodge thought these melons were a kind of cantaloupe, for in the twentieth century the Indians of the Southwest still sliced and dried them in a similar manner. The Spaniards saw tame eagles from which feathers were plucked to be used in ceremonies and festivities. Today the

Hopi and the Zuni keep eagles for their feathers, which they prize highly and hold to be sacred.

Owing to the ruggedness of much of the country they inhabited, the Opata were divided into numerous, isolated, small communities, among which dissension frequently arose, sometimes ending in actual hostility. This situation brought about the construction outside some villages of defensive works of volcanic rock, behind which a settlement or several allied settlements could retreat in the event of inter-tribal eruptions.

In addition to these domestic troubles, they were almost constantly harassed by tribes which later became absorbed by the Apaches.

Although not warlike themselves, the Opata, therefore, knew well the arts of war, and were fierce adversaries in combat. They, and other tribes of their family, possessed a deadly poison with which they treated arrow heads.

Cabeza de Vaca mentions it: "They have a poison from a certain tree the size of the apple. For effect no more is necessary than to pluck the fruit and moisten the arrow with it, or, if there be no fruit, to break a twig and with the milk do the like. The tree is abundant and so deadly that, if the leaves be bruised and steeped in some neighboring water, the deer and other animals drinking it soon burst."

Coronado's men knew the deadliness of the Opata poison. Castañeda tells of a soldier killed by an arrow which had only scratched his hand. A detachment was sent to avenge the soldier's death, and seventeen more Spaniards were killed by the poison in the fight that ensued. "They would die in agony from only a small wound," Castañeda reported, "the bodies breaking out with an insupportable pestilential stench."

Coronado's men fortunately discovered, in some unknown manner, that the juice of the quince was a good antidote. Castañeda continued, "At one place . . . the Indians wounded a Spaniard called Mesa, and he did not die, although the wound of the fresh poison is fatal, and there was a delay of over two hours before curing him with the juice. The poison, however, had left its mark upon him. The skin rotted and fell off until it left the bones and sinews bare, with a horrible smell. The wound was in the wrist, and the poison had reached as far as the shoulder when he was cured. The skin on all this fell off."

The Indians accepted Cabeza de Vaca and the others with him as men of good will and peace, and they knew no trouble as a result, but the Spaniards coming after them quickly destroyed this beneficial situation with their dishonesty, greed and brutality.

The natives who possessed such a vicious poison, and had no compunctions about using it when necessary, were also well versed in personal hygiene. Cabeza de Vaca remarked of this custom with approval, and noted: "Among these people the women are treated with more decorum than in any part of the Indies we had visited. They wear a shirt of cotton that falls as low as the knee, and over it half sleeves with skirts reaching to the ground, made of dressed deerskin. It opens in front and is brought close with straps of leather. They soap this with a certain root that cleanses well, by which they are enabled to keep it becomingly. Shoes are worn."

The soap was amole, the root of the yucca.

The intelligence, friendliness and cleanliness of these people, and their readiness to honor the God of the Christians, not only won Cabeza de Vaca's admiration and regard, but greatly influenced his actions in the days immediately ahead.

Traveling on southward and westward through the narrow valley of the Yaqui, the four men, followed by a large contingent of Indians, reached Guasave. There they left the valley, and made their way behind Indian guides over the great ridges on a foot trail that brought them to Batuc on the Rio Oposura.

It was late in January when they reached Ures, a town on the Rio Sonora that was to have a distinguished place in history from that time forward.

Passing through this rugged land, en route to Ures, they "continually found settled domiciles, with plenty of maize and beans. The people gave us many deer and cotton shawls better than those of New Spain, many beads and certain corals found on the South Sea, and fine turquoises that come from the north."

The coral they received was evidence that they could not be far from the great ocean that rolled its combers against the west coast of Mexico, and in Mexico there were Christians.

Stirred with profound excitement and thankfulness, they pressed onward as fast as circumstances would permit.

It was a magnificent land, not only rich in food and game, but rich in legends and tales.

They ate preserves of a kind they had never before tasted. It was made from the saguara, the great columnar cactus. They saw wild sheep with extremely large bodies, long wool, and immense horns. These animals were very wary, remained high on the cliffs and crags, and were rarely killed by the Indians.

Cabeza de Vaca did not know that he was looking at the famed Rocky Mountain sheep, which were just as difficult to bring down then as they were in the centuries to follow, and which until the day of the telescopic sight and the high-powered rifle were abundant in the mountains of northern Mexico and southern Arizona. They're gone now, destroyed by bold hunters who sneak up and shoot them from the safety of great distance.

A note in the Castañeda narrative attests to the size of the sheep then observed: "Three days after we entered the wilderness we found a horn on the bank of a river that flows in the bottom of a very steep, deep gully, which the general had noticed and left there for his army to see, for it was six feet long and as thick at the base as a man's thigh. It seemed to be more like the horn of a goat than of any other animal. It was something worth seeing."

Two incidents took place in the pueblo at Ures which significantly affected the course of future events.

Among the gifts which the generous people bestowed upon Cabeza de Vaca were five emeralds made into arrowheads and which were used in various ceremonies.

They were probably malachites, but Cabeza de Vaca wrote that they appeared to be precious. "I asked whence they got these; and they said the stones were brought from some lofty mountains that stand toward the north, where were populous towns and very large houses, and they were purchased with plumes and the feathers of parrots."

Once again he heard of the large pueblos in Arizona and New Mexico, the fabulous Seven Cities, which contained buildings four and five stories in height. Now he knew emeralds were to be found in them.

The other important incident was a feast at which the hearts of six hundred deer were served as the main course. Cabeza de Vaca called Ures the Pueblo de los Corazónes— the City of the Hearts.

Its geographical location made it the entrance to the homelands of numerous tribes dwelling on the South Sea. The sea was in reality the Gulf of California.

Cabeza de Vaca did not actually see the gulf, but he received detailed descriptions of both the country bordering it and the inhabitants of the territory.

The Indians painted it as a forlorn and barren country in which maize would not grow and the people lived on flour made of powdered foxtail grass and straw, and on fish which they caught from rafts.

The people were the Seri, some of whom stood more than seven feet tall, the Guaymas, the Upanguaymas and the Tepoca. Cabeza de Vaca spoke of them as being timid and dejected. The adjectives are too polite and they comprise an extraordinary understatement.

Castañeda was less reserved in speaking of them, and he saw them. The country along the gulf, he said, "is inhabited by brutish, bestial, naked people who eat their own offal. The men and women couple like animals, the female openly getting down on all fours."

In the Town of the Hearts, the four men were shown greater respect than they had received in any place on their long journey, if such is possible. They were continually feasted, and celebrations and dances in their honor were given day and night. Inter-tribal dissensions were forgotten. Friendliness and peace dominated the scene.

The great influence Cabeza de Vaca had over these Indians did not die with his departure. He implanted in them an enduring belief in the sincerity and kindness of the Spaniards. He and his companions were the first outsiders these Indians had ever seen, and the examples served to create in them a lasting trust in the strange men of the black and white races.

Coronado could testify to the truth of this. His army, fighting its way north through savages who had tasted the cruelty of the Spanish conquerors, found protection and kindness, not to mention badly needed provisions, among the Indians of Corazónes.

Two short excerpts from Castañeda illustrate the assertion.

In a clash with Indians in northern Sonora, near the present Arizona border, a detachment from Coronado's force was badly beaten. "The Spaniards who survived started off the same day on foot, not having any horses. They went toward Culiacan [that is, toward the south], keeping away from the roads, and did not find any food until they reached Corazónes, where the Indians, like the good friends they have always been, provided them with food."

Of another fight, Castañeda said: "In several places yells were heard and Indians seen, and some of the horses were wounded and killed, before Batuc [a town on the Rio de Ospura] was reached, where the friendly Indians from Corazónes came to meet the army and see the general. They were always friendly and had treated all the Spaniards who passed through their country well, furnishing them with what food they needed, and men, if they needed these."

Cabeza de Vaca was among the Opata probably for three weeks. He was in the Town of the Hearts, however, only three days. When the four men took their leave, the Indians guided them southward over a trail that passed through Metape. It was their intention to avoid journeying through the wastelands immediately adjacent to the Gulf.

Cabeza de Vaca wrote that they traveled southward for a day and then reached the Yaqui River. It was undoubtedly a longer trip, but it does not matter. The element of time is not significant.

Of far greater importance is the event which took place on the bank of the Yaqui.

The river was in flood, and they were forced to wait for fifteen days until the waters receded.

During this period hundreds of Indians visited their camp, and one day the sharp eyes of Castillo caught sight of a buckle that had come from a sword belt hanging on a thong about the neck of one of the visiting natives. Stitched to the buckle was a horseshoe nail.

5

Castillo did not attempt to find out by himself where the Indian had secured the belt buckle and the horseshoe nail. Making an effort to conceal his excitement, he drew Cabeza de Vaca aside and told him of the discovery. They deliberated on a course of action. Wise in the ways of the Indians, they knew that an open and direct approach would be impolitic.

In seeking information from an Indian, it was advisable to move slowly, perhaps by a circuitous route, much as one might do in interrogating a child. The men knew as well that in their roles as gods, or famed shamans, they were required to preserve their calmness and dignity under all circumstances, to display soberness and act in a manner of detachment at all times. Otherwise, they would lose face, and the awe with which the natives regarded them would be dissipated.

Never before had it been so difficult for them to maintain this attitude and this demeanor as it was when they sought out the Indian who possessed the first articles they had seen in all the years since they fled westward from the Texas coast that were unquestionably of Spanish origin. With a casualness they did not feel, they entered into a preliminary conversation with him, and when at last they deemed the moment to be auspicious, they remarked that it would be interesting to know how he had secured the buckle and the nail.

They received an answer of a kind they had fully expected. The buckle and the nail, said the Indian, had come from heaven.

Struggling to hide their emotion, they came gradually to
the point of inquiring who had brought them from heaven.
They heard then the response they knew the Indian must
make if he were to tell the truth.

It was: men who wore beards like theirs had come sometime before to a point on the Yaqui River. The men rode
horses, and they carried lances and swords, and they had
killed two Indians.

In a manner of the utmost indifference we could feign, we
asked them what had become of those men.

The answer came:

They had gone to sea, putting their lances beneath the water,
and going themselves under water; afterwards . . . they were
seen on the surface going toward the sunset.

Cabeza de Vaca and Castillo gave no sign of the disappointment which sickened them. It seemed obvious that
the Spaniards had landed from a ship, and had sailed away
again on the South Sea. God alone could say who they were,
where they had come from, or where they had gone.

The despair they had known so long returned. Yet, the
tarnished buckle and the bent nail remained as pinpoints
of light shining through the darkness of their despondency.
Consolation was to be found in the thought that if Christians had come as far as that river, at least on one occasion,
perhaps others had reached places not a great distance
away toward the south. They held to this splinter of hope,
and

. . . we made greater speed.

With several hundred Indians trailing them, they moved
eagerly on through the rolling country and the valleys
under the western shoulders of the great mountains. Day

after day they pushed relentlessly forward, tarrying in villages no longer than necessary to avoid injuring the feelings of their hospitable hosts, and each day they received intelligence that indicated the correctness of their deduction. Christians had been in the country.

The joy and thankfulness which had filled them at first, however, was soon crushed. They began to see the waste, the desolation, the destruction which the Spaniards had left behind them.

Cabeza de Vaca's own words at this juncture need no interpretation, no paraphrasing. They are clear and unequivocal. "We passed through many territories and found them all vacant; their inhabitants wandered fleeing among the mountains, without daring to have houses or till the earth for fear of Christians.

"The sight was one of infinite pain to us, a land very fertile and beautiful, abounding in springs and streams, the hamlets deserted and burned, the people thin and weak, all fleeing or in concealment.

"As they did not plant, they appeased their keen hunger by eating roots and the bark of trees. We bore a share in the famine along the whole way; for poorly could these unfortunates provide for us, themselves being so reduced they looked as though they would willingly die.

"They brought shawls of those they had concealed because of the Christians, presenting them to us; and they related how the Christians at other times had come through the land, destroying and burning the towns, carrying away half the men, and all the women and the boys, while those who had been able to escape were wandering about fugitives.

"We found them so alarmed they dared not remain anywhere. They would not nor could they till the earth, but preferred to die rather than live in dread of such cruel usage as they received. Although these showed themselves greatly delighted with us, we feared that on our arrival among those who held the frontier, and fought against the Christians, they would treat us badly, and revenge upon us the conduct of their enemies; but, when God our Lord was pleased to bring us there, they began to dread and respect us as the others had done, and even somewhat more, at which we no little wondered."

The terrorized people who had suffered so greatly at the hands of Spaniards received Cabeza de Vaca with kindness and respect and without fear. He was moved to write:

"Thence it may at once be seen that, to bring all these people to be Christians and to the obedience of the Imperial Majesty, they must be won by kindness, which is a way certain, and no other is.

"They took us to a town on the edge of a range of mountains, to which the ascent is over difficult crags. We found many people there collected out of fear of the Christians. They received us well, and presented us all they had. They gave us more than two thousand back-loads of maize, which we gave to the distressed and hungered beings who guided us to that place."

Cabeza de Vaca was filled with indignation and sorrow. How completely blind, how inconceivably stupid were his countrymen! They were bent on the taking of a few slaves, while all about them great fortunes awaited them. Here was a land that could easily be built into a prosperous and wealthy Spanish colonial empire, and it was being devastated and ruined.

"Throughout this region," he wrote, "wheresoever the mountains extend, we saw clear traces of gold and lead, iron, copper, and other metals.

"The people of the fixed residences and those beyond [the Opata and related tribes in northern Mexico] regard silver and gold with indifference, nor can they conceive of any use for them."

It was a land "plentiful of subsistence. Three times a year it is planted with maize and beans. Deer are of three kinds; one the size of the young steer of Spain."

Both Cabeza de Vaca's fury and his disappointment increased until he was consumed by them. He summoned his trusting followers to a council, and he gave them his word that he would pursue the diabolical invaders until he had caught them, and he would command them to halt their cruelty and to take no more slaves. He swore before God that he would restore peace to the land.

Of this the Indians were very glad.

Runners were sent off to carry Cabeza de Vaca's promise to all the people hiding in the hills and the forests.

The procession moved on southward, and those traveling with Cabeza de Vaca lost their fear, convinced that so long as he was with them they would be safe.

They came upon several places where the slave hunters had camped, but the raiders themselves were not overtaken. Moving doggedly on, they were joined presently by several Indians who told them that on the previous night some Spaniards had been observed from behind trees by native scouts. De Vaca noted that, "those who came with us were alarmed at this intelligence; some returned to spread the news over the land that the Christians were coming; and many more would have followed, had we not forbidden it and told them to cast aside their fear, when they reassured themselves and were well content."

Scouts were ordered by Cabeza de Vaca to guide him to the place where the Spaniards had been seen. It was reached on the afternoon of the following day. "We . . . saw at once that they told the truth. We perceived that the persons were mounted, by the stakes to which the horses had been tied."

They were on the Rio Sinaloa, and they were closing in.

6

That night Cabeza de Vaca lay in his robes desperately weary and suffering from a melancholia that not even the knowledge that other Spaniards were near-by could dispel.

Perhaps the reaction was too much for the body he had so heavily taxed. It was as if in some strange way the excitement and joy he had waited so long to experience had created a despondency in him.

Because he felt himself almost incapable of going on the short distance remaining to the goal which they had for so long struggled to reach, he pleaded with Dorantes and Castillo to go on without him. The Indians who had seen the slave hunters would lead the way.

Dorantes and Castillo shook their heads in refusal. They excused themselves, as Cabeza de Vaca recalled, "because of weariness and exhaustion . . . although either might have done better than I, being more youthful."

In the morning, Cabeza de Vaca rallied his waning strength. Estevanico agreed to go with him, and taking eleven Indians as guides, they set out on the trail.

In the course of ten leagues, they came upon three places where the Spaniards had rested.

It was on the next day—sometime in the middle of March, 1536—that twenty Spanish horsemen were startled to see a gaunt bearded white man and an immense Negro dressed in animal skins appear without warning out of the bush. Behind them came eleven Indians.

Cabeza de Vaca wrote:

"They stood staring at me a length of time, so confounded that they neither hailed me nor drew near to make an inquiry."

There were tears in his eyes, and his voice faltered, as he spoke to them in Spanish.

PART SEVEN

Triumph and a Tragic Land

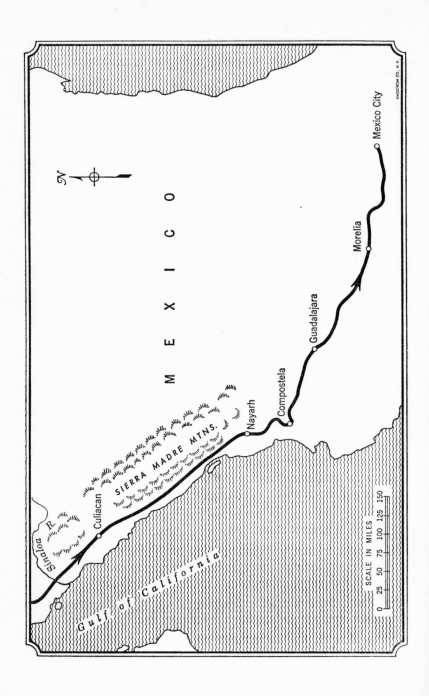

In 1526, a year before Cabeza de Vaca sailed from Spain, Nuño Beltran de Guzmán was appointed Governor of the Mexican province of Pánuco. He took his post in May, 1527, and later that year became President of the *Audencia,* the administrative and judicial board which governed the colony.

It was a position which gave him supreme authority. He used it with wanton disregard for the welfare or the feelings of his subjects, holding himself to be a god to whom all under his jurisdiction, with no regard for race or color, must pay obeisance. In a foul mood one day he hanged several natives who did not sweep the street before him as he passed through their village.

Guzmán, a personal and political enemy of Cortez, was dishonest, arrogant, barbarously cruel and without conscience. Slavery was forbidden by royal decree, but he found means of circumventing that law, as he did most others. He sold hundreds, perhaps thousands, to the operators of mines and to *encomienderos* throughout the West Indies, and pocketed the money he received for them.

The extremities he practiced eventually brought a strong protest to the Crown from high officers of the Church, and he was ordered to mend his ways and govern his territory with justice and in accordance with colonial statutes.

The reprimand was wasted. If Guzmán was obliged to restrain his brutal actions somewhat, he was not precluded from looking about for other ways of gratifying his avarice. It was one of his Indian slaves who gave him information that opened the door to the opportunity he sought.

The Indian was called Tejo. Castañeda tells of the incident this way: "This Indian said he was the son of a trader who was dead, but that when he was a little boy his father had gone into the back country with fine feathers to trade for ornaments, and that when he came back he brought a large amount of gold and silver."

Tejo stated that he made one or two trips with his father, and that he had seen "some very large villages, which he compared to Mexico [City] and its environs. He had seen seven very large towns which had streets of silver workers. It took forty days to go there from his country, through a wilderness in which nothing grew."

Inspired by the dream of conquering these rich cities, Guzmán raised a large force of Spaniards, Aztecs and Tlascaltecs, and set out. Hodge says the army contained ten thousand men, but Castañeda sets the number at four hundred Spaniards and twenty thousand Indians.

The discrepancy is not important. Hodge, more reliable, of course, states that Guzmán started from Mexico City late in 1529, and that he "conquered the territory through which he passed, laying waste the settlements and fields and inflicting unspeakable punishment on the native inhabitants.

"Guzmán built a chapel at Tonalá, which formed the beginning of the settlement of the present city of Guadalajara, named from his native town in Spain; he also founded the towns of Santiago de Compostela and San Miguel Culiacán, in Tepic and Sinaloa respectively, and started on his return journey in 1531.

"Meanwhile a new *Audencia* had arrived in Mexico, and Guzmán was summoned to appear at the capital. This he refused to do. . . . . In May 1533, the king commanded him to submit to the provincial authorities; many of his friends and adherents deserted him, and he was stripped of his title of Governor of Pánuco.

"In 1536 [March 17] the licentiate Diego Perez de la Torre was appointed *juez de residencia,* an officer whose duty was to conduct a rigid investigation of the accounts and administration of government officials—this time with special reference to Guzmán.

"By Torre's order, Guzmán was arrested and confined in jail until 1538. . . . He was banished to Torrejón de Velasco, where he died in 1544, penniless and despised."

The brief history of Guzmán's career is significant, for it reveals that word of the Seven Cities of Cibola had reached Mexico City before the arrival of Cabeza de Vaca.

Castañeda embellishes the story with the statement that upon leaving Mexico City, Guzmán "crossed Tarasca, which is in the province of Michoacán, so as to get into the region which the Indian [Tejo] said was to be crossed toward the North Sea [Gulf of California], in this way getting to the country which they were looking for, which was already named the 'Seven Cities.'

"He thought, from the forty days of which Tejo had spoken, that it would be found to be about two hundred leagues, and that they would easily be able to cross the country."

Matters didn't turn out as Guzmán thought they would, and "they tried to cross the country, but found the difficulties very great, because the mountain chains which are near the sea are so rough that it was impossible, after great labor, to find a passageway in that region."

Not only mountains hindered them. Justifiably vengeful natives had much to do with halting them. Guzmán was not a man of courage, and he had no Cabeza de Vaca to help him. "His whole army had to stay in the district of

Culiacán for so long on this account that some rich men who were with him, who had possessions in Mexico, changed their minds, and every day became more anxious to return.

"Besides this, Nuño de Guzmán received word that . . . Don Hernando Cortez had come from Spain with his new title [*Marqués del Valle de Oaxaca y Capitán General de la Nueva España y de la Costa del Sur*], and with great favors and estates, and as Nuño de Guzmán had been a great rival of his . . . and had done much damage to his property . . . he feared that Don Hernando Cortez would want to pay him back in the same way, or worse."

Guzmán was beaten and discredited, and he was afraid to face the music. When the authorities finally caught up with him, he was jailed, then exiled.

Don Antonio Mendoza, viceroy of New Spain (Mexico), appointed as Guzmán's successor "Francisco Vásquez de Coronado, a gentleman from Salamanca, who had married a lady in the City of Mexico, the daughter of Alonso de Estrada, the treasurer and at one time governor of Mexico, and the son, most people said, of His Catholic Majesty Don Ferdinand, and many stated it as certain."

Tejo had died, and the search for the seven cities had been abandoned. Then something happened that brought the name once more to the lips of everyone in great excitement. "Three Spaniards, named Cabeza de Vaca, Dorantes, and Castillo Maldonado, and a Negro, who had been lost on the expedition which Panfilo de Narvaez led into Florida, reached Mexico."

2

The sound of their own language coming from a wild man of the forest confounded the slave hunters on that historic day beside the Rio Sinaloa in March 1536. When Cabeza de Vaca told them who he was and how he had come there, they seemed to be not only unimpressed but to disbelieve him. The reverence with which the Indians regarded Cabeza de Vaca mystified and frightened them. Not a little angered, Cabeza de Vaca demanded that he be taken to their commander.

They readily agreed to show him the way, mounted their horses and set out along the river bank. A short time later Cabeza de Vaca and Estevanico presented themselves before an astonished Captain Diego de Alcaraz. "We gave thanks to God our Lord for having chosen to bring us out of a captivity so melancholy and wretched. The delight we felt let each one conjecture, when he shall remember the length of time we were in that country, the suffering and perils we underwent."

Captain Alcaraz listened politely to their story, but his eyes betrayed his skepticism. He had never heard of the Narvaez Expedition. He made no commitments, thinking that Cabeza de Vaca was a demented soldier who had deserted and, taking a Negro slave with him, had wandered into the wilderness. It was a matter for the governor to handle, and he decided that it would be best for him to make out that he believed the fantastic tale until he could get Cabeza de Vaca and Estevanico back to headquarters. There was something very queer about the whole thing. These men were traveling unarmed about the country with a retinue of savages who obviously revered them. They displayed a remarkable assurance, and they acted as if they were accustomed to holding positions of great influence. It was apparent that they had been among the natives for some time, for they conversed with great facility in the sign language.

Alcaraz was dense, but he was not stupid enough to put himself in a position in which he might be disciplined for jumping to an unfounded conclusion. There was something —perhaps it was the look of fearlessness and supreme confidence he saw in Cabeza de Vaca's eyes—that prevented him from clapping Cabeza de Vaca and Estevanico in irons and carrying them off to San Miguel Culiacán to be justly dealt with. Every movement Cabeza de Vaca made was marked with dignity. Despite his skins and his long matted hair, he had an air that was almost regal.

Alcaraz was cautious, and he was not a little apprehensive. He was made in the Guzmán mold. He was without honor or integrity. In his twisted, cold mind the capture of slaves by false promises was simply clever strategy, an indication of ingenuity, and a thing to be commended.

Alcaraz was later to serve as a lieutenant under Captain Melchior Díaz in the army of Coronado. Castañeda speaks of him as a "man unfitted to have people under his command." He was to die a horrible death, his flesh putrid and falling from his bones, after being wounded by a poisoned arrow in an Indian fight near the Arizona border.

The more Alcaraz listened, the more he became convinced that Cabeza de Vaca was a religious crackpot who had become fanatical on the subject of justice for the Indians, and he made the mistake of attempting to use the demented wanderer, as they made their way back toward headquarters, to his own advantage.

He confided to Cabeza de Vaca that he was "completely undone" because of his failure to capture any Indians, and "he knew not which way to turn, and his men had well begun to experience hunger and fatigue."

If he expected this sad statement to impress Cabeza de Vaca, he was disappointed. Nor did the recital of his misfortune evoke from Cabeza de Vaca the slightest expression of compassion.

Cabeza de Vaca was occupied with the consideration of the difficult situation he saw himself facing. He knew the time had come when he must make good his pledge to the Indians that he would halt the taking of slaves by the Spaniards.

Alcaraz's eyes grew bright with rapacity as Cabeza de Vaca told him Dorantes and Castillo were waiting, not ten leagues away, with the multitude which had followed them from the north. He quickly offered to dispatch fifty natives who were in his service and several soldiers to bring them all to his camp. Without revealing his intentions, Cabeza de Vaca agreed to the proposal, and sent Estevanico with the detachment as a guide.

Cabeza de Vaca wrote that he and Alcaraz had "many high words" over a period of five days. The basis of their conflict could not have been simpler. Dorantes and Castillo arrived with six hundred Indians. Alcaraz wanted to take them prisoner, and march them off into slavery. It would have been an unprecedented haul, and he envisioned himself being promoted for having brought off such a profitable feat. Only Cabeza de Vaca stood in his way.

It was a clash of irreconcilable minds. Alcaraz might have resolved it quickly by shooting Cabeza de Vaca. Something stayed his hand, something in Cabeza de Vaca's eyes, something in his words. Alcaraz knew a fear that he could not explain.

Cabeza de Vaca says Alcaraz "begged" him to order the people of the country to come out of hiding and bring the Spaniards food, and that he sent out messengers with the request. Alcaraz was dumbfounded when he saw six hundred more natives come out of the hills bringing

> . . . all the maize in their possession. They fetched it in certain pots, closed with clay, which they had concealed in the earth. They brought . . . whatever else they had.

Cabeza de Vaca addressed the great throng. He advised them to return to their homes, to feel no fear, to rebuild their houses and replant their crops.

They refused, not because they wished to defy him nor because they did not have faith in him, but because they did not want to leave him until they had seen him safely delivered into the hands of other Indians farther south. That had been the custom across the entire continent, and they feared that if they broke it they would suffer grave consequences.

> . . . they were afraid they should die, and, going with us, they feared neither Christians nor lances.

Alcaraz had heard enough. His fury became almost uncontrollable. He saw himself facing defeat, his great opportunity being destroyed by a ragged crazy man who had wandered out of the wilderness like a lost dog. In a desperate effort to save himself, he resorted to subterfuge, to what might be termed a psychological strategem.

Through his interpreter he made an angry speech in which he told the Indians that Cabeza de Vaca was not a god, not a genuine medicine man, but merely a lost Spaniard. Cabeza de Vaca possessed no supernatural powers, nor did he have any legal authority. He was an ordinary Spanish soldier who had been wandering in the wild for a long time. Cabeza de Vaca was the same as he, Diego de Alcaraz, the same flesh and blood. Cabeza de Vaca, as well as his companions, were persons of "mean condition and small force." The Indians were stupid to listen to Cabeza de Vaca, for he was nothing, and he could do nothing for them.

On the other hand, he, Diego de Alcaraz, loyal servant of God and the Spanish Crown, had unlimited authority. It was he who must be obeyed, and if the Indians did not do so, they would suffer.

Alcaraz might as well have saved his breath. The Indians only stared at him in stony silence for a time. At last they bluntly called him a liar. Cabeza de Vaca and his friends, they said, had come whence the sun rises. Alcaraz had come whence it goes down. Cabeza de Vaca healed the sick. Alcaraz killed the well. Cabeza de Vaca had come naked and barefoot. Alcaraz had come in clothing and on a horse, and he carried arms. Cabeza de Vaca was covetous of nothing, and returned all that was given him. Alcaraz robbed whoever he met, and he bestowed nothing on anyone.

Alcaraz was driven from the arena in abject defeat. Cabeza de Vaca made another effort to get the Indians to return to their homes. This time he met with success. Seeing that it was his sincere desire that they go, they "told us they would do what we commanded, and would build their towns, if the Christians would suffer them . . . only with great effort and solicitation we got them to go."

The Indians trailed away. They went filled with trust and faith.

In a turn about, Alcaraz made an attempt to show that he could accept his defeat in good grace. He became polite and solicitous, declaring he would see that Cabeza de Vaca was no longer delayed. No doubt Cabeza de Vaca must be anxious to reach civilization. He assigned an *alcalde* named Zebreros to take two soldiers and a contingent of Indians and conduct the four men safely to the vice-governor of the province, Captain Melchior Díaz, who was believed to be in Culiacán.

Cabeza de Vaca went with contentment in his heart. "It is but an instance of how frequently men are mistaken . . .

we set about to preserve the liberty of the Indians and thought we had secured it, but the contrary appeared."

Alcaraz secretly instructed Zebreros to lead the four men on a circuitous route through the wilderness and prevent them from having any contact with natives. At an opportune time, Zebreros was to desert them, leaving them lost and without food or guides. Meanwhile, he, Alcaraz, would capture as many Indians as he could control and drive them directly to Culiacán.

Zebreros obeyed his orders too conscientiously. He went into a country with which neither he nor any of his detachment was familiar, and got lost.

Seven men died of thirst on that terrible march. Only after a circular trek of seventy-five miles through a waterless desert was an Indian town reached. There Zebreros vanished. Perhaps he was overcome with the fear of reprisals from the obviously powerful Cabeza de Vaca, whom the Indians so revered. Perhaps he had no heart for continuing the deception, the plan of Alcaraz to lead Cabeza de Vaca into the desert, abandon him, and let him die of thirst and starvation.

Zebreros abandoned Cabeza de Vaca, but he selected a place only eight miles from the safety of Culiacán. There he fled, and, hoping to save his own skin, he squealed on Alcaraz to Vice-Governor Melchior Díaz.

Castañeda says that although Díaz was not a gentleman by birth, he merited the position he held. Elsewhere Díaz is described as honorable, honest and merciful, a rare combination of qualities in the days of the *conquistadores*.

Díaz was to become an outstanding officer under the banner of Coronado. He was destined to die grotesquely in an accident on the Colorado River in Arizona in 1541. Attempting to protect some sheep from being attacked by a greyhound which belonged to a soldier, he, as Castañeda tells it, "threw his lance at the dog while his horse was running, so that it stuck up in the ground, and not being able to stop his horse he went over the lance so that it nailed him through the thighs and the iron came out behind, rupturing his bladder. . . . He lived about twenty days, during which they [his soldiers] proceeded with great difficulty on account of the necessity of carrying him."

As vice-governor Díaz struggled to comply with the laws, a difficult undertaking under Guzmán. He was opposed to slavery for reasons of humanity, not simply because it was illegal. It was his opinion that the slave hunters, although given sanction by Guzmán, were operating under questionable authority.

The law enacted by the Second Mexican *Audencia* in 1530, and which forbade any form of slavery, was, in Díaz's estimation, clear and precise. Diego Fernando de Proano, Díaz's predecessor at Culiacán, had been tried and found guilty under it for branding and selling gangs of Indians. However, even this stringent action had failed to discourage Guzmán. The governor issued a directive, or opinion, approving the enslavement of native rebels, conspirators, and disturbers of the peace under the pretext that such an ordinance was necessary to preserve order in the province.

The regulation was interpreted by Guzmán's political cronies as a license to take slaves, and they charged virtually every native in the province with being a rebel. Díaz had no alternative but to defy his superior if he wished to enforce the law.

Díaz knew the story of the disastrous Narvaez Expedition. When he heard from Zebreros that the four survivors were camped only a few miles away, he mounted his horse and went to welcome them. It was a happy and an emotional meeting.

Díaz, wrote Cabeza de Vaca, "wept with us, giving praises to God our Lord for having extended over us so great care. He comforted us and entertained us hospitably.

In behalf of the governor, Nuño de Guzmán and himself, he tendered all that he had, and the service in his power."

Díaz escorted the men to his headquarters at Anhacan, adjacent to Culiacán. He was regretful and displeased when he heard how they had been tricked, and he promised that Alcaraz would be disciplined. He was eager to stop the slave-taking, and as a step toward this end, he requested Cabeza de Vaca to stay with him for a time for the purpose of aiding him in getting the Indians resettled in their villages.

Díaz asked Cabeza de Vaca to send messengers into the territory to inform the Indians that the government would tolerate no more cruelty or slave raids. He felt that Cabeza de Vaca's assistance would be of inestimable value, and he implored him to use his influence to bring about the desired results.

Cabeza de Vaca was doubtful that he would be successful.

> We had brought no native of our own, nor of those who accompanied us . . . intelligent in these affairs.

Nevertheless, Cabeza de Vaca agreed to make the attempt. He selected as his emissaries two captives who had been in the Zebreros contingent which had led him into the desert. These Indians had seen the attitude and heard the words of the natives at the time of Cabeza de Vaca's clash with Alcaraz, and from Cabeza de Vaca's followers they had learned of "the great authority and command we carried and exercised . . . the wonders we had worked, the sick we had cured, and the many things besides we had done."

Cabeza de Vaca's message requested all the Indians in the area to come to Anhacan for a great council. To protect the messengers on their mission, he gave them the most powerful spiritual weapon he possessed, one of the magic gourds he had obtained far back in Texas.

For seven days Cabeza de Vaca and Melchior Díaz waited. They were on the verge of abandoning hope that the Indians would come, when the messengers returned. They brought with them only three headmen, and reported that the Indians, although they believed Cabeza de Vaca, were suspicious that he had been forced to send for them against his will. Since Cabeza de Vaca had left the Sinaloa River, Alcaraz had resumed his slave raids. Several Indians had been killed in the fighting, and a number had been captured and chained together. The three headmen had taken a chance with their own lives to learn if Cabeza de Vaca's message was valid. They brought him a quantity of beads, turquoises and feathers to show that their esteem for him had not diminished.

Melchior Díaz immediately took command of the situation, and threw his full support behind Cabeza de Vaca in a public announcement. He told the headmen that Cabeza de Vaca and the three men with him had come to Anhacan in the name of God. De Vaca wrote that Díaz reminded the chiefs "that we had traveled about the world many years, telling all the people we found that they should believe in God . . . that if they desired to be Christians and serve God in the way we required, the Christians would cherish them as brothers and behave toward them very kindly."

Díaz explained that only by accepting the teachings and the commands of Cabeza de Vaca could the Indians find protection from such men as Guzmán and Alcaraz, for Cabeza de Vaca had the power to halt these men in their cruel and wicked activities. Cabeza de Vaca spoke with God in Heaven.

Melchior Díaz was an astute officer. He anticipated events to come. He saw Cabeza de Vaca as a famous man. Cabeza de Vaca and his companions had performed an almost unbelievable feat. In Mexico City, Cabeza de Vaca would be received by the Viceroy and the Marquis del Valle, and he would be honored and fêted, perhaps given a title. The favors he asked would probably be quickly granted. One of those favors would be a request for stricter enforcement of the slave laws.

What was more, Cabeza de Vaca knew all about the mysterious country to the north, the Seven Cities of Cibola for which Guzmán had searched in vain. Now there were indications that Guzmán's goose was cooked. Cabeza de Vaca's reports would be of no use to Guzmán, but they would be of great interest to the Viceroy.

Melchior Díaz was unquestionably sincere in what he did. Cabeza de Vaca's influence with the Indians brought about a peace that no other man in Mexico could have achieved. Melchior Díaz was willing to share in the credit, and he knew that under such circumstances Guzmán could not blame him for halting slavery in the province. He was deeply gratified, and he was happy in the realization that he had achieved the conditions he wanted without endangering his own career.

Indians soon swarmed into Anhacan. There was feasting and dancing, and the council fires burned through the night. Díaz distributed gifts and food.

The basic purpose of the great gathering was not neglected, however. Díaz made an open covenant with God. Henceforth, he would neither invade the Indians' lands, nor would he consent to invasions by others. No person would be enslaved.

Cabeza de Vaca made his final speech of the journey.

Afterward the Indians gave him their pledge that they would be true Christians and serve God. He asked them to build a house for *Dios,* and at its entrance to place a cross, and they told him they would do as he commanded.

The Indians were baptized, and they went back to their

burned fields and razed villages with hearts full of gratefulness and love for the barefoot man who had come out of the sun to help them.

3

Cabeza de Vaca, Dorantes, Castillo and Estevanico could no longer wear clothes. Their skins, burned and scarred by the sun and wind and rain, by the terrible heat and the bitter cold, could not tolerate the gentle touch of linen or silk. No shoes could be found to fit their calloused feet—they could not have suffered the best boots in Mexico, anyway—only well-worn Indian moccasins were bearable. The soft beds provided for them by Melchior Díaz were covered by fine white cotton sheets and downy woolen blankets. They slept on the hard bare floor under buffalo robes. Several weeks passed before they could adjust themselves to the comforts of civilization.

It was April 1, 1536, when they moved from Anhacan to Díaz's quarters in Culiacán. During the next fortnight numerous Indians appeared to make reports. They were extremely gratifying to Cabeza de Vaca. The natives were returning to their homes.

The most gratifying news of all, however, came from the lips of Alcaraz. He returned from the north empty-handed. Called before Díaz he told how the Indians' towns were once more inhabitated. Churches were being built, fields were being planted. He had been greeted by Indians with crosses in their hands. The thing that dismayed him the most was that no Indian seemed to be afraid of him. If he still considered Cabeza de Vaca a demented religious fanatic, he held his tongue on the matter.

Cabeza de Vaca soon afterward was to write the King of Spain: "God in His infinite mercy is pleased that in the days of Your Majesty, under your might and dominion, these nations should come to be thoroughly and voluntarily subject to the Lord. . . . We regard this as certain, that Your Majesty is he who is destined to do so much, not difficult to accomplish; for in the two thousand leagues we journeyed on land, and in boats on water, and in that we traveled unceasingly for ten months after coming out of captivity, we found neither sacrifices nor idolatry."

He added for the enlightenment of the Crown that it was his opinion that the continent was two thousand leagues in width at its widest part, and that the most fertile and richest areas were those adjacent to the South Sea, the Pacific.

For the first time the world knew that a great land mass lay north of Mexico.

The four men left Culiacán on May 15, almost exactly eight years and one month after they had landed on the shore of Florida.

Twenty mounted soldiers, six unidentified Christians, and five hundred Indian slaves comprised their escort for the trip of "a hundred leagues" to Compostela, where Governor Guzmán awaited them.

Guzmán made every effort to be entertaining and hospitable, but his graciousness was not in the least a reflection of inherent gentlemanly instincts. He was aware that Diego Perez de la Torre, holding the powers of a *juez de residencia,* had come from Spain to investigate him. Alcaraz had made a report, and so he was also aware of Cabeza de Vaca's power. In addition, Cabeza de Vaca had witnessed slave raiders in operation, and now Cabeza de Vaca was on his way to Mexico City.

Word of the return of the survivors had already gone south by post and government pouch. Guzmán could expect that the viceroy and Cortez, that whoreson, would be waiting to receive them in the presidential palace. It was altogether a disheartening outlook, but nothing more was to be lost—and perhaps something was to be gained—by showing every courtesy to Cabeza de Vaca. Cabeza de Vaca seemed to be quite gullible and trusting.

Guzmán soon learned the erroneousness of this opinion. Cabeza de Vaca not only was not impressed by the attention paid him, or by the luxuries proferred to him, but he had no intention of sparing Guzmán or accepting his friendship.

In Culiacán, Cabeza de Vaca had managed to obtain from a notary a *testimonio,* or certified copy, of Guzmán's directive authorizing his agents to take as slaves any Indians who were considered rebels. He confronted Guzmán with the document, accused him of violating the law under the dishonest pretext of maintaining peace in the province, and announced that the entire issue would be brought to the attention of the proper officials. These, of course, included the viceroy, the Marquis del Valle, and the *juez de residencia.*

Guzmán's courtesy vanished. If he considered retaliating violently, he made no move in that direction. Either his courage, if he possessed any, failed him, or he realized he had reached the end of his tether.

From Compostela, over the old Camino Real, a triumphal procession moved onward to Mexico City. Thousands of people—Indians, Spaniards, and their bemuddled offspring —lined the streets of towns and villages, and gathered along country roads, to catch a glimpse of the celebrated wanderers, and they gave "thanks to God for having saved us from so many calamities."

They entered Mexico City on July 24, the day before the vespers of Saint Iago—the day of Saint James the Apostle—and were carried with cheers and waving flags along the wide avenues.

We were handsomely treated by the Viceroy and the Marquis del Valle, and welcomed with joy. They gave us clothing and proffered whatsoever they had.

The next day a great celebration was held, and there was a jousting of bulls.

Epilogue

During the delightful summer weeks he rested in Mexico City, Cabeza de Vaca made no unfounded assertions about the country through which he had passed. He made no claims, either orally or in writing, about having discovered a fabulously rich land. Indeed, every statement he uttered was conservative and factual.

When he repeated stories he had heard from the Indians, he did not fail to remind his listeners that they were told to him in the sign language, and that he could not vouch for their accuracy. He had no personal knowledge of the gold and silver mines which native taletellers claimed existed in the northern deserts. He had seen no cities with buildings several stories in height, in which people ate from golden dishes and adorned themselves with priceless jewels. The only evidence he had found that the country contained any mineral resources at all consisted of some scoria of iron, some small bags of mica, some galena with which the Indians painted their faces, some pieces of turquoise, five emerald arrow heads, and a copper bell, which probably by some mysterious means had been transported northward from Mexico.

That was the essence of his report on the subject. Yet, the word spread like wildfire through dry grass that he had actually seen the Seven Cities of Cibola; that if he had had the means of carrying it he would have returned with an inconceivable fortune; that he had crossed streams which flowed in beds of solid gold; that he had seen Indian children playing with diamonds, pearls and emeralds which their mothers had cast away as worthless; that he had passed hills of silver and a mountain which contained so many jewels of all kinds that he dared not look at it in the sunlight for fear of being blinded.

Not a mountain of jewels, but their own dreams and illusions blinded the officials of Mexico. The viceroy himself is said to have proposed that Cabeza de Vaca lead an expedition as his representative to the fabled land. If that is true, Cabeza de Vaca declined. He was thinking of home, of a reunion with his wife, of a patio in Jerez de la Frontera bathed in the blue light of late afternoon. Those were the only riches he desired at the moment.

In October 1536, he made arrangements to sail, but as his ship was about to depart, a hurricane swept the eastern seaboard of Mexico. The vessel, as well as most other shipping, was destroyed. Cabeza de Vaca accepted the advice of navigators that it would be wise to wait until spring before attempting the long voyage, and returned to Mexico City. Such a delay was nothing new to him, and he had only to glance back into his years of captivity to find the patience he needed.

In his comfortable quarters in the capital, he sat down at a desk, took up a quill, and began to write the narrative that would give his name a high place on the roster of the world's greatest pathfinders.

"Sacred Caesarian Catholic Majesty:

"Among the many who have held sway, I think no prince can be found whose service has been attended with the ardor and emulation shown for that of Your Highness * at

* The Emperor Charles V.

this time. The inducement is evident and powerful: men do not pursue together the same career without motive, and strangers are observed to strive with those who are equally impelled by religion and loyalty.

"Although ambition and love of action are common to all, as to the advantages that each may gain, there are great inequalities of fortune, the result not of conduct, but only accident, nor caused by the fault of anyone, but coming in the providence of God and solely by His will. Hence to one arises deeds more signal than he thought to achieve; to another the opposite in every way occurs, so that he can show no higher proof of purpose than his effort, and at times even this is so concealed that it cannot of itself appear.

"As for me, I say in undertaking the march I made on the main by the royal authority, I firmly trusted that my conduct and services would be as evident and distinguished as were those of my ancestors and that I should not have to speak in order to be reckoned among those who for diligence and fidelity in affairs Your Majesty honors. . . .

"To me, one only duty remains, to present a relation of what was seen and heard in the . . . years I wandered lost and in privation through many and remote lands. Not merely a statement of positions and distances, animals and vegetation, but of the diverse customs of the many and very barbarous people . . .

"My hope of going out from among those nations was always small, still my care and diligence were none the less to keep in particular remembrance everything, that if at any time God our Lord should will to bring me where I now am, it might testify to my exertion in the royal behalf.

"As the narrative is in my opinion of no trivial value to those who in your name go to subdue those countries and bring them to a knowledge of the true faith and true Lord, and under the imperial dominion, I have written this with much exactness; and although in it may be read things very novel and for some persons difficult to believe, nevertheless they may without hesitation credit me as strictly faithful.

"Better than to exaggerate, I have lessened in all things, and it is sufficient to say the relation is offered to Your Majesty for truth. I beg it may be received in the name of homage, since it is the most that one could bring who returned thence naked."

During Lent of 1537, Cabeza de Vaca and Dorantes went to Vera Cruz to take ship. They boarded on Palm Sunday, but for fifteen days waited in the harbor for a favorable wind. The vessel leaked so badly that Cabeza de Vaca finally transferred to another that also was waiting to sail. Dorantes declined to make the change, and they separated.

After coming close to foundering in a spring storm off Bermuda, and outrunning French pirates off the Azores, Cabeza de Vaca's ship reached Lisbon on the 10th of August.

His fame had preceded him, and he was granted an audience not long afterward with the king in Seville.

Shortly before the arrival of Cabeza de Vaca in Spain, Hernando de Soto had been awarded the title of Marquis, appointed *adelantado* of Florida, and given a license, much like that Narvaez had held, to explore, conquer and settle that still unknown land. De Soto had become extremely wealthy while assisting Pizarro in the conquest of Peru.

The Gentleman of Elvas, who was de Soto's chronicler, declares that in Seville de Soto lived on a grand scale. He "employed a superintendent of household, an usher, pages, equerry, chamberlain, footmen, and all the other servants requisite for the establishment of a gentleman."

De Soto was not born a gentleman, but a few silver bars stained with the blood of Incas had opened social doors that otherwise would have been closed to him. In the fall of 1537 he was preparing for his great expedition to the New World. At this time, writes the Gentleman of Elvas, "a *hidalgo* arrived at court from the Indias, Cabeza de Vaca by name. . . . He brought with him a written relation of adventures, which said in some places: Here I have seen this; and the rest which I saw I leave to confer of with his Majesty: generally, however, he described the poverty of the country, and spoke of the hardships he had undergone.

"Some of his kinsfolk, desirous of going to the Indias, strongly urged him to tell them whether he had seen any rich country in Florida or not; but he told them he could not do so; because he and another (by name Orantes,* who had remained in New Spain with the purpose of returning into Florida) had sworn not to divulge certain things which they had seen, lest someone might beg the government in advance of them, for which he had come to Spain; nevertheless, he gave them to understand that it was the richest country in the world."

This was sheer poppycock. Cabeza de Vaca never described Florida as anything but the miserable country it was. De Soto offered to make Cabeza de Vaca his second in command, but the offer was declined for two good reasons: Cabeza de Vaca had had all he wanted of the swamps of Florida, and he had sworn to himself that he would never go on any expedition of which he did not have full control. His experiences with Narvaez had been enough to cause him to take that oath.

The Gentleman of Elvas wrote his account of the de Soto Expedition, and of events preceding it, after his return, not from a diary he had kept, not from notes made in the field, but purely from memory. Needless to say, he romanced a good deal. His assertions regarding the statements of Cabeza de Vaca in Seville are palpably erroneous.

Cabeza de Vaca, however, was not to escape in Spain, any more than he had in Mexico, from being branded a spinner of fantastic tales. Castañeda also made the same accusation against him.

* Dorantes.

In his narrative of the Coronado Expedition, written twenty years after the remnants of its once mighty force had straggled back to Mexico, Castañeda charges that Cabeza de Vaca and his companions, upon reaching Mexico City "gave the good Don Antonio de Mendoza [the Viceroy] an account of some large and powerful villages, four and five stories high, of which they had heard a great deal in the countries they had crossed, and other things very different from what turned out to be the truth."

Castañeda had no more evidence to support such a statement than did the Gentleman of Elvas.

Neither the Viceroy Mendoza nor Governor Coronado— nor anyone else in Mexico, for that matter—needed fanciful tales to stir them to action. The fact that Cabeza de Vaca had *heard* about the Seven Cities was enough. It was confirmation of what they had believed for ten years, ever since an Indian slave named Tejo had told Guzmán what he had seen as a boy traveling with his trader father. Guzmán had failed to find them, but Guzmán was a dolt. Cabeza de Vaca's report, the people cried, qualified as it was, indicated that the cities were far north of the country Guzmán had searched.

There is no document to show that Cabeza de Vaca's unnamed wife received him with anything but hysterical joy. It is known, however, that she had waited faithfully for him. An inheritance had made her moderately well-to-do, and she willingly turned the money over to him.

His audience with the king lasted an unusually long time. The monarch was fascinated by his *Relacion,* and he came away with the assurance that he would receive high honors for his service, and that a suitable appointment would be found for him. Cabeza de Vaca, said the king, was the kind of trustworthy and devout servant for which Spain had great need.

Cabeza de Vaca went home to Jerez. Some of his old

friends and members of his family were gone, but the old city had not changed at all. His sister Maria was still there. She had married Ruy Díaz de Guzmán—no relation of the beast of Mexico—and they proudly presented their son Alonso, page and secretary of the Duke of Medina Sidonia whom Cabeza de Vaca had served so many years before.

He was not happy in Jerez. He knew no peace. The curiosity of the people was insupportable. They constantly pestered him, asking his advice, imploring him to find good posts for them in the Indies, begging for loans, imploring him to tell tales of his adventures, believing he had a hogshead of jewels secretly hidden in Seville. The story spread that he had been sworn to secrecy by his three companions because of the fear that the government would deprive them of their riches by levying heavy taxes on them.

The Gentleman of Elvas, dipping once more into his undependable memory, says that two of Cabeza de Vaca's kinsmen, Baltasar de Gallegos and Cristobal de Espindola, announced that his tales had influenced them to join the de Soto company, and that they "besought him to counsel them."

In response to this plea, according to the Gentleman, Cabeza de Vaca declared that he had returned to Spain in the hope of himself becoming governor of Florida, "and though he found it already had been granted to Don Hernando de Soto, yet, on account of his oath, he could not divulge what they [his kinsmen] desired to know; nevertheless, he would advise them to sell their estates and go—that in so doing they would act wisely."

If Cabeza de Vaca entertained the hope of becoming governor of Florida, it was a well-guarded secret. Although such a thing is possible—and certainly no man would have been better qualified to hold the office—the chances are that he did not. He was fully aware that governorships were not awarded on merit, but were sold for money. He was penniless in his own right, and the inheritance of his wife would have been insufficient to finance such an undertaking.

He was apprised, as well, that de Soto had paid handsomely for the appointment. When de Soto had returned to Spain with a fortune, the king immediately had borrowed six hundred thousand *reales* from him. It would have been ridiculous for Cabeza de Vaca to think of himself as playing against such competition. He didn't, for he was not naïve, and neither was he stupid.

He gave counsel to his kinsmen, but not of the kind portrayed by the Gentleman. He told them of his long suffering, of the emptiness and poverty of the country, of his captivity by degraded savages, of eating spiders and worms to keep alive. He told them that if there was gold in those endless reaches of forest and desert, he had not found it, except for a few traces close to the country already occupied by Spaniards. He told them that if they chose to go, they did so after hearing his advice that they could be certain of finding nothing of value, that no fortune awaited them.

Of course, they did not believe him. They smiled, agreeing knowingly that he was not revealing everything he knew. He was a clever one, but they were not to be so easily fooled.

Gallegos and Espandola sold their houses, their vineyards, their fields of wheat, their eight acres of olive trees, and sailed away with de Soto. Both survived the expedition, but one cannot refrain from wondering how often and bitterly, when they were lost, hungry and ragged in the swamps of Georgia and Arkansas, they cursed the name of Cabeza de Vaca.

Idleness weighed heavily on Cabeza de Vaca in Spain. He had spent too many years in the wilderness to adjust himself to the comforts of life there. He felt a strong urge at times to throw off his good clothes, don a piece of deerskin and walk barefoot through the streets. He longed for the sound of Indian drums, for a sight of the great mountains rising beside the South Sea. He had no interest in the political squabbles in which his friends indulged, viewing them as inane and unimportant in the great scheme of things he knew. His blood remained unstirred by such issues as the heretics of Ghent and the imperial rights of Italy. His eyes looked far beyond the crowded, filthy streets, across a great shining sea. There was so much that a man could do out there, so many things to be done that had a meaning.

The months passed into years, and nothing came of the king's promises. Cabeza de Vaca consoled himself with the thought that the court had its hands full of pressing problems. The great patience, tolerance and understanding he had developed in the wilderness saved him from despondency.

In September, 1539, a battered ship came in from South America. It brought word that things were going very badly in the provinces bordering the Rio de la Plata. The natives were in revolt, and the Spanish garrisons could not long hold out against them without relief. Unless a strong fighting force commanded by a capable and experienced administrator were sent at once from Spain, the only two Spanish colonies south of the Equator would be lost. If such a disaster were permitted to occur, the economy of the nation would be grievously injured, uncountable fortunes would be left untouched, and all the work of the padres to win the South American Indians to Christianity would be wasted. A recovery might never be achieved.

Cabeza de Vaca found out that he had not, after all, been forgotten. He was summoned before the Council of the Indies and informed that the king would be pleased to appoint him Governor, Captain-General, and *adelantado* of the Province of Rio de la Plata.

Cabeza de Vaca sailed for South America in November, 1540.

His adventures there, which equaled in many respects those occurring on his long journey from Florida to Mexico, must be recounted in another story. It is enough to say here that he performed remarkable feats of exploration in jungles never before seen by white men.

In the end, the dishonesty, cruelty and greed of his own subordinates and associates defeated him. He was unable to enforce his policies of justice, decency and honesty. It was the Indies all over again. The natives, despite all his efforts, his protests and his orders, were tortured, robbed, raped and murdered.

At last officials, growing tired of his rectitude and his piety, conspired to bring false charges of maladministration against him. In April, 1543, he was arrested and thrown into prison. After a confinement of two years he was sent under guard to Spain.

Perhaps the court didn't take the charges against him very seriously. Political expediency, however, required that he be convicted. He was sentenced to serve eight years in exile in Africa, but the judgment was not carried out. After being held under loose guard for a year in Seville, he was acquitted.

He died in 1557, lonely and disconsolate, feeling he had failed in the mission life had given him to fulfill.

After sailing for some days toward Cuba, Dorantes' ship leaked so badly that it was forced to return to Vera Cruz. He went back to Mexico City.

The viceroy welcomed him cordially, and tendered him an assignment to make a reconnaissance of the country north of the City of Hearts. After his recent sea experience, Dorantes had no stomach for sailing again, at least until he had recovered his courage. Mexico was an agreeable country, and the opportunity to command an expedition under the banner of Mendoza was a strong inducement to remain there. He accepted the commission.

Mendoza appropriated money, men and supplies for the undertaking, but for some unknown reason it was never carried out. Perhaps Mendoza decided it would have been an unnecessary expenditure in view of the fact that Coronado was planning to go himself in search of the Seven Cities.

Dorantes was not forgotten, however. Mendoza arranged for him to marry a wealthy widow, Marie de la Torre, who owned extensive properties and received large rents in the towns of Asala and Jalazintzo. They had eleven children. In addition to rearing such a large family and managing his wife's estate, Dorantes served Mendoza as an officer in the conquest of Jalisco.

He never returned to Spain. The exact date of his death is not known, but there is evidence to show that he lived for a number of years in affluence and comfort, a man of position and respect. One of his sons, Balthasar, is known to have been born about 1550, and became king's treasurer in Vera Cruz. Upon the death of his father he inherited an *encomienda* that produced an income of five thousand pesos a year. Another *encomienda* was inherited by Dorantes' son, Gaspar, at the pueblos of Ocava. A third son, Melchior, became the owner, also by inheritance, of a large number of Indian slaves and properties which brought in sizeable returns.

Direct descendants of Dorantes reside in Mexico City today.

The viceroy was not greatly impressed by the timid, quiet Castillo. He offered him no lucrative posts, but he did not ignore him.

As a reward for his achievement with Cabeza de Vaca,

Mendoza granted Castillo half the income from the Indian village of Tehuacán. He also arranged for him to marry a widow with property.

The Castillos lived quiet and unostentatiously in Mexico City. They had no sons, but Señora Castillo gave birth to eleven daughters.

Like Dorantes, Castillo never returned to Spain, and the time of his death is not known.

Dorantes committed his slave, Estevanico, whom he had treated as a free man on the long journey, to the service of Mendoza. It was a gift that the viceroy greatly appreciated, for Estevanico was not an ordinary slave. If he had been a white man, he would have been honored, and no doubt married off to a wealthy widow, of which Mexico had a great surplus.

Yet, Estevanico was highly regarded, recognized as a man of outstanding accomplishments and noteworthy qualities. Through long years of the most grueling privation neither his loyalty to his companions nor his courage had failed. Moreover, he had proved himself an astute pupil of the great Cabeza de Vaca. The viceroy intended to make good use of him.

While Coronado was considering going in search of the Seven Cities of Cibola, Mendoza proposed that Estevanico be sent ahead with several friars to pacify the Indians and prepare the way for the main expedition. Coronado agreed to the plan.

The friars assigned to the mission were Fra Marcos of Nice, a lay brother named Daniel, and a regular priest, Fra Antonio de Santa Maria. With Estevanico as a guide, they were to break the trail to the Seven Cities and return to report their findings. Estevanico was to emulate Cabeza de Vaca, and assure the Indians that neither the viceroy nor Coronado had any intentions of enslaving them.

Estevanico was commanded to obey the friars in "all and everything" they requested him to do.

Estevanico had no intention of obeying anyone. He knew very well that the friars were completely dependent upon him for the success of the mission, if not for their survival. It would be he, not they, who issued the orders. He saw himself at last in a position he felt he had long deserved. If the friars didn't like what he did, they could whistle up a tree. He alone knew the trail to the City of Hearts. He alone could talk with the Indians. He alone would have their trust. He was no longer subservient, no longer only an assistant god under the command of Cabeza de Vaca. Now he was a god!

The little party set out from Culiacán March 7, 1539, and traveled through country Estevanico well remembered. All along the line of march he was welcomed with enthusiasm and respect by the Indians, who beseeched him to heal them with a touch of his hands.

Estevanico swaggered through medicine ceremonies and performed religious rites which not only amazed the padres but for which they expressed strong disapproval.

Castañeda says Estevanico clashed with them also "because he took the women that were given him and collected turquoises, and got together a stock of everything. Besides, the Indians in those places got along with the Negro better, because they had seen him before."

Fra Marcos, who had seen service in the conquest of Peru, was a wise and practical man, although gifted with a remarkable imagination, as was later to be demonstrated when he returned to Mexico and reported on the wonders of the Seven Cities, which he had not seen. He recognized the futility of attempting to curb Estevanico, and decided that perhaps the mission might be better served if he let the irrepressible Moor go on ahead with a free hand. Estevanico was a big, friendly, immoral child whom the Indians obviously revered. If Estevanico got into trouble, Fra Marcos reflected, it would be just as well if he and his brothers were not on hand. In the main sense, Estevanico was doing his job remarkably well, and perhaps in time he would weary of dancing half the night about a campfire, carrying maidens into his tent, and drinking the vile Indian stimulants. After all, they had a mission to complete, and when that was accomplished there would be time to force Estevanico to mend his ways and atone for his sins.

Estevanico was unleashed completely a short distance before the City of Hearts was reached. It was the opportunity he had hoped for.

There was something familiar about the scene. It was reminiscent of a parade that had taken place on a larger scale in the American wilderness. Everywhere Estevanico went, the Indians came out to meet an old friend, to give him feathers and robes and turquoises, and anything else he desired. All they asked in return was that he touch them with his great black hands, make the sign of the cross over them, and mumble the mysterious words which gave them assurance and comfort.

But Estevanico was not Cabeza de Vaca. He had learned well his mentor's ways, the magic words of a blessing and a Hail Mary, he knew how to display and rattle his magic gourd. After that he was Estevanico; he reverted to the true Estevanico, the unrestrained, ebullient, untamed, gay, lustful, unfettered, undisciplined giant that nature had made him.

Ures was soon left behind, and Estevanico moved on unhesitatingly into strange country, country which no man except the Indians who dwelt in it had ever seen.

It was a colorful, wild procession. Some three hundred Indians accompanied him. On he strode with a regal manner at the head of the column. In one hand he carried the sacred gourd rattle. His powerful ebony legs and arms were adorned with feathers. A crown of plumes accentuated his height. Tiny bells tinkled on his ankles. Turquoises strung on deer thongs dripped over his broad chest. Immediately behind him his harem straggled through the dust of the high desert. These were girls he had found especially pleasing. The others whom he had experimented with and found wanting were left behind. Near him a personal servant carried four large green dinner plates on which his meals were served. Two lean greyhounds trotted by his side.

Crossing what is now the border between Mexico and the United States, Estevanico reached the San Pedro River in Arizona. Descending it as far as the site of the present town of Tombstone—perhaps he went along the river to its junction with the Gila—he turned northeast. His Indian guides knew the way to the city he sought. It was Hawikuh, a Zuni pueblo, in northwestern New Mexico.

Fra Marcos had instructed Estevanico to mark his trail well, and Estevanico dutifully obeyed, but he took pains to see that the padre did not catch up to him. He wanted the glory of discovering the Seven Cities all for himself.

The story goes that Estevanico was to report his progress and discoveries by sending crosses of different sizes back to Fra Marcos. A little cross would mean that things were going well but nothing of importance had been found. If he came into a land that was better than Mexico, he was to send a large cross.

Estevanico, perhaps wishing to keep the good father's spirits high, didn't bother with small crosses. Four days after setting out ahead he sent back a cross the size of a man, with a message for the friars to advance in haste, for he had learned he was only thirty days' journey from the Seven Cities.

One of the padres became ill and turned back. As Fra Marcos and his companion paddled on in pursuit of the swiftly moving Estevanico, they saw more immense crosses mounted on hilltops, and they came to shelters that had been erected for the nightly repose of Estevanico and his comely mistresses. But they never caught up to him.

When Estevanico reached a point only a day's march from Hawikuh, he camped. Following the custom which Cabeza de Vaca had used successfully, emissaries were dispatched to the city. They went armed with the holy gourd, and with instructions to announce that a Child of the Sun had arrived to bring the people good fortune and to heal the afflicted.

Writing of this event, Castañeda penned a potent line: "The people of this country were more intelligent than those who followed Estevanico."

When they received the message, the headmen of Hawikuh failed to register gratefulness or joy. They examined the gourd with a dispassionate eye, and concluded that it had not come from anywhere nearer the sun than a pueblo on the upper Rio Grande River. Some pointed questions were asked of the emissaries, but the answers received were far from satisfactory. After due consultation, the Zuni governors suggested to the emissaries that they admonish their master to take his gourd and himself back whence he came.

When he had been apprised of this attitude, Estevanico laughed. It had happened before. Indians who were unfriendly in the beginning were always the most hospitable and humble in the end. Taking an escort he considered suitable for the occasion, he marched toward Hawikuh.

The city was not quite as large as he had expected it to be, but swallowing this disappointment, he strode toward its gate. The gate was promptly closed against him. Presently some dignified and sober-faced Zunis emerged from behind a wall and courteously offered him a haven for the night on the outskirts of the pueblo.

Castañeda describes well the events which followed:

"They lodged him in a little hut they had outside their village, and the older men and the governors heard his story and took steps to find out the reason he had come to that country. For three days they made inquiries about him and held a council.

"The account which the Negro gave them of two white men who were following him, sent by a great Lord, who knew about the things in the sky, and how these were coming to instruct them in divine matters, made them think that he must be a spy or a guide from some nations who wished to come and conquer them, because it seemed to them unreasonable to say that the people were white in the country from which he came and that he was sent by them, he being black."

The sun was only a lance high on the morning Estevanico stood on a small hillock outside the city in all his splendor and regal bearing, his followers grouped about him. The men of Zuni came out the gate and advanced toward him. He not only demanded turquoises and women, but homage befitting a Child of the Sun, a god who held in his hand the medicine to heal the sick, the power of life and death.

The answer came in a shower of deadly arrows.

Estevanico the black, and all but three of his faithful Indian followers, died there that day.

The Zunis kept the greyhounds and the green dinner plates, but they threw away the gourd.

Selected Bibliography

ADAMSON, H. C., *Lands of New World Neighbors*. Whittlesey House, New York, 1941.

BAKER, J. N. L., *History of Geographical Discovery and Exploration*. Houghton Mifflin, Boston, 1930.

BANCROFT, HUBERT HOWE, *History of Mexico*. The History Company, San Francisco, 1886.

———, *The North Mexican States*. The History Company, San Francisco, 1889.

———, *History of Central America*. The History Company, San Francisco, 1887.

———, *History of Texas*. The History Company, San Francisco, 1886.

BANDELIER, ADOLPH F., *Contributions to the History of the Southwest Portion of the United States*. J. Wilson & Son, Cambridge, 1890.

———, *Investigations Among the Indians*. J. Wilson & Son, Cambridge, 1892.

BANDELIER, FANNY, *The Journey of Alvar Nuñez Cabeza de Vaca*. A. S. Barnes, New York, 1958.

BARTLETT, JOHN R., *Personal Narrative of Explorations and Incidents, Etc.* G. Routledge, London, 1856.

BASKETT, JAMES N., "Study of the Route of Cabeza de Vaca." *Texas State Historical Quarterly*, Vol. 10.

BIEDMA, *Biedma's Narrative*. The Hakluyt Society, London, 1851.

BISHOP, MORRIS, *The Odyssey of Cabeza de Vaca.* Century, New York, 1933.

BOLTON, HERBERT E., *Spanish Borderlands.* Yale University Press, New Haven, 1921.

——, *Colonization of North America.* Macmillan, New York, 1920.

——, *Spanish Explorers in the Southwest.* Charles Scribner's Sons, New York, 1916.

BOLTON, HERBERT E., and MARSHALL, T. M., *The Story of Haiti.* Macmillan, New York, 1920.

BOURNE, E. G., *The Northmen, Columbus and Cabot.* Charles Scribner's Sons, New York, 1906.

BREBNER, J. B., *Explorers in North America.* A. & C. Black, London, 1933.

BRINTON, DANIEL G., *Notes on the Florida Peninsula.* G. P. Putnam's Sons, New York, 1859.

BUREAU OF AMERICAN ETHNOLOGY, *Fourteenth Annual Report.* Smithsonian Institute, Washington, D. C., 1892.

——, *Twenty-fifth Annual Report.* Smithsonian Institute, Washington, D. C., 1907.

——, *Handbook of American Indians.* Smithsonian Institute, Washington, D. C., 1907.

CABEZA DE VACA. (See Nuñez)

CASAS, BARTOLOMÉ DE LAS, *Historia de las Indias.* Academy of History, Madrid, 1874.

——, *Relation of First Voyages Made by Spaniards.* Brown & Bell, London, 1699.

——, *Tears of the Indians.* N. Brook, London, 1656. Reprinted by Stanford University Press, Stanford, 1933.

CASTAÑEDA, PEDRO DE, *Narrative of the Expedition of Coronado.* In Bureau of American Ethnology, *Fourteenth Annual Report.* Smithsonian Institute, Washington, D. C., 1892.

CHURCHILL, AWNSHAM, *Collection of Voyages and Travels.* A. & J. Churchill, London, 1704.

COOPEWOOD, BETHEL, "Route of Cabeza de Vaca." *Texas State Historical Quarterly,* Vols. 3 & 4.

CORONADO. (See Castañeda)

DAVENPORT, HARBERT, "Expedition of Panfilo de Narvaez." *Southwestern Historical Quarterly,* Vols. 27 & 28.

——, "First Europeans in Texas." *Southwestern Historical Quarterly,* Vol. 22.

DIAZ DEL CASTILLO, BERNAL, *True History of the Conquest of New Spain.* R. M. McBride, New York, 1927.

ESPINOSA, ALONSO DE, *The Gaunches of Tenerife.* The Hakluyt Society, London, 1907.

FISKE, JOHN, *The Discovery of America.* Houghton Mifflin, Boston, 1892.

GAGE, THOMAS, *The English-American, A New Survey of the West Indies.* R. Cotes, London, 1648.

GANN, THOMAS, *Discoveries and Adventures in Central America.* Duckworth, London, 1924.

GRISMER, RAYMOND L., *Sailing the Spanish Main.* H. W. Wilson, New York, 1939.

HAKLUYT, RICHARD, *Principal Navigations.* E. P. Dutton, New York, 1907.

——, *Traffiques and Discoveries.* Alfred A. Knopf, New York, 1926.

HALLENBECK, CLEVE, *Journey and Route of Cabeza de Vaca.* Arthur H. Clark, Glendale, 1940.

HAMILTON, L. J., *American Treasure and the Price of Revolution in Spain.* Harvard University Press, Cambridge, 1934.

HARING, G. H., *Spanish Empire in America.* Oxford University Press, New York, 1947.

HODGE, FREDERICK W., *Spanish Explorers in the Southern United States.* Charles Scribner's Sons, New York, 1907. Reprinted by Barnes and Noble, New York, 1959.
   Contains Cabeza de Vaca's *Relacion* and *The Narrative of the Expedition of Hernando de Soto* by the Gentleman of Elvas, edited by T. Hayes Lewis.

HODGE, FREDERICK W., *The Narrative of the Expedition of Coronado by Castañeda*. Charles Scribner's Sons, New York, 1907.

HOLMES, V. B., *History of the Americas*. Ronald Press, New York, 1950.

JARAMILLO, CAPT. JUAN. (See Bureau of American Ethnology, *Fourteenth Annual Report*) (See Winship)

JONES, TOM B., *Introduction to Hispanic American History*. Harper Brothers, New York, 1939.

KIRKPATRICK, F. A., *The Spanish Conquistadores*. A. & C. Black, London, 1934.

LOWERY, WOODBURY, *Spanish Settlements in North America*. Charles Scribner's Sons, New York, 1911.

MACLEOD, WILLIAM C., *The American Indian Frontier*. G. P. Putnam's Sons, New York, 1928.

McFARLAND, BATES H., "Alvar Nuñez Cabeza de Vaca." *Texas State Historical Quarterly*, Vol. 1.

MARCOS, FRAY, "Discovery of New Mexico." *Magazine of Western History*, 1886.

MARSHALL, T. M., and BOLTON, HERBERT E., *The Story of Haiti*. Macmillan, New York, 1920.

MARTIN, P. S., *Indians Before Columbus*. University of Chicago Press, Chicago, 1947.

MERRIMEN, ROGER B., *The Spanish Empire*. Macmillan, New York, 1918.

MORISON, S. E., *Admiral of the Ocean Sea*. Little, Brown, Boston, 1942.

MOSES, BERNARD, *Establishment of Spanish Rule in America*. G. P. Putnam's Sons, New York, 1898.

NUÑEZ, ALVAR CABEZA DE VACA, *Relacion*. Zamora, 1542.

———, *Relacion de los naufragios y comentarios*. Valladolid, 1555.

———, *Navigazioni et viaggi*. Venice, 1556.

———, *Purchas, His Pilgrimes*. London, 1613.

———, *Relacion y comentarios*. Madrid, 1736.

Nuñez, Alvar Cabeza de Vaca, *Historiadores primitivos de las Indias Occidentales.* Madrid, 1749.
——, *Voyages.* Paris, 1837.
——, *Historiadores primitivos de las Indias.* Madrid, 1852.
——, *Coleccíon de libros y documentos referentes a la historia de America.* Madrid, 1906.
Oviedo y Valdés, G. Fernández de, *Historia general y natural de las Indias.* Academy of History, Madrid, 1852.
Payne, E. J., *History of the New World Called America.* Clarendon Press, Oxford, 1892.
Phinney, A. H., "Narvaez and de Soto: Their Landing Places." *Florida Historical Quarterly,* 1925.
Ponton, Brownie, "Alvar Nuñez Cabeza de Vaca." *Texas State Historical Quarterly,* Vol. 1.
Prescott, W. H., *Conquest of Mexico.* J. B. Lippincott, Philadelphia, 1873.
Priestley, H. I., *The Coming of the White Man.* Macmillan, New York, 1930.
——, *The Mexican Nation,* Macmillan, New York, 1923.
Purchas, Samuel, *Purchas, His Pilgrimes.* W. Stansby, London, 1625.
Richman, I. B., *The Spanish Conquerors.* Yale University Press, New Haven, 1919.
Rodman, Seldon, *Haiti: The Black Republic.* Devin-Adair, New York, 1954.
Simpson, L. B., *The Encomienda in New Spain.* University of California Press, Berkeley, 1929.
Smith, Buckingham, *Narrative of Alvar Nuñez Cabeza de Vaca.* George W. Riggs, Washington, D. C., 1851.
Soto, Hernando de. (See Hodge)
Wells, H. G., *Outline of History.* Macmillan, New York, 1920.
Wells, Joseph K., "First Europeans in Texas." *Southwestern Historical Quarterly,* Vol. 22.
Winship, George Parker, *The Journey of Coronado.* A. S. Barnes, New York, 1904.